The early eighteenth century saw a far-reaching financial revolution in England, whose impact on the literature of the period has hitherto been relatively unexplored. In this original study, Colin Nicholson reads familiar texts such as *Gulliver's Travels*, *The Beggar's Opera* and *The Dunciad* as 'capital satires', responding to the social and political effects of the installation of capitalist financial institutions in London. The founding of the Bank of England and the inauguration of the National Debt permanently altered the political economy of England: the South Sea Bubble disaster of 1721 educated a political generation into the money markets. Nicholson traces the ways in which the imaginary motive of business confidence in the stock exchange has profound effects upon imaginative writing that is actively engaged in the art of political propaganda. While they invested in stocks and shares, Swift, Pope and Gay conducted a campaign against the civic effects of these new financial institutions. Conflict between these writers' commitment to reviving an inherited discourse of civic humanism and the transformations being undergone by their own society reconstituting those values, is shown to have radically affected a number of key literary texts.

CAMBRIDGE STUDIES IN EIGHTEENTH-CENTURY
ENGLISH LITERATURE AND THOUGHT 21

Writing and the rise of finance

Writing and the rise of finance

Capital satires of the early eighteenth century

COLIN NICHOLSON
University of Edinburgh

CAMBRIDGE
UNIVERSITY PRESS

Published by the Press Syndicate of the University of Cambridge
The Pitt Building, Trumpington Street, Cambridge CB2 1RP
40 West 20th Street, New York, NY 10011–4211, USA
10 Stamford Road, Oakleigh, Victoria 3166, Australia

© Cambridge University Press 1994

First published 1994

Printed in Great Britain at the University Press, Cambridge

A catalogue record for this book is available from the British Library

Library of Congress cataloguing in publication data

Nicholson, Colin.
Writing and the rise of finance: capital satires of the early eighteenth century /
Colin Nicholson.
p.   cm. – (Cambridge studies in eighteenth-century English literature and thought)
Includes bibliographical references and index.
ISBN 0-521-45323-2
1. English literature – 18th century – History and criticism.
2. Capitalism and literature – Great Britain – History – 18th century.
3. Finance – Great Britain – History – 18th century.
4. Capitalists and financiers in literature.
5. Satire, English – History and criticism.
6. Economics in literature.
7. Finance in literature.   I. Title.   II. Series.
PR448.C34N53 1994
820.9′355–dc20   93-27263 CIP

ISBN 0 521 45323 2 hardback

For Beccy, Matthew and Calum

Contents

Illustrations

All reproduced by permission of the Trustees of the British Museum.

Preface

This book traces literary, political and economic intersections in a clearly defined period. It uses Bernard Mandeville and Daniel Defoe's essays and journalism with other contemporary writing to read Swift, Pope and John Gay in terms of a developing political economy that was permanently changing their world as they wrote. While every age begins to seem revolutionary in one way or another and every social order constantly transforming, the precise origins of those structures of motive and systems of wealth-creation we now denote as capitalist are more elusive than most. Nonetheless, 'modern history in the sphere of government borrowing begins in 1694' Ashton tells us, and P. G. M. Dickson's study of the development of public credit, *The Financial Revolution*, identifies and describes radically innovative changes that took place in England after the Restoration. These practices and procedures set in place elements of an economic order that would in turn finance the industrial revolution of a later period, and the writings of the Hanoverian Opposition testify to the onset of a recognisably modern world whose first appearance they experienced as threatening. They encountered what we now term finance capitalism as a system of credit that expanded and shrank as developing stock and money markets rose and fell. Public Credit, sometimes perceivable as the 'business confidence' or 'market forces' of the time, seemed to them a most mysterious entity that would or would not manifest itself; appearing to possess a will of its own yet apparently open to coaxing into a participatory and enabling movement. As a way of negotiating and controlling this new agency, the representation of Credit as an inconstant, often a self-willed but sometimes a persuadable woman gained a certain cross-party currency. In literary texts already celebrated for their articulation with a public awareness of far-reaching changes in the organisation of society, the rhetoric of Eve as fateful temptress survives in altered usage.

Radical change is predominantly inscribed in the writing as a contest

over the altering constitution of political subjectivity, thought of in the
lexicon of the time as virtuous citizenship; a contest significantly influenced by a revolutionary economics and the market society it brought
into being. The readings of *Gulliver's Travels*, *The Beggar's Opera* and *The
Dunciad* developed here bring into debate the conflict between traditional forms of civic personality grounded in real property and
endowed with classical virtue, and market-oriented perceptions of
individuality where passion and fantasy are encouraged to operate in
constant flux. As the wealth of imaginative construction negotiates
credit-based constructions of imaginary wealth, versions of history are
fought for which in Tory apprehensions repeatedly challenge an
increasingly settled system of usurping dominance. Their writings are
designed as interventions to influence and shape the proper use of
power in an appropriate system of government. Poetry speaks politics in
sometimes fiercely direct ways, while developing stratagems of finance
and commerce infiltrate rival assumptions and effects into literary
structures of argument and response. In such transforming relations of
power, writing and society constitute each other as an economics of the
imagination works to develop discursive systems that might accommodate transitions from household management signified by *oikonomia* to a
state management of *the* economy of more modern usage. So this book is
also and necessarily an interdisciplinary study of the ways in which the
languages and logics of political and economic activity merge and
interact with those of imaginative production. I discovered in writing it
that on several occasions the words of Karl Marx, and particularly
though not exclusively the young Marx, engage with the terms and
issues of a conflict raging a century earlier. In one sense there is nothing
too surprising in this. Marx often challenges writers from the eighteenth
century and for him structural continuities in capitalist processes of
accumulation were virtually a given, though a complex and transmut-
ing one. The recurrent obsession with purchasable goods and artefacts
we find inscribed in neo-classical texts was termed commodity-fetishism
by Marx and in his writings on the money and credit systems which
those texts also represent we encounter tropes that articulate with the
earlier period. I had not initially thought to figure Marx seated in the
audience of *The Beggar's Opera* or to suggest that he might have profited
by reading *The Rape of the Lock*, but again an intertextual dialogue
presented itself linking one transitional period with another. Money as
metaphor and metaphors of money are exchanged in interesting ways.

   As they confronted their discovery of new pluralities of power, new
'associations' in the term that became widely used, writers of the Tory

Opposition in post-Restoration England sought to redirect the culture by which they were being significantly created, a struggle in which inherited terms of humanist discourse become a ground of contest. In the interests of specific power, and formulations of power are their overriding concern, they were reconstructing a past to shape a more congenial history of their present, enabling us to trace in their work developing recognitions that writing does not simply translate systems of domination, but becomes itself a location of power and of resistance to it. Authorising tropes and hierarchies derived from classical culture turn to and are turned by an emergent market society of proliferating possibilities. We in turn confront historical subjectivities actively producing and being produced by the contending discourses of their time. During the half-century after 1688 a complicated dialectic unfolds as change in the economic and social foundations of politics and the political personality reproduce the citizen as both agent and observer of transforming processes fundamentally affecting his or her nature. Any notion that essentialist humanist assumptions of a bedrock, universally shared 'human condition' constituting 'human nature' derive from this part of the eighteenth century is effectively abolished by the writings of Swift, Pope and Gay, where divergence and difference provide creative stimulus. Far from proposing an autonomous, unified identity, they bring the autonomy of human agency into question and expose classical selfhood as being at risk. Opposition writers were actively resisting their own marginalisation from centres of governing power and their drive for discursive centrality discloses fracture and fragmentation.

To help locate and trace some of the shifting linguistic configurations of selfhood and society in Hanoverian England, this book begins with John Pocock's study of political thought,[1] and thereafter touches base with it from time to time. I acknowledge, too, my debt to Isaac Kramnick's *Bolingbroke and his Circle: The Politics of Nostalgia in the Age of Walpole*[2] which suggested several useful lines of enquiry, and I have been helped by the literary-historical work of Howard Erskine-Hill. It will soon become evident how indebted I am to historians of the period, and in particular to the work of H. T. Dickinson.[3] I also wish to record my personal thanks to Harry Dickinson for his encouragement during the early stages of my research.

[1] J. G. A. Pocock, *The Machiavellian Moment: Florentine Political Thought and the Atlantic Republican Tradition* (Princeton, 1975)
[2] Isaac Kramnick, *Bolingbroke and his Circle: The Politics of Nostalgia in the Age of Walpole* (London, 1968)
[3] See Bibliography for a list of works consulted.

My thanks to Maynard Mack must be shared by all readers of Pope for whom he has acted as guide, philosopher and friend. As far as this book is concerned, Mack's study of Pope's private interests and public politics, *The Garden and the City*,[4] has been a continuing – if sometimes daunting – source of information. Mack and his co-editors of the *Twickenham Edition* of Pope's poems,[5] and the editorial labours of Harold Williams, Herbert Davies and others on Swift's poetry and prose have made texts and commentary available in invaluable ways. George Sherburn and Harold Williams have virtually constructed historical archives in their editions of Swift's and Pope's correspondence, and the same could be said for Donald Bond's work on the *Tatler* and *Spectator*. Since this present book is also concerned with self-constructions of social subjectivity, I have drawn on all of these sources in an effort to reproduce the writers' own words wherever appropriate. My thanks are also due to numerous colleagues: to my fellow-members of the 'Eighteenth Century Study Group' at Edinburgh University and to its Department of English Literature and its Institute for Advanced Studies in the Humanities where portions of this book were presented and discussed; to Randall Stevenson for many discussions; to Geoffrey Carnall for his comments on working drafts and for sharing his knowledge over the years that we have taught together; and to Paul Edwards who, when he knew he was not long for this world, gave me his collection of Swift and told me to get on with it. Ronnie Jack took care to preserve the utopian space of sabbatical leave and the arrival of Ian Donaldson at Edinburgh was for me a lucky hit in the commerce of academic exchange: I am grateful for the suggestions he made during the later stages of this book's development. Abdul Majothi of Edinburgh University's Computer Service User Support Group deserves a medal. Lastly, I thank my wife Liz for her exemplary patience and for useful discussion and advice about historical sociology.

Earlier versions of material contained in chapters 3 and 8 first appeared in *Literature and History*, vol. 5:2 (1979) and vol. 12:2 (1986) respectively.

[4] Maynard Mack, *The Garden and the City: Retirement and Politics in the Later Poetry of Pope* (Toronto, 1969)
[5] For full details of the works mentioned below see the Bibliography on pp. 202–11.

Abbreviations

FR   *The Financial Revolution: A Study in the Development of Public Credit 1688–1756*, by P. G. M. Dickson (London, 1967)

P. Corr.   *The Correspondence of Alexander Pope*, edited by George Sherburn, 5 vols. (Oxford, 1956)

S. Corr.   *The Correspondence of Jonathan Swift*, edited by Harold Williams, 5 vols. (revised edition, Oxford, 1965)

S. Life   *Swift: The Man, his Works, and the Age*, by Irvin Ehrenpreis, 3 vols. (London, 1962–83)

SP   *The Prose Writings of Jonathan Swift*, edited by Herbert Davis, Irvin Ehrenpreis, Louis Landa, Harold Williams, 16 vols. (Oxford, 1939–75)

TE   *The Twickenham Edition of the Works of Alexander Pope*, edited by John Butt, E. Audra, G. Tillotson, M. Mack, F. W. Bateson, J. Sutherland, N. Ault and A. Williamson, 11 vols. (London, 1939–69)

Introduction

I tell thee, *Rica*, [the commerce of stockjobbers] is Lying, Political Lying; and tho' each Man knows the other to deal in this Commodity, yet no one Day passes, in which some of these Fellows do not grow rich, and others are undone, as they *out-lye* one another, or as the Lye of *one* gains more credit than that of *another*. They call the chief nominal Commodity which they deal in SOUTH SEA STOCKS. This is worth more or less in *Idea only*, as the *Lye of the Day* takes or does not take. Thou wilt think that I rave, that I talk idly, when I tell thee here are many People, whom I have convers'd with, and who appear, in other particulars, to be Men of *Reason*, and yet, on the first mention of these Syllables *South Sea Stock*, lose at once all reflection and comparison. They told me that, in the Year 1720, they carry'd this Ideal-Value of their Stocks so high, that what, in the beginning of the Year, was not valued at 1000 *Piastres*, mounted to more than 10000 in less than the space of seven moons; that is, every Man had agreed to call himself exceeding rich ... But at last ... the People awoke from their Golden Dreams.

The Craftsman (27 May 1727)

In his remarkable study of political and intellectual movements from the classically derived discourses of European feudalism into those of Anglo-American modernity, John Pocock traces early modern republican theory in the context of an emerging historicism. His preliminary schema enables us to identify three components of what he calls 'the Machiavellian moment'.[1] In the first place it constitutes a problem in historical self-understanding as a crisis develops between personality and society. Secondly and in consequence, 'the Machiavellian moment' denotes a phase in which the republic is seen as confronting its own temporal finitude. During such transitions the republic attempts to remain morally and politically stable in a stream of irrational events

---

[1] Pocock, *Machiavellian Moment*, pp. vii–ix.

1

conceived as essentially destructive of all systems of secular stability. In
the lexicon of the time this conflict was spoken of as the confrontation of
classical humanist cognitions of 'Virtue' with transforming systems of
'Corruption'. We have been cautioned not to hold our breaths until this
moment passes[2] since, thirdly, 'the Machiavellian moment' has a continuing history. A developing secular political self-consciousness continues to pose problems in historical self-awareness, and the early
eighteenth-century form of the problematic sees a growing acknowledgement of the confrontation of 'virtue' with 'corruption' as a pressing problem in the conduct of public and private affairs. In writing
produced to resist revolutionising processes of socio-economic innovation, corruption, increasingly seen in terms of a chaos of appetites
creating dependence and a consequent loss of autonomy, now flourishes
in a society experiencing unprecedented change that is both rapid and
irrational. What is additionally complicating about this phase is that
parliament itself, a governing institution, is seen to be both a corrupting
agency and an object of corruption. By the 1730s, the terms 'legal
slavery' and 'parliamentary tyranny' had become firmly established in
political vocabulary,[3] and Dr Johnson was subsequently to observe that
'the House of Commons is no longer under the power of the crown, and
therefore must be bribed'.[4] Widespread denunciation of parliament
and society for their 'corruption' by fundholders and stockjobbers
living off their share of the public debts testifies to the prevalence of this
perception. For Opposition writers during the Whig ascendancy traditional emphases of a humanist and Machiavellian vocabulary become
the vehicle of a basically hostile perception of early modern capitalism,
a hostility grounded in awareness of the elaborate conventions of public
credit rather than of the more direct interchanges of the market. The
processes observed, and the changes in language consequent upon the
observation, were in a material and secular sense more revolutionary
than anything to be detected in the radical Puritanism of the preceding
Civil War era.[5]

    Neo-classical writing in the Hanoverian era brings into dispute both
civic and private constructions of subjectivity where a destabilising gap

---

[2] J. H. Hexter, *On Historians: Reappraisals of Some of the Makers of Modern History* (London,
   1979), p. 255.
[3] J. A. W. Gunn, *Beyond Liberty and Property: The Process of Self-Recognition in Eighteenth-Century
   Political Thought* (Montreal, 1983), p. 25.
[4] James Boswell, *Boswell's Life of Johnson*, edited by R. W. Chapman (Oxford, 1904, rpt.
   1961), p. 1037.
[5] Pocock, *Machiavellian Moment*, pp. 423, 486.

opens up between individual self-awareness on the one hand and a changing consciousness of property, society and history on the other. The state in its traditional identifications is perceived by some as no longer able to control its own history or resist its own corruption so that by 1740, it has been claimed, political argument had ceased to grant the idea of a politics of public virtue an important place in public dialogue. Writers steeped in the cognitive ideals of civic humanism found it increasingly difficult to grant self-interested individuals enmeshed in credit-driven commercial enterprise the autonomy and breadth of mind necessary for civic virtue. Simultaneously it became possible for the argument to be put (by Addison among others) that market forms of sociability, sympathy and honesty might be developed to redefine citizenship, and this was the project of *The Spectator*. The virtues of sociability in this view are substituted for civic virtues in an attempt to provide ideological coherence for a developing political economy. 'But the individual distinguished by these character traits is no longer a civic being; he is a private individual, a gentleman of manners, finding fulfillment in economic success and personal pursuits, not in deliberation on the public good.'[6] These things were a perceivable slippage from traditional, classical cognitions, and Pope's friend George Berkeley put the altering perception of 'corruption' plainly in an essay he wrote in 1721 as a response to the South Sea Bubble disaster, when he identified bribery as a corruption that has become 'a national crime'. Cozenage and stockjobbing have 'brought forth new and portentous villainies, not to be paralleled in our own or any other history ... We have made a jest of public spirit, and cancelled all respect for whatever our laws and religion repute sacred.' Fearing 'some great catastrophe', and that 'the final period of our State approaches', Berkeley ends his essay by asking God to grant that:

the time be not near when men shall say: 'This island was once inhabited by a religious, brave, sincere people, of plain uncorrupt manners, respecting inbred worth rather than titles and appearances, asserters of liberty, lovers of their country, jealous of their own rights, and unwilling to infringe the rights of others; improvers of learning and other useful arts, enemies to luxury, tender of other men's lives and prodigal of their own; inferior in nothing to the old Greeks and Romans, and superior to each of those people in the perfections of the other. Such were our ancestors during their rise and greatness; but they degenerated, grew servile flatterers of men in power, adopted Epicurean

---

[6] Shelley Burtt, *Virtue Transformed: Political Argument in England, 1688–1740* (Cambridge, 1992), pp. 27, 33, 34.

notions, became venal, corrupt, injurious, which drew upon them the hatred of God and man, and occasioned their final ruin.'[7]

In the face of such apocalyptic visions, however, and while radical and disruptive economic systems were being put in place, it remains a fact that the Whig regime which supervised their installation also presided over an extended period of political stability. Although it was marked by a singular ferocity, the war of words that accompanied these changes was matched by an institutional moment of political integration as England moved towards recognisably modern systems of state management. The battles now conducted 'at home' were discursive not military, and the domestic 'peace and plenty' attributed to a Stuart monarchy in Pope's *Windsor Forest* was in reality the substantial achievement of Hanoverian Whiggism.

By the end of the Nine Years War of 1688–97, no one could deny that England had become a trading nation and at a very rapid pace an entity known as Trade entered the political vocabulary to an extent that all writers engaged with its significance. But as what we now call the 'Financial Revolution' got under way, new instruments of monetary policy – centrally the Bank of England and the National Debt – transformed the relationship of the citizen to the state. In the writing of those who opposed these developments we detect a nostalgia for Aristotelian notions of freehold and real property as the foundations of personality and value. The public pronouncements of Tory neo-classicists, from which their private activities noticeably depart as we shall see, continue to promote landed property as the guarantee of a civic virtue that enabled the citizen as head of his *oikos* or household to rule and be ruled as one of a community of heads making decisions which were binding on all: a classical republic that had developed into an English 'balance of power' between king, lords and commoners. Conversely a process that soon began to assume self-generating proportions engaged the attentions of Swift, Pope, Gay and others in all sorts of ways. By encouraging large and small investors to lend capital to the state, the state accepted an increasing volume of credit which enabled it to undertake a greater range of activities than could be paid for out of current capital. As the volume of investments grew, the state promised to pay its creditors out of revenues yet to be collected and thus gave birth to the National Debt. New forms of property become the currency of social activity and mobility: society opens to wider participation as a

---

[7] George Berkeley, *The Works of George Berkeley, Bishop of Cloyne*, edited by A. A. Luce and T. E. Jessop, 9 vols. (London, 1948–57), VI, pp. 84–5.

consequence of which, in its civic self-identifications, the human personality radically revises its senses of identity and possibility. Uncertainty and flux were threatening to displace fixity and favoured forms and in marked conflict with the hierarchical values promoted in Pope's *Essay on Man*, new kinds of activity were generating inherently unstable procedures:

The volume of investment meant that the shares, tickets, or tallies entitling the possessor to a share of repayment from the public funds became marketable property, whose value rose and fell as public confidence in the state's political, military, and financial transactions waxed and waned. The fundholder and the stockjobber, the bull and the bear, had come upon the stage; and the figure around which they were grouped, the concept which they introduced into the language of English politics, was not Trade but Credit.[8]

The seemingly perverse and unpredictable relationship between opinion and fantasy and business confidence began to assume the dimensions of a social power, and for traditionalists such a leap from the politics of domestic economy and landed integrity to the administrative apparatus of modern finance was not at all palatable. As the far-reaching consequences of these developments make their way into imaginative recognitions, Opposition writers generate answerable figures of alien powers and corrupting forces.

Six years after Pope's birth (and the Revolution Settlement) it had become clear that under conditions of war the London gold-market system was no longer adequate either for wealthy trading merchants or for the increasing demands being made upon it by the state, as Charles Davenant had seen:

For war is quite changed from what it was in the time of our forefathers; when in a hasty expedition, and a pitched field, the matter was decided by courage; but now the whole art of war is in a matter reduced to money; and now-a-days, that prince, who can best find money to feed, cloath, and pay his army, not he that hath the most valiant troops, is surest of success and conquest.[9]

Much of the banking system then operating had grown haphazardly since the Civil War period when wealthy nobles and merchants judged it prudent to lodge their money, plate and jewels in the vaults of the goldsmiths. Once these latter realised that only a small fraction of such deposits were being withdrawn for day to day expenses, leaving most of

---

[8] Pocock, *Machiavellian Moment*, p. 426.
[9] Charles Davenant, 'An Essay upon Ways and Means of Supplying the War', in *Works*, edited by Sir Charles Whitworth, 5 vols. (London, 1771), I, p. 16.

it lying idle, it was a short step to lending money on its security, and thus prefiguring two of the main functions of modern banks. Worried that King William would refuse to pay the debts of his Stuart predecessors, the gold merchants supported neither the war against France nor the new regime: yet the state needed money and loans. When the King asked the London merchants for a loan of £1,200,000 sterling in 1694, they adapted a plan drawn up by the Scot, William Patterson, and used a new body called the Bank of England to raise it. 'Gilbert Heathcote and his syndicate'[10] formed a share-holding association with a capital of £1,200,000, secured against the anticipated revenue of new excise taxes which were to provide the funds to repay the interest on the money loaned to the King. Private individuals were entering into a contractual relationship with the state, and the Bank thus formed issued its contributors with bank notes equal in value to their share of the capital; notes that could be circulated and used in payment, though it was not obligatory to accept them. For its part, retaining the cash put up by shareholders, the Bank could pay out on commercial securities and give advances to individuals. It was therefore a credit institution and since the king's debt was founded on a parliamentary undertaking, the Bank had established a national debt dependant upon public credit. It is common knowledge that the king spent the entire loan pursuing the war against France, and that because the syndicate had such confidence in the Bank they lent him more. As a result, the practice and recording of payment and exchange through various kinds of paper document developed exponentially.[11] The Bank was given the right of receiving money from the public and lending this at interest, as well as the right of making loans in paper, which it brought into being at will.[12] Not only had the national debt been born and entailed upon the future, but when shareholders in the public funds realised that they could trade their shares for profit, the state itself could be perceived as a marketable property.

So even as Opposition writers were proposing various reconstitutions of monarchical, aristocratic and hierarchical forms of government, they were (often unwillingly, sometimes unwittingly) becoming aware that the participating subjectivities they addressed and sought to influence, whether governed or governing, were themselves being constituted by forces and energies increasingly perceived as beyond any human

[10] Howard Erskine-Hill, 'Pope and the Financial Revolution', in *Writers and Their Background*, edited by P. Dixon (London, 1972), p. 204.

[11] Pierre Vilar, *A History of Gold and Money: 1450–1920* (London, 1984), pp. 215ff.

[12] T. S. Ashton, *An Economic History of England: The Eighteenth Century* (London, 1955), p. 178.

control. The paper-money economy of credit significantly developed during the financial revolution changed in decisive ways how people thought and wrote about themselves and their world. The emergence of classes whose property consisted not of land or goods or even bullion, but of paper promises to repay in an undefined future, was seen as entailing the emergence of new types of personality, unprecedentedly dangerous and unstable.[13] What appeared to be a new system of value emerged in which paper money as a single commodity set apart from the world of production came to express the values of the heterogeneous world of commodities then flooding onto London's markets as commerce expanded globally. In discernible ways a newly mysterious phenomenon of equivalence on which exchange value and the very possibility of exchanging one object for another and different one are somehow founded, affects human agency, consciousness and intention. Across society, subjects and objects were relating to each other in complicated patterns of valorisation and transference, and while the single transactions of this movement evidently arose from conscious and particular individual will and purpose, the wider process could be conceived as an interrelation which seemed to arise spontaneously from nature. Their own collisions with one another produce a mutual interaction often seen as a system and power independent of them.[14] It became possible to consider whether the prime structure of agency in social affairs was human subjectivity or the objects and practices that had been constructed. Did the shaping of society proceed according to the will of a determining subjectivity or was the human increasingly a determined subject? When private and personal fantasy coincided with the market the former could appear to be the case, but not so when they met market resistance. Not surprisingly, these considerations find radicalised articulation in contemporary linguistic representations of resemblance and identity. What we encounter in Opposition and other writing is a complicated inscription of developing subjectivities constituting as they are being constituted by a developing political economy. By 1710 amid rumours of peace with France, Daniel Defoe could develop Davenant's perception to assert that:

Our ruining that National Credit, which really is the Support of the War, and without which, it cannot live ... will give *France* the advantage; this will give us all up a Prey to Tyranny, and Slaves to a Conquer'd, Reduc'd Enemy – Who

[13] J. G. A. Pocock, *Virtue, Commerce, and History: Essays on Political Thought and History, Chiefly in the Eighteenth Century* (Cambridge, 1985), p. 235.
[14] Karl Marx, *Grundrisse* (Harmondsworth, 1973), pp. 196–7.

by the Force of this very Credit was brought to offer Incredible Things ... Yet if your Credit Dies, he revives ... He that proposes to carry on the War without Credit, proposes Impossibilities, and indeed talks Nonsense.[15]

It has been suggested[16] that the linguistic condition of existence for these financial practices and their participating human subjects is an assumed transparency of discourse, the discourse of 'common sense': as Stanley Fish asserts, after 1660 the plain style brought about largely during the Revolutionary period 'wins the day'.[17] Defoe made effective use of it, but insofar as a transparent discourse was common because immediately available to and shared by such figures as John Locke's 'reasonable gentleman' ('the general maxims we are discoursing of are not known to children, idiots and the greater part of mankind'),[18] Swift's manipulations of plain style are read in turn as a subversion of that common-sense subjectivity and of the transparent language deployed to articulate its preferred perceptions. And insofar as the 'gentleman' was believed to be the only member of society who spoke a language universally intelligible,[19] then his textual construction also becomes a matter of imaginative contention. Because what was at issue in these rival figurations was the demise of classical notions of selfhood during a period when investment expectations and profit-taking were redesigning the order of social life. The social and ethical supremacy of the traditionally valorised landed gentleman was being decisively challenged by his monetary counterpart.

By means of the space for public discourse opened up by the very processes and adaptations against which they argued, Opposition writers were able publicly to resist the ensuing onslaught against those hierarchies of meaning and power within which they identified themselves. According to Leslie Stephen, Pope's subscription technique meant that he 'received a kind of commission from the upper class' to produce his writing, and effected a break with past practice by replacing the individual patron with a 'kind of joint-stock body of collective patronage'.[20] By 1725, Defoe had noticed that writing 'is

---

[15] Daniel Defoe, *A Review of the State of the English Nation* (London, 1704–13), edited in 22 facsimile books by A. W. Secord (Columbia, 1938), VII, no. 62, p. 242 (facsimile book 17).

[16] Antony Easthope, *British Post-Structuralism: Since 1968* (London, 1988), p. 203.

[17] Stanley Fish, *Self-Consuming Artifacts: The Experience of Seventeenth Century Literature* (Berkeley, 1974), p. 379.

[18] John Locke, *An Essay Concerning Human Understanding*, edited by P. H. Nidditch (Oxford, 1975, rpt. 1990), p. 63.

[19] John Barrell, *English Literature in History 1730–80: An Equal, Wide Survey* (London, 1983), p. 34.

[20] Leslie Stephen, *English Literature and Society in the Eighteenth Century* (London, 1963), p. 51.

becoming a very considerable Branch of the English Commerce. The
Booksellers are the Master Manufacturers or Employers. The several
Writers, Authors, Copyers, Sub-Writers and all other operators with
Pen and Ink are the workmen employed by the said Master-Manufac-
turers.'[21] Pope would have had no truck with such a description, but he
knew the developing systems of publishing better than most: what we
have come to call the emergent 'public sphere' was something he and
his friends exploited with audacity and panache. Conceived as an ideal
discursive realm where exchange without domination is possible, the
public sphere was held to be a place where reason rather than power
held court, since carrying one's opinion is more an act of collaboration
than of competition.[22] Crucial in this process were the London coffee-
houses which served as places of cultural and political debate and
exchange, but also as nubs of finance and insurance where the stockjobbers set up in business and the South Sea Bubble débacle was largely
transacted.[23] Here, again in Stephen's words, a 'characteristic fraterni-
sation of the politicians and the authors' happened every day 'in a kind
of tacit confederation of clubs to ... form the whole public opinion of
the day'.[24] A newly politicised culture was calling into being a cultural
politics responsive to its needs, and on the Tory side of the divide Swift,
Pope and Gay entered the lists with verve and sometimes with venom.

   The paper-money systems of public credit and the commodities
thereby circulated seemed to be assuming sole and overwhelming
command of all social valuation, leaving Opposition writers with the
Herculean task of resisting forces apparently moving beyond any civic
control. Perhaps inevitably the conflict in which they engaged produces
a series of unpredictable imaginative impacts. In a further hybridi-
sation of already established serio-comic conjunctions in the mock-epic,
The Rape of the Lock links commodity fetishism with psychic fetishism;
the one an effect of the social formation in terms of political economy,
the other an effect of the subject in terms of the subconscious. When
Pope describes his Baron's irresistible attraction towards Belinda's
'bright Locks' he shows us stimulated fantasy – 'He saw, he wish'd, and
to the Prize aspir'd'[25] – shortly to effect a displaced possession. Natural

---

[21] Quoted in Ian Watt, *The Rise of the Novel* (Harmondsworth, 1966), p. 55.
[22] Terry Eagleton, *The Function of Criticism: From 'The Spectator' to Poststructuralism* (London,
   1984), p. 17.
[23] Ibid., p. 23.   [24] Stephen, *English Literature and Society*, p. 23.
[25] Geoffrey Tillotson, *The Poems of Alexander Pope: Vol. II, The Rape of the Lock and Other Poems*
   (London, 1940, rpt. 1954), p. 159. Subsequent quotations are given in the text parenthetically.

desire is rerouted into fetishised acquisition. The resulting minor brawl among London's smart set may analogise other reactions and manifestations in a credit-based trading society: not least the disappointment and frustration when rival ideas of self-interested activity materially trespass upon the opinion and expectation of others, concerning appropriate behaviour and results. The contrapuntal explorations of *Gulliver's Travels* generate narrative strategies almost as nomadic as its hero's wanderings to acknowledge that in a new world of speculative fantasy any construction of its narrating subject in a position of dominance is itself a delusory fiction given that promissory notes of paper-credit are increasingly the alienating agency which positions and enables economic individualism. Through the diverse formal elements it draws together in comic equivalence, *The Beggar's Opera* pursues a sense of money transformed from its role as the medium of circulation for goods into the Lord and God of the world of commodities, autonomously arising out of circulation to become the arbiter of value, and its acquisition the aim of all endeavour. A growing sense that classical valorisations are losing their purchase on his world is disclosed in Pope's poetry of the 1730s; poetry that still seeks to articulate society in the ethical terms of a humanist vocabulary thereby stretched to breaking point. Hierarchic signifiers come into conflict with democratising signifieds and in satirical rebuttal the final *Dunciad* sardonically mocks the assumption of power by an alien deity to which everything else in the world of the poem is subordinate, not least its hybrid hero Colley Cibber, Walpole's laureate and cultural paradigm of market morality. As citizens of a transforming market society refocus ethics and reconstruct value, forms of imaginative materialism arise where text-based fictions coalesce with the speculative varieties operating daily on the stock exchange. The intertextuality discovered with the force of revelation in late twentieth-century critical theory is for this political culture part of an assumed pattern of cross-discursive identification.

Across the fantastic worlds that Swift fashions it seems that all value-systems are called into question, and we can read Gulliver's initial inflation in size and subsequent miniaturisation as a defining trope for the monetary dispositions visibly extending property-ownership and wealth-acquisition by which perceptions of individual worth came to measured by the rise and fall of the stock market. If Pope's Queen of Dulness embodies public credit as cultural agency, Swift departs from a fashion of the time which saw credit as female inconstancy. The instabilities of credit-based commerce and exchange significantly constitute Swift's celebrated protagonist. Setting accept-

Figure 1   'The Bubblers Medley, or a Sketch of the Times, being Europes Memorial for the Year 1720'

able boundaries between print and practice for the imaginary and the speculative proved ultimately to be futile and by the time of Pope's death in 1743, the political economy he sought to temper and redirect had demonstrated its irreversible triumph: his favoured couplet-form exposed as unequal to the task of disciplined restraint he had set for it. *Gulliver's Travels*, on the other hand, inscribes formal heterogeneities that subsequent fiction-writing would productively exploit.

What Swift called the 'Money'd Interest' had arrived and had made itself institutionally indispensable. In the years immediately following the incorporation of the Bank of England, overseas trade developed phenomenally. The expansion of commerce to distant quarters of the globe stimulated a restless spirit of economic innovation in England and particularly in London. There was also a growing interest in insurance to lessen the hazards of shipwreck, fire and premature death, and a rash of joint-stock companies flourished and died, particularly around the South Sea year of 1720. The crucial factor in joint-stock companies was the right and ability to sell shares, thus allowing the company concerned to continue trading without having constantly to repay its capital, thereby retaining capital liquidity, while its shareholders had income in the form of dividends. It has been estimated that during the speculative boom which culminated in the South Sea Bubble, over 200 insurance companies were floated in London alone; clear evidence that a world was being turned upside down as new systems of finance changed the basis upon which not only trade but national government organised itself and its responsibilities. While the inauguration of a National Debt secured by taxation yet to be levied, and an accompanying proliferation in insurance brokerage was fundamentally altering traditional practice, the lives and writings of Pope and Swift correspond in an almost exact chronology with this institutionalising phase of an economic differentiation progressively dismantling and restructuring the ways in which individuals saw themselves and their society.

Making due allowance for its antagonistic perspective, Swift's is still one of the best accounts for understanding why and how the revolution in national finances struck alarm and fear into traditionalists:

By all I have yet read of the History or our own Country, it appears to me, that National Debts secured upon Parliamentary Funds of Interest, were things unknown in *England* before the last Revolution under the Prince of *Orange* ... But, when this Expedient ... was first put in practice; artful Men in Office and Credit began to consider what Uses it might be apply'd to; and soon found it was likely to prove the most fruitful Seminary, not only to establish a Faction ... but likewise, to raise vast Wealth for themselves in particular, who were to be the Managers and Directors in it. Thus, a new Estate and Property sprung up in the hands of the Mortgagees, to whom every House and Foot of Land in *England* paid a Rent Charge free of all Taxes ... So that the gentlemen of Estates were in effect but tenants to these New Landlords; many of whom were able in time to force the Election of Burroughs out of the Hands of those who had been the old Proprietors and Inhabitants.   (*SP* II, pp. 68–70)

Beyond his partisan stance Swift is recording structural shifts in economic and political power, concerns that were naturally and increasingly to occupy writers of diverse political persuasion, giving point to Pope's threat in 1733:

> Yes, while I live, no rich or noble knave
> Shall walk the World, in credit, to his grave.
>
> (*Satire II, i,* 119–20)

And it is to the pre-revolutionary world since displaced by credit and its new forms of paper-payment that Pope is looking back with mock-yearning but serious concern in the *Epistle to Bathurst*:

> Oh that such bulky bribes as all might see,
> Still, as of old, incumber'd villainy![26]

A convenient way of registering the emergence of the new apparatus of power is by recalling that in conjunction with the exchequer bill system built up by Walpole after the South Sea collapse, on eight occasions between 1721 and 1742 the government floated a variety of loan-schemes, some of them part lotteries, in which the Bank of England played a leading part. A radical dislocation of traditional practice was made more distressing for some because a mania for trading in lottery tickets could also be perceived as putting the state up for auction. The public loans of the 1740s were entirely administered by the Bank, whose ascendancy by this time was unchallenged; its control over government borrowing complete. Wars had been waged and won without any attempt to balance the books: the attempt to construct a Tory rival to the power of the Bank, in the shape of the South Sea Company, had disintegrated ignominiously with the Bank swallowing up the wreckage. Since government revenue was now being raised on the security of taxation yet to be levied, credit finance and deficit finance had become signs of economic strength rather than frailty and everywhere, it could seem, like the goddess of *The Dunciad*, Public Credit 'rul'd, in native Anarchy, the mind'.[27] We might more readily appreciate the profound senses of misgiving displayed in Pope's

---

[26] F. W. Bateson, *The Poems of Alexander Pope: Vol. III, ii, Epistles to Several Persons (Moral Essays)*, (London, 1951), p. 86. Subsequent quotations are given in the text parenthetically.

[27] James Sutherland, *The Poems of Alexander Pope: Vol. IV, The Dunciad* (London, 1953), p. 270. Subsequent quotations are given in the text parenthetically.

and Swift's mature work and in the writings of those who shared their fears if we recall the excitement with which Karl Marx welcomed the society being introduced:

All fixed, fast-frozen relations, with their train of ancient and venerable prejudices and opinions, are swept away, all new-formed ones become anti-quated before they can ossify. All that is solid melts into air, all that is holy is profaned, and man is at last compelled to face with sober senses, his real conditions of life, and his relations with his kind.[28]

Not for the only time in Marx, political desire overemphasises the completeness of change: ancient and venerable prejudices and opinions were to demonstrate a remarkable resilience as they accommodated to more acceptable transitions. But what was solid for Pope and his friends was land, against which the airy substance of paper-credit was a mockery of all they professed to hold dear, and one of the perceptions they shared was of rapidly expanding and shrinking values of currency actively undermining once stable values associated with the blood-ties of family and with a propertied stake in the country. Each of them acknowledges the presence of a different kind of agency in society identified in Swift's *Examiner* warning: 'that *power*, which, according to the old maxim, was used to follow land, is now gone over to money; and the Country Gentleman is in the condition of the young heir, out of whose estate a scrivener receives half the rent for interest, and hath a mortgage on the whole' (*SP* III, p. 5). As he watched the engrossing operations of the Bank, including its arrangement of government long-term borrowing from the private sector upon the security of future taxation which allowed it to spend on the War of Spanish Succession out of all proportion to its current revenue, Swift was equally clear about other effects of the socio-economic process unfolding around him:

Several persons who had small or encumbered estates, sold them, and turned their money into those funds to great advantage; merchants, as well as other monied men, finding trade was dangerous and growing more expensive, taxes were increased, and funds multiplied every year, till they have arrived at the monstrous height we now behold them. And that which was first a corruption, is at last grown necessary. By this means, the wealth of the nation, that used to be reckoned by the value of land, is now computed by the rise and fall of stocks.
(*SP* III, p. 6)

These were sentiments that were to be echoed time and again in the period. 'Our Gentry', wrote Richard Steele in *The Spectator*, 'are, generally speaking, in debt; and many families have put it into a kind of

[28] Karl Marx, *The Revolutions of 1848* (Harmondsworth, 1973), pp. 70–1.

method of being so from generation to generation.'[29] Conditions of widespread mortgaging encourage the recognition that a social order was shifting, and its traditional frameworks for action and discourse dissolving. Pope associates this general drift of property in the sixty years after 1680, which according to Habakkuk marks one of the great shifts in English land-ownership,[30] with an irresistible and sedulous fraud and deception: 'What's *Property*? Dear Swift! you see it alter / From you to me, from me to Peter Walter' (*Satire II (ii)*, 167–8). Walter, the grasping New Man of aristocratic household finance and steward to Newcastle, Walpole's Secretary of State,[31] was one of the moneylenders and fraudsters in the service of the new finance whose dealings were exposed.

It is a question how far these revolutionary changes were actually understood by those who engineered and embraced them, let alone those who opposed them. Certainly the great business flotations of the 1690s had brought in their wake a massive influx of tellers, scriveners and stockjobbers (stockjobbing soon became a general term of abuse for anything to do with money markets), and with them an invading strangeness of terms and jargon. In his 1701 pamphlet 'The Villainy of Stock-Jobbers Detected', Defoe was sure of a sympathetic response when he criticised how 'these people can ruin silently, undermine and impoverish by a sort of impenetrable artifice, like poison that works at a distance, can wheedle men to ruin themselves, and fiddle them out of their money, by the strange and unheard of engines of interest, dis-counts, transfers, tallies, debentures, shares, projects, and the devil and all of figures and hard names'.[32] Evidently the hardest of them all was Public Credit: 'what all people are busy about,' Defoe wrote in his 1710 essay on the subject, 'but not one in forty understands: every man has a concern in it, few know what it is, nor is it easy to define or describe it'.[33] A year later Swift was describing it as 'such a complication of knavery and cozenage, and such an unintelligible jargon of terms to involve it in, as were never known in any other age or country in the world' (*SP* III, p. 6). Both writers have political ends in view but they are testifying to pressures and practices in social life that were instruc-

---

[29] *The Spectator*, edited by Donald F. Bond, 5 vols. (Oxford, 1965), I, p. 352.
[30] H. J. Habakkuk, 'English Landownership 1680–1740', *Economic History Review*, 10 (1939–40), p. 3.
[31] Maynard Mack, *The Garden and the City: Retirement and Politics in the Later Poetry of Pope, 1731–1743* (Toronto, 1969), p. 183.
[32] Daniel Defoe, 'The Villainy of Stock-Jobbers Detected' (London, 1701), p. 22.
[33] Defoe, 'An Essay Upon the Public Credit' (London, 1710), p. 13.

ting their perceptions as they wrote. There were few who did not recognise that a revolution of some kind had taken place since William III's accession. 'How could they have failed to do so', Geoffrey Holmes remarks, 'when by 1710 a single word inserted in the Queen's speech could cause a flutter on the Exchange, and politicians assessed a ministry's prospects as much on the basis of fluctuations of the stock market and the state of credit as on a reading of the signs at Court or in Parliament.'[34]

'I know it is a *disputed point*,' Defoe cagily allowed when discussing the interdependence of personal and national credit early in 1711, 'whether this Levying Money by Loans, upon Funds of Interest, be a Service to the Nation or a Prejudice.'[35] He had earlier acknowledged that by definition credit was 'in no way dependent upon Persons, Parliaments, or any particular Men, or set of Men, as such, in the world, but upon their Conduct and just Behaviour',[36] and throughout 1710 he frequently returned to the topic in his *Review*. As his pen produces to the order of Harley his paymaster, Defoe assumes into his argument identifications of the private and public that were deeply troubling to others:

I have, I think, plainly lay'd down the great Foundation of Credit among us. I have shewn how the Funds *however* they are call'd Publick, and *however* having Money in them, is call'd having money in the Government, *are our own*, and that the Government are, in this Case, no more than our *Rent gatherers*, Stewards and Tellers of the Money – It is strange, this consideration should not move us – What is it, Gentlemen, that you are doing? What, are you resolv'd to Ruin and Destroy your Selves?[37]

'At this Time', he argues, '*The Credit of the Nation* is ... *its Politick Life* – Money is the Sinews of the War; Credit is Money – Money is the Life and Soul of all our Opposition to *Popery*; of all our Alliance against *France*, and at this Time, *No Credit, no Money*.'[38] In this respect, he insists, 'the whole Nation has but one Head, and he that would destroy the Credit, Poisons the whole Frame, let the People divide into what Factions or Parties they think fit'.[39] But divide into factions and parties they did, often in confused and confusing ways. Swift's views straddled the Whig/Tory dichotomy, using country rhetoric to address Tories in the *Examiner*, yet professing a belief in contract theory, not in an

---

[34] Geoffrey Holmes, *British Politics in the Age of Anne* (London, 1967), p. 152.
[35] Defoe, *Review*, VII, no. 137, p. 545 (facsimile book 18).
[36] Defoe, *Public Credit*, p. 26.   [37] Defoe, *Review*, VII, no. 104, p. 413 (facsimile book 18).
[38] Ibid., no. 142, p. 565.   [39] Ibid., no. 119, p. 474.

'ancient constitution',[40] and when Robert Harley recruited them for the Tories, Swift and Defoe had both been active for the Whigs.

In the decades following the Revolution Settlement everyone claimed God and civic virtue for their side and when Swift abused antagonistic journalists as 'outrageous Party-Writers' he also records a suppressed self-recognition (*SP* III, p. 15). 'They have scoundrels enough to write for their passions and designs,' Swift was to hear Pope say, 'let us write for truth, for honour, for posterity' (*P. Corr.* II, pp. 412–13). Swift and Defoe, working for the same political master without acknowledging each other, took energetic part in a process of argument and persuasion that brought politics and print, and writing and society, into significantly different relations. The forces and allies of Puritanism and Dissent, though they had not succeeded in establishing a lasting English republic, did not leave the field: they spun and toiled. While significantly extending the forum at Westminster as a framework of reference for the conduct of the nation's affairs, the Parliamentarians continued to develop their business experience and went into their schools and academies to elaborate programmes of learning that would sustain and articulate cultural and commercial values appropriate for a new world in the making. Some of their brethren were thriving in America, too, while in England the Republic of Letters was firmly established as a site of political engagement, and Bolingbroke recognised his enemy when with his Schism Act of 1714 he attempted to destroy the education system of the Dissenters. And when Swift satirised the plain style it favoured, he was also paying its effectiveness a compliment. He took the style into some weird and wonderful areas to express his sometimes savage indignation at new systems of power, allegiance and management then emerging, but his radical techniques relate to dissenting modes of discourse in ways that Pope's and Gay's do not.

Pope knew their power and efficacy, though, and sought to methodise his writing in ways that promoted an answerable clarity and concision. His *Epistle to Bathurst* insists that the riches introduced by England's developing commercial society are 'No grace of Heav'n or token of th'Elect', and in railing against Dissenting pieties which sanctioned the rise in society of new men of business and administration, Pope, too, is testifying to the power of an insurgent ideology. But all public writing serves at some court of power or other and Pope, Swift

[40] J. A. Downie, *Robert Harley and the Press: Propaganda and Public Opinion in the Age of Swift and Defoe* (Cambridge, 1979), p. 128.

and Gay came to know well the power exercised by expanding markets. Gay's bid for a monetary fortune on the stock exchange seems to have permanently damaged his health, whereas Pope has been described as the first English writer to achieve financial independence from the sale of his work; and Pope was adept at juggling his market to personal advantage. While publicly opposing the rapidly expanding financial systems and institutions of his time, like his friends and colleagues Pope participated in them and profited from the opportunities they pre-sented. So it becomes an interesting reflection upon subsequent literary canon-formation and the cultural valorisations it encodes that some of the most remembered voices from a time of the greatest explosion of financial and commercial activity England had hitherto seen, publicly set themselves determinedly at variance with what was happening, while privately seeking profit from it. If Walpole justifiably attacked Bolingbroke for setting himself up as 'Anti-Minister' during the Whig ascendancy, Pope has as just a claim to be considered the 'Anti-Laureate' to Hanoverian England. The installation of modern struc-tures of finance and investment and the shifting configurations of power they represented and entailed were vigorously contested by the writers who famously grouped themselves around Bolingbroke, initially in the Brothers Club founded in the summer of 1711. Swift was a member from the beginning; Pope and Gay soon joined. Out of the Brothers Club grew the Scriblerus Club, and from them came their capital satires *Gulliver's Travels*, *The Beggar's Opera* and *The Dunciad*.

The texts they produced repeatedly express a struggle for meaning and value in what was for them an era of devastating change. Unable to accept that the system of public credit and the rise of the moneyed interest had been a natural consequence of the revolution of 1688, they sought and promoted a political alignment that came to be called the Country Party with themselves as leading figures in it. 'Utterly futile [and] ridiculously unrealistic'[41] as these aspirations had become, and particularly so after the failure of the Tories to unseat Walpole in the general election of 1734, they were aspirations that during the long years of Whig rule held the loyalty and determination of the writers we may still conveniently call the Scriblerians. Their satires were con-ceived and devised as instruments of political persuasion in the service of a platform and a programme increasingly remote from the exercise of power. Bolingbroke was at the centre of this opposition. When he became a neighbour of Pope's in 1725, he turned Dawley Farm into a

[41] J. H. Plumb, *The Growth of Political Stability in England, 1675–1725* (London, 1967), p. 129.

gathering place for government opponents and there the idea for the *Craftsman* newspaper was born.[42] At Dawley Farm Pope's *Essay on Man* was significantly developed, and Bolingbroke's ideas and emphases feed into Pope's writing during a time when the latter's poetry was attracting a wide readership. Convinced that politics was still capable of being moulded and shaped to their preferred perspectives, this group fought for the hearts and minds of others in a self-conscious programme of propagandising art. As their campaign unfolded, Swift could tell Gay that he hoped to see Pope's Queen of Dulness knock down *The Beggar's Opera*, just as the *Opera* had knocked down *Gulliver's Travels*; but not, Swift added, until the *Opera* had 'fully done its job'. A few weeks later Swift judged it opportune to prompt Pope into publishing *The Dunciad*: 'There is now a vacancy for Fame; the Beggar's Opera has done its task' (*S. Corr.* II, pp. 278, 286). From the wrong side of history, as it were, the Scriblerians set their writing against political and economic trans-valuations that were permanently altering inherited structures and habitual priorities of private and social experience. Those trans-valuations were promoted and supported every bit as vigorously, and often far more legitimately than the opposition they aroused.

Less than two years after Pope's birth, John Locke published his *Treatises of Government*[43] which helped to establish discursive parameters for much of what was subsequently said and thought about the revo-lution in human affairs that continued after the apparent demise of English republicanism signalled by the restoration of a monarchy in 1660. The Protestant identification of individual salvation with its material manifestation in economic individualism was too firmly rooted to wither on the vine, and a peculiarly English contractual arrange-ment between sovereign and parliament was brought into being: part monarchy, part republic. Locke emphasises market relations between individuals as the natural order of things, argues for the sanctity of property rights, contrasts patriarchal power with the manifest justice of a balance held in political or civil society, and considers the proper boundaries to be placed upon the executive and upon legislative power. His last five chapters measure the relative merits of 'Paternal, Political, and Despotical Power, considered together'; examine in turn 'Con-quest', 'Usurpation' and 'Tyranny', and conclude with a consideration

---

[42] Brean Hammond, *Pope and Bolingbroke: A Study of Friendship and Influence* (Columbia, MI, 1984), pp. 38 ff.

[43] John Locke, *Two Treatises of Government*, edited by Peter Laslett (Cambridge, 1960, rpt. 1992).

of appropriate circumstances for the 'Dissolution of Government'. As a leading apologist of the Revolution Settlement, Locke systematically assumes into the structure of his argument a legally tenable relationship between persons, in effect rewriting natural law as modern juris-prudence, and in the decades following the publication of his *Two Treatises* the political economy of the new English state he inscribed was to become the stuff of imaginative literature in any number of ways.[44] Theatre audiences divided into Whig and Tory seating arrangements, often wearing partisan insignia, and John Loftis has charted the poli-tical affiliations of drama in the period, from the Whig sympathies of Richard Steele and the actor-managers of Drury Lane Theatre to the suspicion of Tory and even Jacobite inclinations of its rival estab-lishment at Lincoln's Inn Fields. By the reign of George I, the dramatic declamation of Whig principles had become widespread: 'The steady iteration of the apostrophes to liberty and freedom in times and places that are fictionally remote ultimately establishes the illusion that Whig political philosophy is founded on immutable natural law. The drama-tists could after all control the political forces operating in their trage-dies; and they made them operate in the manner described by Locke in *The Second Treatise of Government*.'[45] By their metaphorical and analogi-cal identifications, Whig writers were helping to seal and certify the Revolution Settlement as 'literal' reality.

The terms and traditions of social hierarchy with their concomitant sense of a 'proper place', socially fixed and determined in the scheme of things were being significantly redesigned and extended: Swift, Pope and Gay each sought advantage from these opportunities and each came to cast a jaundiced, frequently a reactionary, but also a highly entertaining and satirically acute eye upon what they saw happening to the society in which they lived. But their public attitudes and private actions diverge, so that while Pope's later poetry expresses an ideology whose character is that of a family-based, Christian aristocrat or landed gentleman, voicing hostility to an arriviste élite of, as he saw it, corrupt financiers, bankers and brokers and the government they constructed,[46] his personal decision-making suggests more ambivalent orientations. Publicly propounding what has come to be known as the gloom of the Tory satirists (with the precise nature of his own Toryism, like everything else about his convictions and attitudes, still the subject

---

[44] R. Ashcraft and M. M. Goldsmith, 'Locke, Revolution Principles, and the Formation of Whig Ideology', *The Historical Journal*, 26, 4 (1983), pp. 773–800.

[45] John Loftis, *The Politics of Drama in Augustan England* (Oxford, 1963), pp. 82–3.

[46] Brean Hammond, *Pope* (Brighton, 1986), p. 3.

of animated debate), Pope treated the advent of the new order with a mixture of fear, suspicion, moralising contempt and feigned incomprehension – and opportunism. Quick to subject the mercenary spirit of his times and the characters who embodied it to his sometimes lacerating satire, he was not slow to exploit the potentially enriching facilities of a newly burgeoning trade in stocks and shares. One of the few things we can say with certainty about the social and political relationships and orientations of the Scriblerians is that they are marked by perplexing contradictions.

It was never likely that such extraordinary individuals as these would be easily constrained within party labels, particularly at a time when political divisions were still in the active process of defining and composing themselves, and Isaac Kramnick borrows a phrase from Karl Mannheim to suggest instead that what these writers shared with Bolingbroke, their acknowledged leader at crucial points in the early decades of the century, was a set of attitudes and predispositions that might more properly be described as a common 'style of thought'.[47] While the clash of the Whig and Tory parties was the prime, if not always the prevailing element during the extended moment of the Scriblerians, their precise political dispositions were complicated and fluid:

The Whigs were certainly not as conservative as the Tories, but only a minority of them were committed to political principles which might be regarded as genuinely liberal. Most Whigs were certainly opposed to absolute monarchy and were ready to support the right of subjects to resist an arbitrary tyrant, but in many other respects they were deeply conservative. It is essential to remember that the Whigs shared many of the prejudices, assumptions and ultimate objectives of their Tory opponents. Most active Whigs were also men of substance who wanted political power to be exercised by responsible men of their own type and who wanted a stable, orderly, even hierarchical society which would protect the privileges and property of the wealthy and influential.[48]

But these facts and emphases should not obscure very real allegiances and mobilisations in which public political identification was a serious matter. The rhetoric of order, hierarchy and stability that Pope utilises related more comfortably and naturally to a traditional, landed society than it did to an innovative, capitalist one, so the claim that nothing in

---

[47] Isaac Kramnick, *Bolingbroke and his Circle: The Politics of Nostalgia in the Age of Walpole* (London, 1968), p. 3.
[48] H. T. Dickinson, *Liberty and Property: Political Ideology in Eighteenth-Century Britain* (London, 1979), p. 298.

the gamut of Pope's writing specifically indicates that he disapproved of the revolution (as opposed to developments which took place *after* 1688), or that Pope supported either James II or the Old Pretender, is both salutary and potentially misleading.[49] It is hardly likely that Pope would have committed himself unambiguously to print in support of causes and individuals that could have brought serious repercussions to a Roman Catholic writer struggling to make his way independently in a hostile world. On the other hand, there is now a substantial measure of agreement that what most Whigs and Tories were arguing about was in fact how they might best protect and preserve their own – shared – privileged position in society. It was a prime function of the expanding public sphere of debate to enable and confirm this preservation. The spoils of war had been divided, and no matter how furiously the reins of government were subsequently striven for, there was a wider sense in which respect for the security and stability of liberty and property for an ascending bourgeoisie effectively promoted a cross-political identification of assumed mutuality and interest. Domestically, the battles for ideological supremacy and political power were no longer to be military, and when Pope wrote in the *Essay on Man* that as far as government is concerned, 'whate'er is best administer'd is best',[50] he was implicitly testifying to a class-based commonalty that after the Civil War upheavals was under no circumstances to be brought into question again.[51] Nonetheless, the Scriblerians condescended to particulars whenever they addressed themselves to specific issues, constructing ideological contexts for them and allying themselves with the Tory and against the Whig interest. And when we recall that before the Revolution, the Tories had stood for the divine right of kings to rule and hereditary succession and non-resistance, in opposition to the Whig theory of monarchy based upon consent which allowed the people to resist an arbitrary monarch, we remember, too, how retrograde were many aspects of the programme generally supported by the Scriblerians. After the accession of William III, the Tory rank and file expressed their hostility to the King's expensive foreign policy, to the scale of the concessions to the Dissenters, to the expansion of govern-

[49] J. A. Downie, '1688: Pope and the Rhetoric of Jacobitism', in *Pope: New Contexts*, edited by David Fairer (London, 1990), pp. 21–2.

[50] Maynard Mack, *The Poems of Alexander Pope: Vol. III, i, An Essay on Man* (London, 1950), p. 124. Subsequent quotations are given parenthetically in the text.

[51] Brean Hammond refers to 'the unconscious ideology of class' in Pope's poetry (*Pope*, p. 5). It is difficult to determine the borderlines of intention conscious or otherwise, but I know of nothing in the gamut of Pope's writing to suggest that he was not aware of what he was doing.

ment administrative power and to the creation of the National Debt and the system of Public Credit associated with the newly formed Bank of England. Unable to uphold their former principles of divine right and hereditary succession as openly as they might, the Tories claimed, instead, that they were defending the interests of the whole nation, the 'Country', in opposition to the dangerous policies of the Court.[52] It was natural for them to see themselves as the defenders of a landed interest perceived as under threat from a Whig-inspired financial revolution, since the great majority of the Tories were themselves landed gentlemen having little or no contact with the new money markets; and the prejudices and genuine fears of the landed interest as embodied in and represented by the Tory squires became a major element in the political controversies of the period.[53]

The sometime Scriblerians formed a leading cohort in this debate, and with Pope increasingly at their head as Bolingbroke's effectiveness and influence waned during the 1730s. Obsessed with the all-too-visible establishment of the political power of money, one of the constant charges of Bolingbroke and his friends was that this power *had* been institutionalised, and had been able to command the commonwealth. The financial revolution of 1690–1750 was the most meaningful social experience in the lives of Bolingbroke and his circle, informing all their writings on politics and society and feeding their gloom, their satire and their indignation: 'they saw an aristocratic social and political structure being undermined by money and new financial institutions and they didn't like it.'[54] The personal, literary and ideological relationships between Bolingbroke and the Tory wits were long-standing and intimate and when, in the late 1720s, Bolingbroke's newspaper *The Craftsman* became a central platform for the anti-Walpole opposition, terms, images, and structures of argument which appeared there also figure in the writing of Swift, Gay and Pope. What has been said about Pope and Bolingbroke applies more generally to the associated group: 'They held in common ideals, concepts, a specialised vocabulary containing key words like liberty, corruption, and constitution, and a myth for the times that derives from their mutual alienation from the direction being taken by progress.'[55] During the 1730s, Pope edited Patriot plays and continued to hero-worship Bolingbroke, although he was to become increasingly disabused and even cynical about the possibility, let alone

[52] H. T. Dickinson, *Bolingbroke* (London, 1970), pp. 15–16.   [53] Ibid., p. 19
[54] Kramnick, *Bolingbroke and his Circle*, p. 4.
[55] Hammond, *Pope and Bolingbroke*, p. 9.

the likelihood, of a Patriot opposition displacing Walpole. As we attempt to re-assemble sometimes cross-party ideological preferences and assumptions that could be promoted as a cohesive fabric of civic and political identification, we realise that by associating themselves with and significantly articulating the fears and prejudices aroused during the long years of Whig dominance, and thus placing their writing at the service of those who opposed the financial and political power then expanding, Opposition writers were directly challenging an evolving modernity and progress. While they specifically opposed Walpole's lengthening record of public dishonesty, in a wider perspective this writing was produced to oppose the English Revolution as it went on to install itself in power and construct a cultured and civil society congenial to its interests. So I would apply to others the suggestion that the political impulse in Pope was deep-set and tenacious, living along the line of almost everything he put to paper,[56] but with an emphasis on politics in an older, Aristotelian sense where *zoon politikon* signified a social, rather than a subsequently more narrowly defined party political orientation for public action and concern. The *politea* originally referred to the structure of civic relationships within the City and given that broader remit, the Scriblerians' literary reactions to the entry of finance capitalism into social affairs becomes a matter of correspondingly broader cultural enquiry. As recurring tropes in their writing, stock markets, share-dealing, paper money and public credit significantly shape their textual responses in a conflict of attitude and action where discursive and practical economies intersect. Passion and fantasy inscribe themselves divergently in public and private consciousness.

As far as his poetry is concerned, Pope does not engage directly with monetary processes until well after the South Sea Bubble had forcefully educated a wide section of public opinion into some of the mysteries and iniquities inherent in the new scheme of things, and not until the 1730s does he develop a comprehensive opposition. He was, though, living and writing while the revolutions in finance and commerce got under way, and as early as *Windsor Forest* (1704–13)[57] was singing the praises of an English trading empire on its way to exploiting as much of the world's resources as it could reach. It has become clear that besides

---

[56] John Aden, *Pope's Once and Future Kings: Satire and Politics in the Early Career* (Knoxville, TN, 1978), p. 177.

[57] E. Audra and Aubrey Williams, *The Poems of Alexander Pope: Vol I, Pastoral Poetry and An Essay on Criticism* (London, 1961), pp. 145–94. Subsequent quotations are given parenthetically in the text.

being written in praise of Queen Anne's Stuart rule, *Windsor Forest* is freighted with political sub-texts of various kinds,[58] and is additionally complicated by the fact that at the time of writing the forest itself was by no means as calm and settled as Pope would have us believe.[59] The poem may, then, be a piece of political myth-making, but it suggests an early alertness to the possessive egoism that an ethic of conspicuous consumption develops and strengthens. As England's ships colonise markets wherever they find them, commodities flood into London, so that in place of the old wants, satisfied by the productions of the country, we find new wants, requiring for their satisfaction the products of different places. In place of the old local and national seclusion and self-sufficiency, we have intercourse in every direction as a particular form of global interdependence begins to establish itself.[60] Accordingly, Old Father Thames proclaims:

> For me the Balm shall bleed, and Amber flow,
> The Coral redden, and the Ruby glow,
> The Pearly Shell its lucid Globe infold,
> And Phoebus warm the ripening Ore to Gold.
> The Time shall come, when free as Seas or Wind,
> Unbounded *Thames* shall flow for all Mankind,
> Whole Nations enter with each swelling Tyde,
> And Seas but join the Regions they divide;
> Earth's distant Ends our Glory shall behold,
> And the new World launch forth to seek the Old.
> Then Ships of uncouth Form shall stem the Tyde,
> And Feather'd People crowd my wealthy Side,
> And naked Youths and painted Chiefs admire
> Our Speech, our Colour, and our strange Attire!   (393–406)

In a poem ostensibly a paean to peace, there are various mystifications at work; notably the co-ordination of military conquest (106–10) with the hunting pastimes of a landed aristocracy, and subsequently the separation of naval power (220–22) from the trading operations of England's maritime fleets that will paradoxically liberate those 'naked Youths and painted Chiefs' it introduces as spectacle. Beginning and ending in English woods and fields, *Windsor Forest* is a powerful act of textual colonisation, and can be read as early glimmerings of what by the end of the century would become recognisable as a Whig interpre-

---

[58] J. R. Moore, 'Windsor Forest and William III', *Modern Language Notes*, 56 (1951), pp. 451–4; Laura Brown, *Alexander Pope* (Oxford, 1985), pp. 28–45; Hammond, *Pope*, pp. 33–8.
[59] E. P. Thompson, *Whigs and Hunters: The Origins of the Black Act* (London, 1975), pp. 27–115.
[60] Karl Marx, *Early Writings* (Harmondsworth, 1975), p. 71.

tation of historical progress flowing to all from the beneficent operations of commerce between nations. Already, Pope is displaying an attraction towards the world produced by trade and traders in ways that connect with Joseph Addison's contemporary celebration of the merchant class as most useful members of the commonwealth:

They knit mankind together in a mutual intercourse of good Offices, distribute the Gifts of Nature, find Work for the Poor, add Wealth to the Rich, and Magnificence to the Great. Our *English* Merchant converts the tin of his own country into Gold, and exchanges his Wooll for Rubies. The *Mahometans* are clothed in our *British* Manufacture, and the Inhabitants of the Frozen Zone warmed with the Fleeces of our Sheep.[61]

In *Windsor Forest* we watch an ideology in the making that is not easily constrained within party political paradigms. The times were fluid, and writing is sensitive to change: combining preference for the values of a landed aristocracy with praise for a Tory peace concluded on behalf of a Stuart monarch reigning over expanded trade, the poem constructs a royalist adaptation of progress in the economic and social foundations of society to traditional hierarchies. As the world comes to London, London is changed itself and learns to see the world differently: looking out to a transforming society leads to alterations in self-perception. During the experimentation and confusion out of which it established itself as the centre of the world's money-markets as well as the locus of world trade, in the City of London civic relationships were being massively reordered by a scale of change never before experienced. How the political character in civil society was affected by all of this becomes the matter of the Scriblerus satires: how the private personality fared is the subject of *The Rape of The Lock*.

---

[61] *The Spectator*, ed. Bond, I, p. 296

1

A culture of commodities: 'trivial things' in *The Rape of the Lock*

> What tho' no Credit doubting Wits may give?
> The fair and Innocent shall still believe.
>
> *(Rape of the Lock*, I, 39–40)

When Geoffrey Tillotson comments in the final paragraph of his Twickenham introduction to *The Rape of the Lock* that 'the second version is inexhaustible',[1] we pause. If the wealth of annotation he provides initially appears to undermine his remark, a continuing proliferation of commentary on the poem demonstrates how right he is. We have been invited to recover its political subtext as an exercise in repressed emotional Jacobitism,[2] shown how it stylishly subsumes a library of Renaissance attitudes,[3] and asked to reconsider some of its perspectives in the light of feminist critiques.[4] Yet Pope so successfully balances the mock-epic's jesting irreverence towards and ironised respect for classical precedent that we are still able to read his first major work as 'the mock-epic of a mock-world, the make-believe celebration of a society of play-actors'.[5] That too has gathered different emphases and there is more to say about the make-believe aspect of the poem's performance. But I want first to go back to Tillotson's doubt that 'though no reader can fail to be "conscious of the rich Brocade" of the 1714 version, the story itself is not so proportionate in 1714 as in 1711'

---

[1] Tillotson, *Rape of the Lock*, p. 124.

[2] Howard Erskine-Hill, 'Literature and the Jacobite Cause', *Modern Language Studies*, 9 (Fall 1979), pp. 15–20.

[3] Alastair Fowler, 'The Paradoxical Machinery of *The Rape of the Lock*', in *Alexander Pope: Essays for the Tercentenary*, edited by C. Nicholson (Aberdeen, 1988), pp. 151–65.

[4] Felicity A. Nussbaum, *The Brink of All We Hate: English Satires on Women, 1660–1750* (Lexington, 1984), chapter 8; Ellen Pollack, 'Rereading *The Rape of the Lock*: Pope and the Paradox of Female Power', *Studies in Eighteenth-Century Culture 10*, edited by H. C. Payne (Madison, WI, 1981), pp. 429–44; Valerie Rumbold, *Women's Place in Pope's World* (Cambridge, 1989), pp. 67–85.

[5] J. S. Cunningham, *Pope: 'The Rape of the Lock'* (London, 1961), p. 14.

(*TE* II, p. 124), to develop the suggestion that additions to a work of art can so modify the earlier structure as to create a new overall pattern which is equally satisfactory.[6] In light-hearted mood Pope could describe the five-canto version as 'a pretty complete picture of the life of our modern ladies in this idle town' (*P. Corr.* I, p. 211), and his alterations imply that what the poem has to come to terms with is change itself; change which then has to be interpreted as natural or normal, or else as unnatural, artificial and grotesque.[7] Historians have interpreted the period in considerable detail, so while Pope's affectionately indulgent attitude towards the 'beau monde' of Queen Anne's reign and his sheer delight in satirising high society together produce a glittering surface, we can hear other resonances.

Louis Landa's treatment of 'Pope's Belinda' persuasively places her in the economic contexts of her time. Belinda as a consumer, the embodiment of luxury, whose ambience is defined by the wealth of objects with which she surrounds and decks herself is presented as the focal point in a vast nexus of enterprises, a vast commercial expansion which stirred English imaginations to dwell on thoughts of greatness and magnificence. Landa is also sensitive to a defining ambiguity in the poem whereby Belinda might be construed affirmatively, as a celebration of the new riches she uses and wears, but also negatively, as a coded threat to English produce because of the foreign imports she has purchased.[8] We can initiate a differently emphasised reading by recalling that two years after the complete version of *The Rape* appeared Defoe was writing *Robinson Crusoe*, and that three years after *Crusoe* appeared, *Moll Flanders* was for sale. With his curious amalgam of landed estate and improving individualism, Crusoe is an epitome of economic man whose island existence shields him from the mystifying transactions of exchange in a market society, but whose stock-book contains a catalogue of the useful objects he possesses. Because he is sovereign lord over all he surveys and owns, the relations between Robinson and the objects that form his wealth are relatively simple and transparent. But until she becomes a plantation-owner in Virginia, Moll Flanders lives largely in an urban environment, and her relationship to her possessions is correspondingly more involved:

---

[6] Howard Erskine-Hill, 'The "New World" of Pope's *Dunciad*', *Renaissance and Modern Studies*, 6 (1962), pp. 46–67. Rpt. in Maynard Mack, *Essential Articles for the Study of Alexander Pope* (London, 1964), p. 751.

[7] Ralph Cohen, 'Transformation in "The Rape of the Lock" ', *Eighteenth Century Studies*, 2, no. 3 (1969), p. 206.

[8] Louis Landa, 'Pope's Belinda, the Great Emporie of the World, and the Wondrous Worm', in *Essays in Eighteenth-Century English Literature* (Princeton, NJ, 1980), pp. 178–98.

We notice, for instance, that Moll's world contains many things – tangible things such as watches and wigs and yardage and goods and necklaces and dresses and barrels and bales and bottles and trunks ... In *Moll* there is a relatively great frequency in the naming of that kind of object which constitutes material wealth ... Schematically what has been happening here is the conversion of all subjective, emotional and moral experience – implicit in the fact of Moll's five years of marriage and motherhood – into pocket and bank money, into the materially measurable.[9]

Compare that with Tillotson's recognition that 'the epic is thing-less beside Pope's poem with its close-packed material objects' (p. 119), and we begin to detect commodities flooding textuality. Of course, Belinda is wealthier than Moll, and across the gulf of social rank that separates them nothing so vulgar as money is allowed to trouble Pope's heroine. But they move in the same city nonetheless, and it could even be argued that their social separation had a topographical foundation since London was itself a double town: one end being a royal and parliamentary capital, governed, so far as it had a government, by an obscure condominium of palace officials and nominees of the Dean and chapter of Westminster, while the other was virtually a mercantile republic.[10] So when Pope, in the letter to the Mariott ladies just quoted, suggests that: 'people who would rather [*The Rape*] were let alone laugh at it, and seem heartily merry, at the same time that they are uneasy' (*P. Corr.* I, p. 211), we are left wondering whether the uneasy laughter stems in part from an unwilled recognition that the Molls and the Belindas of the period differed not so much in kind as in degree. Because it socially contextualises the wit and grace with which Pope embellishes his perceptions of the times the degree, as for Shakespeare's Ulysses, becomes crucial: but they were times of profound change and the mock-heroic functions ambivalently in a poem that also seeks to individualise some of the effects of contemporary events. If heroic satire reproduces the stability and security of classical order to structure its perceptions and provide them with a hierarchy of status and value, then the strategy of attaching a contemporary narrative to classical frames of reference, could aim to stabilise in a preferential scale and system of subordinations a modernity that was burgeoning, disruptive and decisively redefining value and practice in everyday life.

Dryden had acknowledged a traditional incorporation of monarchy into heroic form when he dedicated his *The Conquest of Granada* (1672) to

---

[9] Dorothy Van Ghent, *The English Novel: Form and Function* (New York, 1953), p. 34.
[10] John Carswell, *The South Sea Bubble* (London, 1960), p. 2.

the Duke of York: 'Heroique Poesie has alwayes been sacred to Princes and to Heroes',[11] he declared, and in his heroic drama the aristocratic mode of conceiving political experience, where the fate and fortune of the state depends upon the prowess and magnanimity of nobly born leaders, appears in exaggerated form.[12] Since then for Tory poets the heroic tradition, 'always Royalist (the king's Divine Right made the best magic symbol), had died on their hands'.[13] But Dryden had shown a way to develop mock-heroic forms too, and Pope often alludes to *MacFlecknoe*: he builds upon Dryden's example and acknowledges his debt, but he had other designs in mind. Where systems of credit promote individual expectations that restructure fixed forms into a generalised mobility, the mock-heroic could play instead with expansions and diminutions of other kinds and, in playing, could display different orders of ambivalence. Pope seems anyway to have had a love–hate relationship with his society and in *The Rape of the Lock* any nostalgic yearning for classically cognisable boundaries for history and personality is tempered and transmuted through an affectionate critique of the present. It then becomes possible for us to read the form of *The Rape* as an ambiguous strategy of containment, with Pope at this early stage of his career still able to find comic equivalence for the separations and conjunctions a developing social market entails. At any rate, when Dorothy Van Ghent goes on to notice that the tangible, material objects with which Moll is so passionately concerned are not at all vivid in texture,[14] she is indicating the different registers used to present these characters, since the opposite is true of the luminous, vibrant things that compose Belinda's universe: Pope produces a linguistically luxurious text whereas the unambiguous celebrant Defoe does not. Defoe shows us a functional inventiveness and comes to us as an emblem of the projecting spirit of self-interested individualism. Pope had more than his share of this, but he reveals other aspects of its psychology. While poor Crusoe has no sex-life in his island domain, Moll displays a combative kind of initiative in her pursuit of material security; Belinda, on the other hand, lives a life of relative passivity. Moll's vigorous scramble for the goods of living is transformed in Belinda's couplet-world of ease and elegance. As the 'thing-hood'

[11] *The Works of John Dryden*, edited by E. N. Hooker, H. T. Swedenberg Jr, V. A. Dearing, G. Guffey, E. Miner, S. H. Monk, A. Roper, 20 vols. (Berkeley, CA, 1956–89), XI, p. 3
[12] Loftis, *Politics of Drama*, p. 14.
[13] William Empson, *Some Versions of Pastoral: A Study of the Pastoral Form in Literature* (London, 1935, rpt. 1950), p. 200.
[14] Van Ghent, *English Novel*, p. 34.

which Moll sees as the index of success and makes the aim of many of her relationships is internalised in Belinda's subjectivity, the energetically achieved satisfactions of the one become the fetishised sexuality of the other. In a society of fashionable spectacle, Belinda, a 'classic' portrait of woman in the new *rentier* class, becomes an object of voyeurism for others – 'evr'y Eye was fix'd on her alone' (II, 6) – as well as for herself: 'A heav'nly image in the Glass appears, / To that she bends, to that her Eyes she rears' (I, 125–6). In a creative display of pre-Marxian perceptions of modern economics, an object-dominated consciousness begins to reveal itself, with practically every couplet inferring connections between a personal and social life and the world of traded artefacts. Patterns of imagery and metaphor ingeniously propose ways in which human life is 'lived' by means of an extension into the purchasable possessions that significantly animate the narrative. 'Trivial things' operate powerfully in the world Pope constructs and human determinations are correspondingly adapted. In a society where credit-payment was dissolving the social frame into a shifting mobility of objects that were desired and expectations that were fantasised about, a comic displacement of values in the famous line from the equally famous toilet scene, 'Puffs, Powders, Patches, Bibles, Billet-doux' (I, 138), satirises the collapse of traditional religious associations as an accommodation to the new order. Similarly, jarring beliefs and values are rhythmically harmonised in the couplet: 'On her white Breast a sparkling *Cross* she wore, / Which *Jews* might kiss, and infidels adore' (II, 7–8), where the epithet 'sparkling' harks back to the 'glitt'ring spoil' with which Belinda has just been decked at her dressing-table, and suppresses any specifically Christian connotations adhering to the image of crucifixion. The cross is reduced to an item of jewellery and its power equated with Belinda's breast, after either of which, along with the Baron, Jew or infidel may 'legitimately' lust. All the trading nations of the world met daily around the Royal Exchange, but the Baron is foremost among those who are enchanted by Belinda's decorative charms; and if fetishised rape is a corrupt intensification of desire, then a perverted lust motivates the Baron's assault upon Belinda. As far as he is concerned the moral of *The Rape* may well be the already ignored warning not to treat woman as an object to be obtained and possessed. We first meet him in a dream-fantasy while she sleeps – he enters as distracting presence before their botched physical encounter, to become a signifier in different ways.

Pope's festive inventiveness initially distracts us much as the characters he creates are distracted from themselves. A giddy world of

gilded chariots, garters and stars dazzles our attention, and these
deflections, arising in part from an evidently pleasurable indulgence
towards the world being constructed, combine with the complicating
oppositions and interactions between classical allusion and a present
thus parodied to elicit a kind of ambivalence in our response. By
shaping a comic surface with serious resonances as analogue for the
divisions and self-divisions the poem exposes, the form of the mock-
heroic suggests a nervous tension between past and present codes of
value, and becomes a suitable frame for connecting commerce with
changing ways of feeling and evaluation:

> With varying Vanities from ev'ry Part,
> They shift the moving Toyshop of their Heart;
> Where Wigs with Wigs, with Sword-knots Sword-knots strive,
> Beaus banish Beaus, and Coaches Coaches drive.
> This erring Mortals Levity may call,
> Oh blind to Truth! the Sylphs contrive it all.
>
> (I, 99–104)

In the fantastic fiction of Belinda's dream the heart has become the
production centre of a kind of puppet-life: her subconscious is open to
suggestion, and the world in which she is that day to move with such
apparent freedom is comically exposed as significantly moved by forces
beyond the human. As objects proliferate, London citizens are metony-
mically displaced. We catch a glimpse of fashionably presented young
males jostling vigorously for a share of Belinda's glancing smile and feel
something of their effort in a difficult passage of sibilants: 'with Sword-
knots Sword-knots strive'. Coaches are driving themselves too, in a
further high-spirited expropriation of human agency. Purchasable artefacts render the human agent, the beaus, and the aural pun is delight-
ful, inseparable from, because identified through, the things which
make their intentions known and effective. Subsequent interpenet-
rations of the personal and the artificial are so consistently developed
that by the time we read 'But now secure the painted Vessel glides' (II,
47), we are momentarily disconcerted as to whether Belinda or her boat
is passing by.

   In the construction of his leading character Pope incorporates his
perceptions of how the world of things refashions a world of subjectivity
in its own image, and Tillotson quotes from a contemporary account (in
The Guardian, a newspaper to which Pope also contributed), evidence
that some of these perceptions were already established in the world of
print:

As I cast my Eye upon her Bosom, it appeared to be all of Chrystal, and so wonderfully transparent, that I saw every Thought in her Heart. The first Images I discovered in it were Fans, Silks, Ribbonds, Laces, and many other Gewgaws, which lay so thick together, that the whole Heart was nothing but a Toy-shop. These all faded away and vanished, when immediately I discerned a long Train of Coaches and six, Equipages and Liveries that ran through the Heart one after another in a very great hurry etc. etc.[15]

Pope was to joke with friends about similar fantasies and expectations during the year of the South Sea Bubble, while in *The Rape* the listed commodities of popular journalism come to life, generating activity and responses themselves and becoming part of the movement of the world he assembles. They are 'mighty contests' rising from 'trivial things' here because they concern in mocking ways the restructuring of human agency, and in lines from what may be a rejected 'preface' to the poem Belinda is invited to consider 'How things are priz'd, which once belong'd to you', and warned of the 'artifice of mind' which leads to her undoing (*TE* VI, pp. 107–8). In polished and memorable cadence *The Rape of the Lock* offers a poetic grammar of the process whereby relations between people assume the characteristics of being relations between things, and it becomes an insight into Pope's understanding that when Marx struggled with this movement of what has come to be called reification, the terms he used can be adapted to describe the sylphs.

The first sentence of *Capital* calls the appearance of wealth in capitalist societies an 'immense collection of commodities', but soon Marx is negotiating some of the difficulties we encounter in *The Rape*. 'A commodity', he writes, 'appears at first sight an extremely obvious and trivial thing. But its analysis brings out that it is a very strange thing, abounding in metaphysical subtleties and theological niceties.' As he tracks the shift from use to exchange via paper money in what he called 'the metamorphosis of commodities', Marx is soon referring to their newly acquired 'mystical', 'enigmatic' and 'mysterious' character.[16] Down in their salons and coffee-shops, early eighteenth-century Londoners were learning that credit-based promissory notes could change material circumstance. Individuals were negotiating, relating and doing business together towards profitable expectations they could not immediately translate into hard cash. But they have to *believe* that this will happen, otherwise they will not venture in the first place. In a generalised slippage from metal specie to paper forms, belief and

---

[15] *Guardian*, p. 106. Quoted in part by Tillotson, *Rape of the Lock*, p. 152, 99n.
[16] Karl Marx, *Capital*, 3 vols. (Harmondsworth, 1976), I, pp. 125, 163, 164, 198.

personal opinion are at a premium where notes of credit postpone the day of reckoning onto an indefinite and uncertain future, so that subsequent transactions can then take place, often to spectacular individual enrichment. As they watched credo slip into credit, Pope and his friends were to become genuinely alarmed at the speed with which valuations of individual worth came to depend on an assessment of personal self-confidence and the quality of fashionable self-presentation. Purchasable appearance was nudging older forms of recognition and estimation aside as stock markets brought into sociable form the buying and selling of enrichment where not what you saw but what you believed would come to pass could and did transform actuality. Marx was so exasperated by citizens of an energetic bourgeois culture for happily relating to each other in such ways that he turned to what he called the misty realms of religion for an appropriate analogy: 'There, the products of the human brain appear as autonomous figures endowed with a life of their own, which enter into relations both with each other and with the human race. So it is in the world of commodities with the products of men's hands. I call this ... fetishism.'[17]

Marx should have read *The Rape of the Lock*. What he has to say feeds into it uncannily at times, including an appropriate description of the Baron's transgression of the laws of things:

In order that these objects may enter into relation with each other as commodities, their guardians must place themselves in relation to one another as persons whose will resides in those objects, and must behave in such a way that each does not appropriate the commodity of the other, and alienate his own, except through an act to which both parties consent.[18]

The Baron breaks that rule, and Pope plays inventive games with the seemingly autonomous figures of his sylphic machinery. But he nonetheless names his deities after objects:

> Haste then ye Spirits! to your Charge repair;
> The flutt'ring fan be *Zephyretta's* Care;
> The Drops to thee, *Brillante*, we consign;
> And, *Momentilla*, let the watch be thine;
> Do thou, *Crispissa*, tend her fav'rite Lock;
> *Ariel* himself shall be the Guard of *Shock*. (II, 111–16)

In a comic division of labour the sylphs attend only to the objects that name them, and at the moment of violent appropriation they are as ineffectual in their task 'in air' as the notion of honour is inoperative in

---

[17] Ibid., p. 165.　　　[18] Ibid., p. 178.

the mundane realm. While in the air, though, the sylphs are glorious, drawing from Pope some of his most attractive lines:

> Some to the Sun their Insect-Wings unfold,
> Waft on the Breeze, or sink in Clouds of Gold.
> Transparent Forms, too fine for mortal Sight,
> Their fluid Bodies half dissolv'd in Light.
> Loose to the Wind their airy Garments flew,
> Thin glitt'ring Textures of the filmy Dew;
> Dipt in the richest Tincture of the Skies,
> Where Light disports in ever-mingling Dies,
> While ev'ry Beam new transient Colours flings,
> Colours that change whene'er they wave their Wings.

(II, 59–68)

A sky glittering with the new wealth on display forms something of an apotheosis for the ambivalently celebrated riches elsewhere in the poem. Both tied to objects and living an apparently independent existence, the metamorphic brilliance of Pope's mock-deities relates them to a world where all that is solid melts into other dimensions; into a world that is experienced as real and unreal at the same time. By prompting circumstance, a machinery of agency 'too fine for mortal sight' stimulates a passion for possessions that have acquired a partial autonomy. The question of who or what is controlling human affairs in the world of the poem is left provocatively unresolved, but the sense of something out there, some hidden hand in the heavens, or 'light *militia* of the lower sky' (I, 42) guiding opportunity and provoking response was a sense explored in a variety of ways during the early years of the eighteenth century, including by some who were politically opposed to Pope, as newspaper readers were discovering.

Richard Steele's sometime protagonist in *The Tatler*, Isaac Bicker-staff, walks towards the Royal Exchange with his friend Pacolet, and listens to explanations of possibility, opportunity and disappointment that often seem to present themselves as random chance. Pacolet is concerned to explain this 'unseen hand', as he calls it, and in doing so he describes a version of Pope's light militia. 'Beings of a superior rank to mankind', Pacolet tells Isaac, 'frequently visit the habitations of men' to change their behaviour, so that what they think of as chance and accident are due, rather, to 'interventions of aerial beings, as they are benevolent or hurtful to the nature of man, and attend his steps in the tracts of ambition, of business, and of pleasure'. When mood and activity are perceived as being manipulated in this way, then a kind of phantom subjectivity is seen operating with and upon, and significantly altering, individual response. Still in Pacolet's company, Bickerstaff is then introduced to two merchants who 'are not real men, but are mere shades and figures' called Alethes and Verisimilis, allegories of Conscience and of Honour respectively whose names suggest truth and appearance. When the man of conscience parts from honour his appearance changes into one 'that attracted a sudden inclination for him and his interests in all who beheld him', and trading takes place. When conscience and honour come together again in Exchange Alley, no one approaches them, and when they go into the Exchange itself, Bickerstaff and Pacolet follow them and see a third figure, a great merchant to whom everyone is paying court. 'This person', Pacolet explains, 'is the demon or genius of credit: his name is Umbra. If you observe, he follows Alethes and Verisimilis at a distance; and indeed has no foundation for the figure he makes in the world, but that he is thought to keep their cash; though at the same time, none who trust him would trust the others for a groat.' When these 'three spectres', of honour, of conscience and of credit are 'jumbled into one place' business picks up around them on the Exchange. But soon conscience withdraws, being unwilling to trade 'further than he had immediate funds to answer', and Verisimilis, while claiming 'revenues large enough to go on his own bottom' stops doing business because it is 'below one of his family to condescend to trade in his own name'. Watching this, Bickerstaff is troubled at the thought of the London Exchange in thrall solely to the figure of Credit, Umbra, until Pacolet reassures him that traders have nothing to do with the honour or conscience of their correspondents as long as their behaviour does nothing to damage 'their credit or their purses'. It is made clear to Bickerstaff that among merchants, 'honour and credit are not valuable possessions in themselves or pursued out of a principle of justice; but merely as they are serviceable to ambition and to commerce'. Bickerstaff learns to see the market as a generator of fictional confidence, a source of value and motive without any basis other than a shared belief in a shared credit-worthiness powerful enough to bind Parliament and trade together: 'For', says Pacolet: 'you may in this one tract of London and Westminster see the imaginary motives on which the greatest affairs move, as well as in rambling over the face of the earth'.[19]

The Rape's sylphic metamorphoses become multiply suggestive as part of a social effort to understand and interpret the remarkable effects of credit in London's expanding money markets, and in this respect the

---

[19] *The Tatler*, edited by Donald F. Bond, 3 vols. (Oxford, 1987), I, pp. 342–7.

self-transforming powers of the sylphs look forward in one direction to Marx's description of money as representing 'the divine existence of commodities, while they represent its earthly form'.[20] Marx remonstrates with this order: 'All things are other than themselves ... and ... an *inhuman* power rules over everything',[21] whereas in Pope's comic transubstantiations nothing is quite what it seems. If duties are miscarried, the profusion of objects and materials cluttering Belinda's dressing-table will take their revenge on the sylphic world:

> *Gums* and *Pomatums* shall his Flight restrain,
> While clog'd he beats his silken Wings in vain;
> Or Alom-*Stypticks* with contracting Power
> Shrink his thin Essence like a rivell'd Flower.   (II, 129–32)

In Belinda's house similar instruments and substances cause her pain as she prepares her appearance:

> Was it for this you took such constant Care
> The *Bodkin*, *Comb*, and *Essence* to prepare;
> For this your Locks in Paper-Durance bound,
> For this with tort'ring Irons wreath'd around?
> For this with Fillets strain'd your tender Head,
> And bravely bore the double Loads of Lead?   (IV, 97–102)

Things glide referentially from one realm to another, now separating subject from object, now merging them, and in this shifting kaleidoscope of richness and representation any separation of powers in the constitution of subjectivity is elided, leaving us with contradictory senses of who or what is determining motive and action at any given time; sometimes the sylphs, sometimes the objects they present for our attention, and sometimes the human characters as they relate to both. At any rate, it soon becomes clear that the object-spirits of an object-world cannot protect Belinda herself. The elaborate fiction of their several duties and responsibilities collapses when she succumbs, 'in spite of all her Art', to the natural occurrence of sexual desire for an earthly lover (III, 143), desire which abolishes Ariel's power at a stroke. Until that single, isolated moment, and then subsequently on to the poem's conclusion, sexuality is repressed, attenuated, fetishised – a surrogate performance in the game of Ombre, or a fantasy of erotic substitution as in the Baron's need for the lock of hair itself. We have glowing cheeks, evening temptations and the glance and whisper of erotic dreams, until

[20] Marx, *Grundrisse*, p. 221.   [21] Marx, *Early Writings*, p. 366.

the lap-dog Shock, who thought Belinda slept too long, 'Leapt up, and wak'd his Mistress with his Tongue' (I, 116), after which *The Rape of the Lock* systematically traps sexual passion in the inert.

   In keeping with this strategy Belinda's hymen figures as the 'frail *China* Jar' that might 'receive a Flaw' in Canto II (106) to become one of many 'rich *China* Vessels, fal'n from high' that 'In glittring Dust and painted Fragments lie' (III, 159–60) after the Baron's seemingly successful assault. Later, Umbriel's prayer to the Goddess of Spleen will suggest externally stimulated suspicions of sexual intrigue: 'If e'er with airy Horns I planted Heads, / Or rumpled Petticoats, or tumbled beds' (IV, 71–2). But by then we have already played the game of Ombre where military imagery weaves in and out of the sexual conquest it both stages and displaces. Emerging from 'Throngs promiscuous', when the King of Hearts 'falls like Thunder on the prostrate *Ace*' (III, 98), no doubt deploying to conquering effect the rest of whatever 'his many-colour'd Robe concealed', we realise how much the '*Trick*' upon which a whole state depends, has engineered a violent and anyway momentary possession that is elsewhere only aspired to and ultimately denied. The card-King achieves what the Baron, 'Who sought no more than on his Foe to die' (V, 78), does not. At the beginning of the game Belinda 'Burns to encounter two adventrous Knights' (III, 26); during it, sexual activity is suggestively transferred to figures on cards: after the coffee-making ritual which celebrates her success at play, Belinda's ravished hair is fleetingly in the Baron's possession. Between appetite and acquisition, between the Baron's first sight of Belinda's hair and his expropriation of it, the narrative inserts a series of fanciful encounters. We watch the Baron worshipping at his altar, witness the sylphs disporting in colourful self-celebration, play the shadowy game of cards and enjoy the ritualised coffee-making. Then the Baron cuts off the hair which vanishes. A theatre of trope enacts the desire it alienates. But if the ravisher hoped to fashion the lock into a ring he may then display, 'While the Fops envy, and the Ladies stare' (IV, 104), he is to be disappointed. Nor is the lock destined to join the 'three Garters, half a Pair of Gloves; / And all the Trophies of his former Loves' (II, 39–40) which the Baron adores in the privacy of his own home. At the end of the poem everything and nothing has happened; the hair that was fraudulently to symbolise a rape that was *never* on the cards floats off into space unseen by anyone, except the poet and his readers.

   The fetishism that is the hall-mark of the Baron's sexuality is more fully explored as self-estrangement in the character of Belinda, with the famous toilet-scene which closes the first Canto deriving its significance from the comedy of transference around which the whole poem is structured. When Belinda 'intent adores / With Head uncover'd, the *Cosmetic* Powers', her dressing-table prefigures the Baron's altar: she is idolising herself through the medium of the objects that will transform her appearance, that will 'create' her public image:

> And now, unveil'd, the *Toilet* stands display'd,
> Each Silver vase in mystic Order laid.
> First, rob'd in White, the Nymph intent adores
> With Head uncover'd, the *Cosmetic* Pow'rs.
> A heav'nly Image in the Glass appears,
> To that she bends, to that her Eyes she rears;
> Th'inferior Priestess, at her Altar's side,
> Trembling, begins the sacred Rites of Pride.
> Unnumber'd Treasures ope at once, and here
> The various Off'rings of the World appear;
> From each she nicely culls with curious Toil,
> And decks the Goddess with the glitt'ring Spoil.
> This Casket *India's* glowing Gems unlocks,
> And all *Arabia* breathes from yonder Box.
> The Tortoise here and Elephant unite,
> Transform'd to *Combs*, the speckled and the white.
> Here Files of Pins extend their shining Rows,
> Puffs, Powders, Patches, Bibles, Billet-doux.
> Now awful Beauty puts on all its Arms;
> The Fair each moment rises in her Charms,
> Repairs her Smiles, awakens ev'ry Grace,
> And calls forth all the Wonders of her Face;
> Sees by Degrees a purer Blush arise,
> And Keener Lightnings quicken in her Eyes.
> The busy *Sylphs* surround their darling Care;
> These set the Head, and those divide the Hair,
> Some fold the Sleeve, whilst others plait the Gown;
> And Betty's prais'd for Labours not her own.   (I, 121–48)

A potentially riotous assembly of object-agency is subdued to the end of individually enriching appearance, and as Belinda surrenders herself to it, the surrounding cosmetic paraphernalia rises to an active presence: a casket 'unlocks' its jewels, perfume 'breathes', and 'Files of Pins' transitively extend themselves, so that an abstraction, 'awful Beauty', can assume command over the contrived dawn of Belinda's attractions. There is only one Belinda, but a mirror reflexion accurately conveys the artificially constructed appearance that is the object of all her devotions.

In *The Rape*'s perversely enchanted world it is not only Betty's labour that is 'not her own'. In order for Belinda to be 'deck'd with all that Land and Sea afford' (V, 11), England's 'Imperial Race' (II, 27) has been hard at work. If *Windsor Forest* diplomatically preserves poetic distance between commercial rapacity around the globe and the 'Peace and Plenty' it domestically secured, it does at least envisage a world subordinated to London's trading pre-eminence:

> There mighty Nations shall inquire their Doom,
> the World's great Oracle in Times to come;
> There Kings shall sue, and suppliant States be seen
> Once more to bend before a *British* QUEEN. (*Windsor Forest*, 381–4)

As the goods of a commercial empire are traded and consumed in Belinda's city, these more specific relationships of subordination, like so much else in the poem, are etherealised; left to 'Hang o'er the *Box*, and hover round the *Ring*' (I, 44) as an organising principle largely unacknowledged by a society intoxicated with its own good fortune. But in an equally disquieting return of the repressed, *The Rape* shows market values confounding a traditional ethics as they refashion the human personality, accommodating it to different priorities. In Pope's construction a commercialised society rewrites virtue and leaves Belinda without any anchoring sense of morality: the oblation of her self into the new order of things co-ordinates her sexual fate with material display:

> Whether the Nymph shall break *Diana's* Law,
> Or some frail *China* Jar receive a Flaw,
> Or stain her Honour, or her new Brocade,
> Forget her Pray'rs, or miss a Masquerade,
> Or lose her Heart, or Necklace, at a Ball;
> Or whether Heav'n has doom'd that *Shock* must fall.
>
> (II, 105–10)

We have already seen human hearts reproducing the values of objects, and Pope's placing of these lines immediately before the naming of the deities points to his awareness. By disclosing a world where private and social action takes the form of the action of objects, *The Rape of the Lock* makes manifest a displacement of the rule of the person over the person by the rule of things over people, so that human behaviour and the values it constructs appear to be not the productions of human activity at all, but 'laws of nature' imposed from elsewhere. Or, as the poem slyly puts it, ''Tis but their *Sylph*, the wise Celestials know, / Though *Honour* is the Word with Men below' (I, 77–8). Pope's echo of a Dryden couplet here (from *The Hind and the Panther*), is not without significance:

'Immortal pow'rs the term of conscience know, / But int'rest is her name with men below.'[22] Public awareness that political affairs contained a logic of 'interest' was already widespread by the time of the Interregnum, and very soon 'Interest' had become the accepted framework of political discussion.[23] Pope personalises the connection through the changes he makes to Dryden's couplet, leaving 'honour' emptied of substance and deprived of moral agency in the social world of his invention.

The extent of the condition he describes is indicated with the third Canto's introduction of politicians as concerned with sexual conquest as they are with affairs of state, and its equation of respect for monarchy with admiration of filigree woodwork. There then follow the lines that have been described as a momentary glimpse of the world of serious affairs, of the world of business and law, an echo of the 'real' world:[24]

> Mean while declining from the Noon of Day,
> The Sun obliquely shoots his burning Ray;
> The Hungry Judges soon the Sentence sign,
> And Wretches hang that Jury-men may Dine
> The Merchant from th'*Exchange* returns in Peace,
> And the long Labours of the *Toilette* cease.   (III, 19–24)

It is part of Pope's individualist design on the classical unities for Belinda's eyes to open with the rising sun and close at the poem's end with its setting, while during the poem's narrative progress 'like the Sun, they shine on all alike' (II, 14). So it seems perverse to separate Belinda's world from another, 'glimpsed' here, which somehow exists outside the poem but is nonetheless its organising perception. The link between the comic brutality of hanging people for the convenience of consumption here and the seeming frivolity everywhere else is part of *The Rape*'s grand illusion, again suggested by a conflating use of italics. The scramble for commodities which defines Moll Flanders as economic woman is suggestively equated with the objects on Belinda's dressing-table, and Pope's earliest readers would have recognised a connection between 'Exchange' and 'Toilette' since the architectural design of the Royal Exchange at the time gave immediate point to the couplet. A contemporary description runs: 'Above stairs there are *Walks*, with near 200 shops, full of choice Commodities, especially for

---

22 *The Poems and Fables of John Dryden*, 4 vols., edited by James Kinsley (London, 1962), II, p. 524.
23 Felix Raab, *The English Face of Machiavelli* (London, 1964), p. 238.
24 Cleanth Brooks, 'The Case of Miss Arabella Fermor', in *The Well-Wrought Urn: Studies in the Structure of Poetry* (London, 1964), p. 83.

Mens and Womens Apparel, besides other *Shops* below the portico.'[25] Further evidence to suggest how alert the poem is to the equations being made derives from the fact that twelve months before the first version of *The Rape* appeared in Lintot's *Miscellany*, Addison published a *Spectator* essay in which he confessed himself ravished by the prospect of a busy day at the Royal Exchange and which provides a useful gloss for significant elements in *The Rape of the Lock* – to the extent that at certain points in the poem it can seem that Pope had Addison's eulogy in mind:

Almost every *degree* [of trade] among mankind produces something peculiar to it. The Food often grows in one Country and the Sauce in another. The Fruits of Portugal are corrected by the Products of *Barbadoes*; the Infusion of a *China* Plant sweetned with the Pith of an Indian Cane; the Phillipick Islands give a Flavour to our *European* Bowls. The single Dress of a Woman of Quality is often the Product of an hundred Climates. The Muff and the fan come together from the different Ends of the Earth. The Scarf is sent from the Torrid Zone, and the Tippet from beneath the Pole. The Brocade Petticoat rises out of the mines of *Peru*, and the Diamond Necklace out of the Bowels of *Indostan*.[26]

Belinda springs irrepressibly to mind as what Addison calls 'a kind of Additional Empire' lands in profusion upon her dressing-table. And the series of transparent verbal and thematic similarities is continued:

Nor has traffic more enriched our Vegetable World, than it has improved the whole Face of Nature among us ... Our ships are laden with the Harvest of every Climate: Our Tables are stored with Spices, and oils, and Wines: Our Rooms are filled with Pyramids of *China*, and adorned with the Workmanship of *Japan*: Our Morning's-Draught comes to us from the remotest Corners of the Earth: We repair our Bodies by the Drugs of America, and repose ourselves under *Indian* Canopies. My Friend, Sir Andrew, calls the Vineyards of *France* our Gardens; the Spice-Islands our Hot-Beds; the *Persians* our Silk-Weavers, and the *Chinese* our Potters ... Traffick ... supplies us with everything that is Convenient and Ornamental.   (pp. 295–6)

This *Spectator* paper gained some currency as a defence and promotion of the merchant class, with Addison considering to be improvements what Pope celebrates more ambiguously as a programme of glittering and gorgeous transformations, though with some grotesque implications. In the same essay, Addison blandly asserts what Pope, in the opening lines of the third Canto, chooses to leave at the level of satiric suggestion: 'Factors in the Trading World are what Ambassadors are in

[25] Guy Miège, *The Present State of Great Britain* (London, 1707), p. 159.
[26] *The Spectator*, ed. Bond, I, pp. 292–3.

the Politick World: they negotiate Affairs, conclude Treaties, and maintain a good Correspondence between those wealthy Societies of Men that are divided from one another by Seas and Oceans' (p. 293). Pope similarly collapses the distinctions between these two worlds but in high comic spirit:

> Here *Britain*'s Statesmen of the Fall foredoom
> Of Foreign Tyrant's, and of Nymphs at home;
> Here Thou, Great *Anna*! whom three Realms obey,
> Dost sometimes Counsel take – and sometimes *Tea*.   (III, 5–8)

The trader and the politician are one, and the social reference is self-evident, as Defoe reminds us when celebrating 'the Circulation of our Manufactures among our selves': '*Coffee, Tea*, and *Chocolate* ... it is well known are now become the Capital Branches of the Nations Commerce.'[27] On the back of this trade, a new class of business men were finding it worth their while to find and occupy seats in Parliament. By 1702 there were at least sixty of them in the Commons,[28] and what some of them were trading in was caffeine for a London high on this narcotic novelty: the coffee-shops were doing a roaring trade. Down in Gin Lane the tipple may have been different, but Pope was learning lessons about social addictions as some of Britain's national drinking habits were established. It is not tea, or the 'Fumes of burning Chocolate' which glow in Canto II (line 135) that Pope isolates for a demonstration of his more ambivalent perception of the new riches celebrated by Addison; it is his comically inflated presentation of the coffee-making ritual in Canto III:

> For lo! the Board with Cups and Spoons is crown'd,
> The Berries crackle and the Mill turns round.
> On shining Altars of *Japan* they raise
> The silver Lamp; the fiery spirits blaze.
> From silver Spouts the grateful Liquors glide,
> While *China*'s Earth receives the smoking Tyde.
> At once they gratify their Scent and Taste,
> And frequent Cups prolong the rich Repast.   (III, 105–12)

A sense of the marvellous is richly maintained, while ambiguities functioning in the grammar are indicated by a scene Pope records from a visit to Swift where there was 'likewise a Side Board of Coffee which the Dean roasted with his own hands in an Engine for the purpose, his landlady attending, all the while that office was performing' (*P. Corr.* I,

---

[27] *Review*, IX, no. 43 (facsimile book 22).   [28] Carswell, *South Sea Bubble*, p. 23.

234). When the same ritual enters *The Rape*, this human control over coffee-making tends to vanish, since what is occurring in the poetic version is the inference of partial autonomy for the objects under view, blurring the issue of who or what is in control. Cups and spoons agentively 'crown' the table: it is the berries which crackle, the mill which turns round. Liquors which by transferred epithet can be described as grateful, glide, while the cups, with equal stress on their performing abilities, both receive and prolong. Parallel to this technique is the treatment of the Baron's actual assault upon Belinda, where Pope's resources in revitalising stock notions of poetic diction succeed in directing attention to the instrument itself with which the Baron carries out his designs. The 'Two-edged Weapon', the 'little Engine', the 'glitt'ring *Forfex*' and the 'fatal Engine' all serve to maintain a sense of object predominance until the grammar suggests that the 'Instruments of Ill', a pair of scissors, complete the assault on their own: 'The meeting Points the Sacred Hair dissever / From the fair head, for ever and for ever!' (III, 153–4). The couplets also sustain a pattern of inanimate noun-phrases cast in an agentive role, while human activity finds its equivalent in non-human agency ('Nymph shall break ... Jar [shall] receive', or perhaps more ambiguously, 'the nice Conduct of a *clouded Cane*'). And Belinda's own words indicate the prevalence of this comic transfer of power: 'Thrice from my trembling hand the *Patch-box* fell; / The tott'ring *China* shook without a Wind' (IV, 153–4), where in the first of these lines the box seems to act independently (it was not dropped, it fell), and the second, picking up an image which forms part of the larger pattern of estranged and displaced sexuality, confronts us directly with the automatic drama of object-life.

Such an ambience may help to explain Belinda's angry complaint at the end of the fourth Canto: 'Oh hadst thou, Cruel! been content to seize / Hairs less in sight, or any Hairs but these!' (IV, 175–6). Her assaulted coiffure is visibly in disarray: retrospectively, actual rape at least offers the protection of an invisible discomposure. The comedy eases without quite masking the unsettling surprise of these lines, while the elaborate presentation of a social order devoted to appearances and to the elevation of things over people does at least contextualise them. And if Belinda's words still seem to cross a little too unnervingly from comic to grotesque violence, then their placing is particularly apt, because it is earlier in the fourth Canto that Pope represents most fully the alienated subjectivity at the heart of his poem. A parodic descent into the particular grotesquerie of this hell is wittily designed to tell the truth of the preceding Cantos; to reveal nakedly what has hitherto been suggested. There are patterns across the five Cantos connecting human life to the sylphs ('Thence, by a soft Transition, we repair / From earthly Vehicles to these of Air' (I, 49–50)); the sylphs to objects (in the protection of Belinda's appearance and elsewhere), and objects to human life throughout. Figures in Pope's invented world internalise the values of objects, reproducing those values as their own and in the fourth Canto's Cave of Spleen this 'human' is in turn reproduced as object-life:

> Unnumber'd Throngs on ev'ry side are seen
> Of Bodies chang'd to various Forms by *Spleen.*
> Here living *Teapots* stand, one Arm held out,
> One bent; the Handle this, and that the Spout:
> A Pipkin there like *Homer's Tripod* walks;
> Here sighs a Jar, and there a Goose-pye talks;
> Men prove with Child, as pow'rful Fancy works,
> And Maids turn'd Bottels, call aloud for Corks.   (IV, 47–54)

One hardly needs the benefit of a Freudian method to detect a previously repressed and fetishised sexuality now producing its own pantomime of derangement: in this cave we witness the workings of the unconscious and the structure of displaced desire. But again it is the mode of this production that is interesting. If earlier the world of objects has challenged human sway, threatening to displace it and sometimes doing so, here, at a subterranean level of psychological farce the non-human assumes complete control of once-human beings: objects perform their 'danse macabre' at will.

By disclosing more extremely in this fourth Canto what his poem is about, Pope is also revealing something of 'the truth' about the origins of Belinda's coquettish nature, and by way of approach to it we can borrow another observation from John Pocock: 'The personification of Credit as an inconstant female figure, it is startling to discover, is a device of Whig rather than Tory writers, and in particular of Defoe and Addison at the time when they were undergoing the assaults which Swift, in the *Examiner*, had launched against all forms of property except land as "only what is transient or imaginary".'[29] But Defoe was working for Robert Harley when he described 'My Beautiful Countess, my Charming Mistress, the Lady CREDIT', and he provides a different kind of context for the contribution Pope's Clarissa will make when he continues:

[29] Pocock, *Machiavellian Moment*, p. 452.

Credit is too wary, too Coy a Lady to stay with any People upon ... mean
Conditions; if you will Entertain this Virgin, you must Act upon the nicest
Principles of Honour, and Justice; you must preserve Sacred all the Foun-
dations, and build regular Structures upon them; you must answer all
Demands, with a respect to the Solemnity, and Value of the Engagement; with
respect to Justice, and Honour, and without any respect to Parties – If this is
not observ'd, Credit will not come; No, tho' the Queen should call; tho' the
Parliament should call, or tho' the whole Nation should call.[30]

In a series of conjunctions we are made aware that the power of the
imaginary was becoming a moving force in secular and material transformations of human relationships and circumstance. If biblical faith
could move mountains then business confidence, through systems of
credit, would sail ships and drive an economy. As faith is increasingly
placed in paper forms pledging invisible futures for the sake of returns
which may or may not materialise, the medium of exchange, money
itself (but now not even metal specie, but paper notes of credit), and not
the goods that money supposedly exists to circulate, increasingly signified the substance of wealth. And again Defoe brings into the light of
day the issues being raised. 'Is it a Mystery', he asks, 'that Nations
should grow rich by War? ... Why do *East India* Company's Stock rise,
when Ships are taken? Mine Adventures raise Annuities when Stocks
fall; lose their Vein of Oar in the Mine, and yet find it in the Shares; let
no Man wonder at these Paradoxes, since such strange things are
practised every Day among us? If any Man requires an Answer to such
things as these, they may find it in this Ejaculation – Great is the Power
of Imagination!'

Through its own explorations of the 'artifice of mind', the moving
powers of the imaginary are very much a part of *The Rape*'s interior
design, and in ways beyond its comic contrast with Clarissa's reasonable reminder of life's brevity. 'Gay Ideas crowd the vacant Brain' (I,
83) in a waking world of blithe, conspicuous consumption, and the
'mystic visions' (IV, 166) Belinda regrets not attending to are pre-
figured in the 'Strange Phantoms' and 'Visions of expiring Maids' that
rise in the Cave of Spleen. This is Belinda's spleen being stoked up by
Umbriel, and it may be relevant to recall that when Pope alluded more
directly to Steele's figure 'Umbra', it was to construct an echo of the
figure of credit as a social parasite and 'The constant Index to all
Button's wits' in a poem that names both Addison and Steele (*TE* VI, p.
140). Given that in Belinda's social circle 'At ev'ry Word a Reputation

---

[30] *Review*, VII, no. 116, pp. 461, 463 (facsimile book 18).

dies' (III, 16), this figuration of female inconstancy seems worth pursuing further, particularly since a lengthy exerpt from Addison's third *Spectator* paper, 'The Bank of England: Vision of "Public Credit"; her friends and enemies', forms the frontispiece to Dickson's *The Financial Revolution*. In a dream Addison sees in the great hall of the Bank of England 'a beautiful virgin seated on a Throne of Gold. Her name (as they told me) was *Publick Credit* ... with the Act of Uniformity on the right Hand, and the Act of Toleration on the Left'. The dreaming spectator sees heaped bags of gold behind the throne, piled to the ceiling, and learns that the lady in question 'could convert whatever she pleased into that precious Metal'. However, at the approach of 'Tyranny', 'Anarchy', 'Bigotry' and 'Atheism', the virgin queen of credit faints and dies away. There are already connections between Pope's wayward 'Goddess with a discontented Air' (IV, 79) and Addison's 'troubled with Vapours'. 'To hear some of these worthy Reasoners talking of *Credit*', Swift had written in the year of the shorter *Rape*'s appearance, 'that she is so nice, so squeamish, so capricious; you would think they were describing a Lady troubled with Vapours ... to be only removed by a *course of Steel*.' (*SP* III, p. 134). Clarissa will supply the necessary steel, but in lines from the *Spectator* essay not included by Dickson, Addison goes on to describe further effects of Credit's capricious nature:

There was as great a change in the Hill of Money Bags, and the Heaps of Money; the former shrinking and falling into so many empty Bags, that I now would have found not above a tenth part of them had been filled with Money. The rest that took up the same space and made the same Figure as the Bags that were really filled with Money, had been blown up with Air, and called into my Memory the Bags full of Wind, which Homer tells us his Hero received as a present from Aeolus. The great heaps of Gold on either side the Throne now appeared to be only heaps of Paper, or like little piles of Notched Sticks, bound up together in bundles, like Bath Faggots.[31]

The notched sticks are wooden tallies that since the twelfth century had been in use by the Exchequer as receipts. Frequently used as a type of cheque payable to the bearer, they were a means of transacting Exchequer business without using coin. As it accommodates to the changes it presents, Addison's essay is concerned to promote harmony and security: Pope concentrates upon volatility:

> A wondrous Bag with both her Hands she binds,
> Like that where once *Ulysses* held the winds;

[31] *The Spectator*, ed. Bond, I, p. 14.

> There she collects the Force of Female Lungs,
> Sighs, Sobs, and Passions, and the War of Tongues.
>
> (IV, 81–4)

Addison's imagery correlates with the social and psychological mutations explored by Pope while *The Rape of the Lock* writes the figure of inconstant Credit in its own way, with the interest here lying not so much in whether Pope is actively satirising Addison's essay, but rather that new forms of finance become a literary subject for Addison in ways that show affinities with the methods employed by Pope for his own more ambivalent purposes. We note a common stock of imagery differently deployed in two writers who were soon publicly to represent political antagonisms.

There was, moreover, an already established tradition of representing the inconstancy of credit. As early as 1698 Davenant had written: 'of all beings that have existence only in the minds of men, nothing is more fantastical and nice than Credit; it is never to be forced; it hangs upon our passions of hope and fear; it comes many times unsought for, and often goes away without reason, and when once lost, is hardly to be quite recovered'.[32] Defoe's *Review* made feminine identifications more vigorously: 'Money has a younger Sister, a very useful and officious servant in Trade, but if she be never so little disappointed, she grows sullen, sick and ill-natur'd, and will be gone for a great while together: Her Name in our Language is call'd Credit, in some Countries Honour, and in others, I know not what.' As relevantly, Defoe describes the antic disposition of trading arrangements floated upon credit:

Trade is a Mystery, which will never be compleatly discover'd or understood; it has its Critical Junctures and Seasons, when acted by no visible Causes, it suffers Convulsion Fitts, hysterical Disorders, and most unaccountable Emotions ... today it obeys the Course of things, and submits to Causes and Consequences; tomorrow it suffers the Storms and Vapours of Human fancy, operated by exotick Projects, and then all runs counter, the Motions are excentrick, unnatural and unaccountable ... and no Man can give a rational Account of it.[33]

Such tricks has the imagination in the world of Pope's poem, that Clarissa's attempted rationalisation is doomed from the outset. In *The Rape* though, Pope is nonetheless warmly engaged in a world of luxurious excess that trade and an expanding paper money-supply helped to

[32] Charles Davenant, 'Discourses on the Public Revenues', in *Works*, ed. Whitworth, I, p. 151.
[33] *Review*, III, no. 4 (facsimile book 6).

procure, sharing with Addison a delight in exotic possessions; and it is even possible that Addison had suggested a prototype for Pope's Belinda:

I consider woman as a beautiful romantic animal, that may be adorned with fur and feathers, pearls and diamonds, ores and silks. The lynx shall cast its skin at her feet to make her a tippet, the peacock, parrot, and swan shall pay contributions to her muff; the sea shall be searched for shells, and the rocks for gems; and every part of nature furnish out its share towards the embellishment of a creature that is the most consummate work of it.[34]

The Whig Addison would have agreed, too, with the sentiments Clarissa expresses in Pope's last addition to the poem. As the narrative returns to the by now splintering elegance of the mundane realm in the final Canto, her 'classic' statement of domestic 'good sense' would charm any *Spectator* reader. But its significance reaches further than the suggestion that Pope would also find these sentiments attractive: he, after all, is shaping a construction that has earlier (III, 127–30) made Clarissa unwittingly provide the Baron with the weapon for his assault. Moreover, her calm reasoning produces action which first ignores and then noisily contradicts what she has to say: but what she has to say responds to attitudes that were shared by others. When Bickerstaff walked to the Royal Exchange with Pacolet, the moral drawn in the essay was that 'the world will never be in any manner of order and tranquillity, till men are firmly convinced, that conscience, honour, and credit, are all in one interest; and that without the concurrence of the former, the latter are but impositions upon ourselves and others'. Steele's essay also ends with a female figure, Lais, distressed by her inner battles with conscience and honour, so that the final sentence can be turned in her defence:

Were men so enlightened and studious of their own good, as to act by the dictates of their reason and reflection, and not the opinion of others, Conscience would be the steady ruler of human life; and the words, Truth, Law, Reason, Equity, and Religion, would be but synonymous terms for that only guide which makes us pass our days in our own favour and approbation.[35]

Reasonable consciences are evidently overwhelmed by the influx of wealth the poem satirises and given its nugatory effect, Pope's insertion of Clarissa's defence of classical verities is a way of acknowledging that the world he has constructed is already moving beyond the regulatory terms of civic humanism as his like-minded contemporaries still sought

[34] *The Tatler*, ed. Bond, II, p. 195.   [35] Ibid., p. 195.

to mobilise them. The poem's characters can no longer be contained by these terms, given that they are themselves so often unnaturally 'contained' by the objects through which they identify themselves. The poetic heaven which provides the final resting place for Belinda's much-abused hair offers closing images of the human contained within the inanimate:

> There Heroes' wits are kept in pondrous Vases,
> And Beaus' in *Snuff-boxes* and *Tweezer-Cases*.
> There broken Vows, and Death-bed Alms are found,
> And Lovers' Hearts with ends of Ribands bound.   (V, 115–19)

Pope would return to the categories of humanist civic discourse in a determined effort to bring his world into a system of ethics, but the pessimistic gloom that settled upon him in his later years might paradoxically be traced to the exuberant perceptions playing beneath the surface of *The Rape*. For his final version of *The Dunciad*, he would devalue the brilliance of his sylphs into an emblem of the graft prominent in a decayed political economy. When Walpole extends his cup of corruption, we trace one destination for Pope's younger and more ambiguous celebrations:

> On others Int'rest her gay liv'ry flings,
> Int'rest, that waves on Party-colour'd wings:
> Turn'd to the Sun, she casts a thousand dyes,
> And, as she turns, the colours fall or rise.   (IV, 537–40)

But in his mid-twenties he felt able to end the poem with a celebration of the breadth of his poetic vision; to revel in the controlling abilities of his own 'quick Poetic Eyes'. Since the deeper meanings of Belinda's personal and social life are insights necessarily denied to her, the structure of the five Cantos brings them into focus for the reader.

2

Cultivating the bubble: some investing contemporaries

'Mr Harley', Swift wrote at the beginning of May, 1711, 'was yesterday to open to the House the ways he has thought of, to raise funds for securing the unprovided debts of the Nation, and we are all impatient to know what they are' (*S. Corr.* I, p. 226). War with France had raised the country's annual expenditure to thirteen millions, the government was heavily in debt, and if he did not know before, Swift was soon to discover that Harley had proposed to Parliament that a South Sea Company, endowed with a promised monopoly on the slave trade with Spanish America from which enormous profits might be expected, should incorporate the National Debt and pay six per cent interest on it to the government's creditors. While the attractions of a Tory corporation to counter the influence of the Whiggish Bank of England and East India Company were obvious enough to an embattled ministry, the Company's original capital was entirely fictitious, consisting of the government debts to be exchanged for South Sea stock, and the Company was therefore from the first more a financial than a trading institution. Nonetheless, Swift served his political master well, blaming the Whigs for the debts already incurred and enthusiastically welcoming the new project:

The Public debts were so prodigiously encreased, by the Negligence and Corruption of those who had been Managers of the Revenue; that the late Ministers, like careless Men, who run out their Fortunes, were so far from any Thoughts of Payment; that they had not the Courage to state or compute them ... The late Chancellor of the *Exchequer* [Harley], suitable to his transcendent Genius for Publick Affairs, proposed a Fund to be Security for that immense Dept, which is now confirmed by a Law; and is likely to prove the greatest Restoration and Establishment of the kingdom's Credit. (*SP* III, p.134)

Swift knew more than he was saying. He had already exploited fears of unaccountable power operating in the political life of the nation during the crisis of 1710, when because of a supposed deleterious effect upon the stock market, directors of the Bank of England personally urged

51

Queen Anne not to dismiss Godolphin and appoint Harley in his stead. 'What people then are these in a corner', Swift charged, 'to whom the constitution must truckle? ... Must our laws from henceforward pass the *Bank* and *East India Company* or have their *Royal Assent* before they are in force?' (*SP* III, p. 134). As finance progressively reconstituted the state the answer was increasingly yes, and recent experience had been instructive in other ways. An earlier Tory attempt to challenge the Bank of England at its own game through the Sword Blade Bank had also been an operation in credit involving the financier John Blunt, whom Pope was to pillory in his *Epistle to Bathurst*. Harley had sought advice from Blunt about setting up the South Sea Company, and Swift had incorporated into his *History of the Four Last Years of Queen Anne's Reign* information supplied by Blunt (*SP* VII, pp. 71–2). Within less than a decade this leading figure in the money markets stimulated by government-sponsored systems of banking and debt-management would come to typify for Opposition writers much of what they suspected and feared about newly ascendant financial institutions. As a leading architect of the South Sea proposals that led to the Bubble of 1720, Blunt would be widely anathematised and legally condemned.

Reflecting in 1711 upon the period from 1690 to 1700, Swift had also described the concentration of 'a sort of artificial Wealth of Funds and Stocks in the hands of those who for ten years had been plundering the Publick', and was disturbed by the loss of balance when a debtor Parliament interlocks with creditor citizens. Once people are tempted by great premiums and high rates of interest into lending their capital to the state, it becomes their concern 'to preserve that Government which they trusted with their money'. To emphasise his point (and implicate Marlborough in the Whig way of doing things), Swift told the story of Eumenes, one of Alexander's captains, who persuaded his fellow-officers to lend him great sums of money following Alexander's death: 'after which they were forced to follow him for their own security' (*SP* III, p. 6). For contemporary Londoners Swift coined the phrase that was to enjoy wide currency for years afterwards when he identified the chief beneficiaries of this process as 'the Monied Men; such as had raised vast sums by trading with Stocks and Funds' (*SP* VI, p. 10). But this was Swift the political writer in the public sphere. A few months earlier, and in a private capacity, he was urging Stella to buy Bank of England stock and resolves to buy in himself to the value of three hundred pounds.[1] Swift was then close to the centre of political

---

[1] Jonathan Swift, *Journal to Stella*, edited by Harold Williams, 2 vols. (Oxford, 1948), I, p. 74.

events, excited (in September, 1711) by his efforts at persuading Harley
to name Francis Stratford as a director of the South Sea Company, and
pleased at his success in getting John Barber (who printed *The Examiner*) appointed printer to the Company. Early in 1712, Stratford
purchased £500 of South Sea stock on Swift's behalf. They had been
school-friends, and remained close all their lives. Close enough,
anyway, for Swift to engage in what might now be recognised as
insider-trading to Stratford's advantage, though at the time stock
market regulation and financial codes of propriety were virtually
unknown: 'I gave him notice of a Treaty of Peace', Swift tells Stella,
'while it was a secret; of wch [sic] he might have made good use, but
that helpt to ruin him.' Stratford had duly bought stocks on the
strength of the information supplied in expectation of a rise in the
market which did not materialise, causing Swift a sleepless night on his
own account persuaded that he, too, had lost money in Stratford's
misfortune. 'This has been a scurvy affair', Swift remarked, 'I believe
Stella would have half laughed at me, to see a suspicious fellow, like me,
over-reached.'[2] He seems never to have lost a deep-seated suspicion of
money markets, partly, no doubt, because their inflation of opinion and
fantasy and their inherent uncertainty and instability exploded
classical rationality. He had felt on his own pulse a growing interdependence of political and financial power that was to herald the
demise of classical preferences for landed independence and the virtuous personal integrity it supposedly guaranteed; and while he commen-
ted upon this growing social and economic hegemony in alarmed and
antagonistic ways on numerous occasions in his role as polemicist, he
was evidently a participator in, as well as an observer of, stock market
systems that were introducing different scales of value into the ethical
scheme of things. As an observer he could always be satirically acute,
referring sarcastically to the manoeuvres of the Whigs in using the word
'Pretender' to frighten their countrymen and affect stock market values
to their own speculative advantage: 'Half a Score Stock-Jobbers are
playing the Knave in *Exchange-Alley*, and there goes *The Pretender* with a
Sponge' (*SP* III, p. 17). When Matthew Prior returned from Paris to
London in October, 1712, amid rumours of an imminent peace, Swift
noted that the stock market 'rose upon his coming'.[3] He watched
finance and politics interacting again when rumours of Queen Anne's
illness in 1713 caused a fall of '6 or 7 per cent' on the stock market: 'And
it is a plain Argument', he added, 'how much they would fall if she

[2] Ibid., pp. 351, 463, 502.   [3] Ibid., p. 566.

really had died' (*S. Corr.* II, p. 10). When she really did die in the following year the markets reacted differently to changed political circumstances then obtaining and rose by three per cent.

Swift was at the time managing for three friends £1000 invested in South Sea stocks, and twice arranges for loan repayments to be made out of the dividends accruing. Years later, that share-management would cause him considerable heart-ache. 'I believe there are hardly three men of any figure in Ireland', he was to tell Knightley Chetwode long after the Bubble had been blown and burst, 'whose affairs are so bad as mine, who now pay interest for a thousand pounds of other people's money ... without receiving one farthing myself, but engaged in a lawsuit seven years to recover it' (*S. Corr.* II, pp. 74, 94, 114; III, pp. 333–4). Evidently Swift had his problems, and Pope also experienced investment-related anxieties, initially in connection with French bonds which the poet's father had invested on his son's life (*P. Corr.* I, pp. 155, 180, 208).[4] But Pope developed his own expertise as a market-analyst, sometimes seeing opportunities where Swift expressed doubt and misgivings. Towards the end of 1716, Pope gauges that South Sea stocks would fall rather than rise with the sitting of Parliament, and against that eventuality he reserves £1,500 to buy at the next opportune moment. There were rumours that Parliament intended to tax the funds and Pope sought to take advantage of such a move by arranging for the purchase of £500 worth of stocks as soon as the price fell (*P. Corr.* I, 379). While developing a certain astuteness as a player of the market, Pope also reveals a sense that the bagatelle is ultimately unpredictable: in March, 1717, he regrets selling stock shortly before the price rose, and a few months later he is looking for more secure forms of return on his capital, asking Caryll's advice about opportunities for a life annuity in which Pope could invest £1,000.

Except that the words and represented feelings of Swift and Pope are recorded in some detail, there was nothing unusual in what they were about. Anyone with surplus capital was investing it, thereby helping to develop as they were being stimulated by a profound culture-change that was unfolding while the Financial Revolution made speedy headway. Inevitably it was to extend into most areas of experience and would visibly affect personal and social perceptions accordingly, processes in which a newspaper like *The Spectator*, launched a month before the South Sea Company, self-consciously played both a responsive and

---

[4] When French interest rates were lowered in 1713, Pope worries about the effect this will have on his insurance policy, and repeats his concern in the following year.

a shaping role. One of the more successful periodicals of its time, *The Spectator* was very much a product of the financial and commercial world of London, as its list of subscribers reveals. Among them were directors of the Bank of England while others were goldsmiths, private bankers or moneylenders. Eight were East India Company directors, and twenty were directors of the South Sea Company. Moreover, the largest single group of subscribers included the 'great body of secretaries, commissioners, clerks, and agents in the various branches of government, civil and military, required to carry on the war abroad and manage affairs at home'.[5] Given such a constituency, it became a natural concern of Addison and Steele to promote a polite and civilising sense of participation in the new society being developed, acclimatising its readers to market priorities and procedures and familiarising them with codes and conventions of recognition and self-recognition appropriate to their place in a burgeoning world. More than anything else, a main function of *The Spectator* was to make its readers feel that they *were* a social constituency and one of growing significance, for whom polite culture could mediate as a validating and confidence-building network of relationships. Politeness becomes an active civilising agent:

By observation, conversation, and cultivation, men and women are brought to an awareness of the needs and responses of others and of how they appear in the eyes of others; this is not only the point at which politeness becomes a highly serious practical morality ... It is also the point at which Addison begins to comment on the structure of English society and the reconciliation of its diverse 'interests.' In the Spectator circle, Sir Roger the country gentleman and Sir Andrew the urban merchant meet and polish one another, and Mr. Spectator comments on the merits and shortcomings of each. His observation is his practice; by observing his friends he heightens their awareness of self and other, and the sociable role is more important, both morally and socially, than any he could play as a politically engaged activist.[6]

The Spectator*, like *The Tatler* before it, cultivated and developed these changes in perception and self-perception. It told its readers why they should not be angry in public, and what the effects of good humour were. It explained the virtues of sociability and taught good manners for polite society: it also talked about books and poems and gave its readers things to say about them when in company. Here was the public sphere in operation and a culturally desirable and necessary

[5] *The Spectator*, ed. Bond, I, pp. xc, xcii.
[6] J. G. A. Pocock, *Virtue, Commerce, and History: Essays on Political Thought and History, Chiefly in the Eighteenth Century* (Cambridge, 1985), pp. 236–7.

aspect of its project of social reinforcement and integration would
involve an accommodation with new capital structures of investment.
'There is no Place in the Town which I so much love to frequent',
Addison tells his readers a few weeks after Harley brought in his South
Sea proposals, 'as the Royal Exchange. It gives me a secret Satisfaction,
and, in some measure, gratifies my Vanity, as I am an *Englishman*, to see
so rich an Assembly of Country-men and Foreigners consulting
together upon the private Business of Mankind, and making this
Metropolis a kind of *Emporium* for the whole Earth.' As it sought to
universalise its appeal *The Spectator* made a bid for political neutrality
by aligning two of the characters it used to debate and represent
different social and economic attitudes, Sir Roger de Coverley and Sir
Andrew Freeport, with different interest-groups: 'the first of them
inclined to the *landed* and the other to the *moneyed* Interest'.[7] But
Addison confirms Swift's sense that the loci of power and decision-
making were significantly shifting, and with a decidedly Whig appreci-
ation of these new dispositions, when he looks upon the bustling
stock exchange as: 'a great Council, in which all considerable Nations
have their representations'.[8] As they record for us the world of their
preferred constructions, these writers are engaging in a struggle for the
meanings of what was happening and for appropriate scales of value in
which to stabilise and order their responses to the changes taking place.
Processes of cultural change become literary sites of adversarial interpretation.

We are usefully reminded that what Bernard Mandeville has to say
about the seductive if sometimes vacuous charm of Richard Steele's
stylish 'praises of his sublime species' applies also to Addison's panegyric on the Royal Exchange.[9] Given the 'usual Elegance of [Steele's]
easy style ... with all its Embellishment of Rhetoric ... it is impossible
not to be charm'd', says Mandeville, 'with his happy Turns of Thought,
and the Politeness of his Expressions'.[10] In 1714, Mandeville was
concerned to probe beneath the superficial sheen with which *The Tatler*
and *The Spectator* represented 'taste' and behaviour for a rising middle
class. Addison, meanwhile, was as concerned to celebrate a world of

---

[7] *The Spectator*, ed. Bond, II, p. 3.   [8] Ibid., I, pp. 292–3.
[9] R.H. Hopkins, 'Some Observations on Mandeville's Satire', in *Mandeville Studies: New
Explorations in the Art and Thought of Bernard Mandeville (1670–1733)*, ed. I. Primer (The
Hague, 1975), p. 178.
[10] Bernard Mandeville, *The Fable of the Bees: Or, Private Vices, Public Benefits*, ed. F, B, Kaye, 2
vols. (Oxford, 1924), I, pp. 52–3. Subsequent quotations are given parenthetically in the
text.

increased prosperity and expanding opportunity and in doing so he recognised and gave expression to material shifts in the structure and balance of social relationships and power. Calling to life one of the former kings of England whose statues stood in niches around the paved court of the Royal Exchange, Addison marvels at how surprised he would be to hear 'all the languages of *Europe* spoken in this little Spot of his former Dominions, and [seeing] so many private Men, who in his Time would have been the vassals of some powerful Baron, Negotiating like Princes for greater Sums of Money than were formerly to be met with in the Royal Exchequer'. For Addison trade is the engine that drives these social changes, producing 'a kind of additional Empire [which] has multiplied the Number of the Rich, made our Landed Estates infinitely more Valuable than they were formerly, and added to them an Accession of other Estates as Valuable as the Lands themselves'.[11] When Addison's cousin Eustace Budgell writes an essay on *The Ways to raise a Man's Fortune*, or *The Art of growing Rich*, he records his pleasure at having observed, 'since my being a Spectator in the World, greater Estates got about *Change*, than at *Whitehall* or *St James*'.[12] These things were galling to Swift and his friends, and six months before Addison's celebration of trading merchants, Swift had angrily traced the advancement of political lying to the monetary influence of people whose 'Principle and Interest it was to corrupt our Manners, blind our Understandings, drain our Wealth, and in Time destroy our Constitution both in Church and State'. What Addison greets with affability tends to the ruin of the landed social order Swift was engaged to represent: 'We have seen a great Part of the Nation's Money got into the Hands of those, who by their Birth, Education and Merit, could pretend no higher than to wear our Liveries' (*SP* III, p. 12).

In contrast, it was intended that *The Spectator*'s readership should identify with and take pride in what was happening to London, and as part of a cultural acclimatisation to developing order and practice an easy familiarity with, and of course a participatory flutter on, the state lotteries that had just been re-introduced in a further effort to ease the country's problems of war-debt, also becomes a natural concern. In *The Spectator*'s predecessor *The Tatler*, Steele reported crowds of people turning down towards the Bank and jostling to be among the 'first [to] get their money into the new-erected Lottery'. Six months later he is mingling in the crowd during the lottery draw, fascinated by the

---

[11] *The Spectator*, ed. Bond, I, p. 296.   [12] Ibid., III, p. 2.

calculations being scribbled down as expectations rise and fall, and pointing to a monetary moral to be drawn from the scene: 'Were it not for such honest fellows as these, the men who govern the rest of their species would have no tools to work with.'[13] Together with Addison, Swift went in 1710 to watch a lottery draw at the Guildhall, and was rather less than enchanted: 'The jackanapes of blue-coat boys [i.e. from Christ's Hospital] gave themselves such airs in pulling out the tickets, and shewed white hands open to the company, to let us see there was no cheat.'[14] Soon lotteries were being regularly organised and when two smaller ones were launched in 1719, a proposal was laid that the holders of the earliest Lottery Orders should exchange them directly for South Sea stock. These moves could justifiably be described as conjuring tricks (*FR*, p. 89), merging lottery tickets and share subscriptions so that gambling and investment procedures became indistinguishable for a widely participating public. Stockjobbers inevitably became involved in both kinds of transaction because very soon lottery tickets were being divided up and sold onward.[15] Since unsold tickets passed as currency, though creditors were not obliged to accept them, boundaries and conventions in other areas of payment and exchange were blurring. During a rash of privately organised operations, including several 'one thousand pounds for a penny' schemes, Lady Wentworth wrote from Twickenham that her daughter Elizabeth had won a pair of silk stockings on a half-crown lottery in the same month that Elizabeth asked her brother for ten pounds to buy a state lottery ticket. She was unlucky; but in August her mother reports after the first 'Classis' lottery (also known as the 'Two Million Adventure') that 'some very ordenary creeture has got 400ll a year'. She gossips that: 'thear is a lady gave her footman ... mony for a lot, and he got five hundred a year, and she would have half, and they had a law suit, but the lawyers gave it all to him'.[16] Out in civil society attorneys were growing fat, while government legislation against imitations of its own forms of money-making proved difficult to police and merely served to provoke a further outbreak of gambling on state lottery results.

Like *The Tatler* and other newspapers, *The Spectator* regularly carried advertisements for lotteries, and we can trace developing senses of fantasy and of imaginary expectations that came increasingly to fascinate writers on both sides of the political divide. Steele mused that:

---

[13] *The Tatler*, ed. Bond, II, p. 229; III, p. 82.   [14] *Journal to Stella*, I, p. 19.
[15] *The Tatler*, ed. Bond, II, p. 249, n. 1.
[16] *The Wentworth Papers*, edited by J. J. Cartwright (London, 1883), pp. 126, 129, 130.

'When a Man has a mind to venture his Mony in a Lottery, every Figure of it appears equally alluring ... and no manner of Reason can be given why a Man should prefer one to the other.' Under the pressure of promissory wealth and a growing confidence in these fictional designs on personal futures, rationality gives way to fad, fancy and personal conceit. In choosing a lottery-ticket number, Steele continues: 'Caprice very often acts in the Place of Reason, and forms to itself some Groundless Imaginary Motive, where real and substantial ones are wanting.'[17] That sense of capriciously differentiating futures expands with a growing awareness of private and secret realms involved in speculation. 'Is it possible', Steele asked his readers in 1712: 'that a young Man at present could pass his Time better than in reading the History of the Stocks, and knowing by what secret Springs they have such sudden Ascents and Falls in the same Day? ... Nothing certainly could be more useful, than to be ... diffident when others exalt, and with a secret Joy buy when others think it in their Interest to sell.'[18]

Interior springs of action, and concealed desires and intentions give rise to fantastic notions that simultaneously seem and do not seem to purchase on an empirically observable reality. Stock-purchases and lottery-tickets stimulated illusions that both inflated and undermined the traditionally property-based securities of identity and relationship, and two months after Steele's encouragement to his readers to familiarise themselves with the tandem arts of speculation and concealment, he explores from another angle the increasingly unstable boundaries between fact and fantasy. In a vision, the Spectator enters the Palace of Vanity and notices that the rounded top of the building 'bore so far the resemblance of a Bubble'. He sees Vanity enthroned and attended by Ostentation, Self-Conceit, Flattery, Affectation 'and *Fashion*, ever changing the Posture of her Cloathes'. At the intrusion of a voice bemoaning the condition of a society so in thrall to whim and opinion, 'Broken Credit' appears alongside Folly and causes consternation. Those who stayed in the palace although 'their merits neither matched the Lustre of the Place, nor their Riches its expenses' are thrown into confusion when they 'plainly discern'd the Building to hang a little up in the Air without any real Foundation ... But as they began to sink lower in their own Minds, methought the Palace sunk along with us, till they arrived at the due point of *esteem* which they ought to have for themselves; then the part of the Building in which they stood touched the

---

[17] *The Spectator*, ed. Bond, II, p. 249.   [18] Ibid., IV, pp. 4–5.

earth.'[19] Steele's is finally a soothing, settling vision, whereas the absence of any solid or observable foundation for these expectations of wealth particularly troubled Opposition writers, for whom expanded opportunities of individual enrichment surreptitiously rendered untenable the hierarchies of power and value they represented.

The Spectator's hope for moderation of desire among aspirants to a share in the magical new riches was to prove as forlorn as any expectations the Tories may have entertained that the South Sea Company might grow into a countervailing power against Whiggish financial institutions. The Bank of England was used as receiver for government lotteries, and it soon became evident that the Bank's support was as necessary for the functioning of the South Sea Company. After the demise of Harley's administration, Swift worries about the manifest convergence of Whig politics and finance when he tells Bolingbroke in 1714 that if in the next election 'the Court, the Bank, East-India and South-Sea act strenuously, and procure a majority, I shall lie down and beg Jupiter to heave the cart out of the dirt' (*S. Corr.* II, p. 129). St John, meanwhile, was nervous on other accounts. In the summer of 1714 he had moved to defend his friend Arthur Moore (who had, incidentally, won £3,000 in the third 'Classis' lottery a couple of years earlier),[20] and who now stood accused of defrauding the South Sea Company. Fearful that the House of Lords would reveal his own complicity, Bolingbroke persuaded the Queen to prorogue Parliament.[21] So there was already an articulate awareness and experience of what was potentially involved when in 1719 the experiment with the South Sea Company was repeated and public creditors again offered the opportunity to exchange government for South Sea stock. But because Parliament did not fix the rate of exchange ('by what must have been a deliberate and criminal neglect'),[22] the Company was encouraged to inflate the price of its stock. If public creditors could be persuaded to exchange their government stock for South Sea stock at three or four times its nominal level, then the Company could sell large amounts of stock on its own account. Having helped to negotiate this arrangement, John Aislabie, the Chancellor of the Exchequer, who was subsequently to describe it as 'setting the nation up to auction', purchased and sold £77,000 worth of stock at the same time as he was

[19] Ibid., IV, pp. 122–4.
[20] C. L. Ewen, *Lotteries and Sweepstakes in the British Isles* (London, 1932), p. 140.
[21] H. T. Dickinson, *Bolingbroke* (London, 1970), p. 13.
[22] J. H. Plumb, *Sir Robert Walpole: The Making of a Statesman* (London, 1956), p. 299.

investing heavily in the Bank of England. Aislabie was also involved in the massive bribery which helped secure parliamentary approval for the South Sea Company's proposals (*FR*, p. 96). The wholesale nature of the excitement and temptation which now began to seize anyone with cash to venture is not easy to recall, nor is the novelty of what was happening. London society had before it the fantastic success of the Scotsman John Law's scheme in France, which seemed to justify a widespread belief that the credit resources of the nation had not been fully exploited. Backed by the authority of the state, credit, they thought, was capable of almost infinite expansion.[23] If contemporary accounts are to be believed, this was evidently the case with Blunt himself:

The progress of the Mississippi Company about that time having intoxicated, and turned the brains of most people, [Blunt's] mind was thereby wonderfully affected, and from his natural inclination to projects, so inflamed ... [he] carried on his views for taking in at once all the National Debts, the Bank and East India included: saying, 'That as Mr LAW had taken his pattern from him, and improved upon what was done here the year before in relation to the Lottery of 1710, he would now improve upon what was done in France, and out-do Mr LAW.'[24]

Law had created a vast financial monopoly, using the Banque Royale to take over the entire public debt in France, securing a monopoly over all foreign trade, and circulating paper money on the strength of that monopoly. 'The effect had been magical; from the economic doldrums France had passed straight into wild inflationary prosperity. So delusive was Law's sleight of hand that hard-headed Dutch and English financiers were tumbling over themselves to get shares in the Mississippi Company which controlled his venture.'[25] In the winter of 1719–20 the market price of shares issued by the Mississippi Company at 500 livres reached 18,000 livres and speculators made huge profits. Apparently on the advice of Law himself, Bolingbroke invested successfully enough for Swift to congratulate him as 'our Mississippi friend' (*S. Corr.* II, p. 341), and St John agreed that he had made 'a great deal of money in these fonds' and claimed to have gained by 'the rise of [the French stocks] ...

---

[23] Ibid., p. 296.
[24] 'The Secret History of the South Sea Scheme', in *A Collection of Several Pieces of Mr [John] Toland: With Some Memoirs of his Life and Writing* (London, 1726), pp. 406–7. A footnote (p. 404) informs us – 'This piece is not Mr Toland's, but it was found amongst his MSS and is enlarged and corrected throughout with his own hand.'
[25] Plumb, *The Making of a Statesman*, pp. 296–7.

att least as much as I have been hitherto robbed of'. With his profits he acquired property at La Source, near Orleans, as a retreat.[26]

In London, following the presentation of John Blunt's plan in 1720 to incorporate into the South Sea Company the whole of the national debt, a scheme was proposed to convert £31,000,000 of government debt currently held in private hands in the forms of annuities. The key idea was that the holders of annuities for terms of years, which the government could not buy out or reduce to a lower rate unless the holders consented, should voluntarily exchange them for a capital sum in the form of new South Sea stock (*FR*, p. 122). As with the previous year's plan the company would profit according to the difference between the par value and market value of its stock. That is to say, if £100 of its stock sold for £200 it need only assign £15,500,000 to the holders of the £31,000,000 of annuities: the other 'half' of the arrangement could be sold as stock on the Exchange, and the Company therefore used all means, both fair and foul, to drive up the market value of its stock. Everything depended upon the 'rise of the stocks', and since its actual trade did not justify such a rise the scheme put a premium on stockjobbing.

While it was floating loans, the Company also raised four money subscriptions during 1720, each of which was heavily over-subscribed. By alternating loans with issues of new stock, John Blunt had in effect 'constructed a financial pump, each spurt of stock being accompanied by a draught of cash to suck it up again, leaving the level higher than before. As fast as stock issued ... the money received for it was returned to the market to support the prices and take up fresh issues at the higher price.'[27] In breach of its bye-laws, the Company was pumping its own funds into Exchange Alley to keep the market buoyant, illicitly buying £332,250 of its own stock between April and November.[28] Loans on subscription receipts were sometimes verbally authorised by directors without being entered in any books; scrip was proliferating exponentially, and in the Alley fantasy became a part of routine buying and selling as trading in futures rapidly developed with money changing hands several times for stock not yet in anyone's possession. Very few people had any clear idea of what was going on as the public took up the South Sea Company's offers with 'a blind enthusiasm reminiscent of the Gadarene swine' (*FR*, p. 133). Meanwhile, under the guise of 'loans' secured by entirely fictitious stock, a great part of the bribes paid

[26] *Letters of Jonathan Swift to Charles Ford*, edited by D. Nichol Smith (Oxford, 1935), pp. 234–5.
[27] Carswell, *South Sea Bubble*, p. 135.   [28] Ibid., p. 169.

to politicians could be discharged in cash collected directly from the public. Funds well in excess of £1 million were transferred in this way to politicians from the pockets of subscribers.[29] The list for the third money subscription on 17 June shows that half the House of Lords and more than half of the Commons were included,[30] while the extent of the mania might be further assessed by a letter written from Dublin and quoted by Swift's biographer:

I have enquired of some that have come from London, what is the religion there? they tell me it is South Sea Stock; what is the policy of England? the answer is the same; what is the trade? South Sea still; and what is the business? nothing but South Sea.   (*S. Life* III, p. 154)

Swift told Vanessa later in the year that: 'Conversation is full of nothing but South Sea, and the ruin of the kingdom, and scarcity of money' (*S. Corr.* II, p. 361): increasing numbers of people were engaged in share dealings in circumstances and on a scale of which they could have no prior experience.

South Sea stock began the year 1720 above par, £100 of stock bringing £128 on the Exchange. On the second of February the House of Commons accepted the Company's proposals, and early in the same month Alexander Pope writes to his friend and agent James Eckersall about the rising price of stock: a week or two later Pope is leaving other trading decisions up to him: 'When I put the Lottery orders into your hands, I knew they were at a discount. Pray believe me I am fully pleas'd with adventuring in so good company' (*P. Corr.* II, p. 32). By tracing Pope's mood-shifts as confidence and expectation fluctuate, we hear ambition and desire being stimulated as the markets moved. Although the first major operation of the revised South Sea scheme was not launched until, as it happens, 1 April, rumour and expectation were already at work pushing up stock prices, and in a letter probably written before the end of February we catch something of Pope's good-humoured fantasy, as well as a touch of emotional urgency:

I daily hear such reports of advantages to be gaind by one project or other in the Stocks, that my Spirit is Up with double Zeal, in the desires of our trying to enrich ourselves. I assure you my own Keeping a Coach & Six is not more in my head than the pleasure I shall take in seeing Mrs Eckersall in her Equipage. To be serious, I hope you have sold the Lottery orders, that the want of ready mony may be no longer an Impediment to our buying in the Stock, which was very unlucky at that time. I hear the S. Sea fell since, and should be glad we

[29] Ibid., p. 135.   [30] Dickson publishes tables of these subscriptions (*FR*, p. 108).

were in: I also hear there is considerably to be got by Subscribing to the new African Stock, Pray let us do something or other, which you judge to be the fairest prospect, I am equal as to what Stock, so you do but like it. Let but Fortune favor us, & the World will be sure to admire our Prudence. If we fail, let's e'en keep the mishap to ourselves. But tis Ignominious (in this age of Hope and Golden Mountains) not to venture.   (*P. Corr.* II, p. 33)

Prudence is already slipping from its classic configurations, and was soon to go by the board entirely. A couple of days later Pope is further involved: 'I . . . desire if you have not actually disposd of the Lottery orders, to let me have em sent before eleven or twelve to morrow morning to Mr Jervas's (your's & all if you please) for I believe I can sell 'em, or do what is equivalent' (*P. Corr.* II, p. 35). On 21 March, Pope advises Teresa Blount that he has borrowed money to buy £500 of South Sea stock at 180: 'It is since risen to 184. I wish us all good luck in it' (*P. Corr.* II, p. 38). It was not, though, all plain sailing, and soon doubts are being voiced about when it might be most appropriate to sell, and when to hold on in the hopes of further gains. Anxieties which market fluctuations produce and accentuate are being expressed in a conscious attempt to assess whether or not the effects of political activity on the price of stocks will be personally profitable. On 23 March, the House of Commons was to debate a motion that the Company should define in advance the amount of new stock it would give the government creditors in exchange for their stock and annuities, and Pope is concerned that the decisions he is then making over stock transactions may not be timed to best advantage:

I was advised to make use of the Rise of the S. Sea Stock which was got above 200 & then sell, and wait to buy again on the coming of the Bill on Munday or Tuesday, when they expected some Ruffle on the Debate. I left my desires with a Friend who was going into the City, being hugely joy'd at the thought of having got Mrs Eckersall at least some coffee mony, notwithstanding all our rubs & impediments for want of getting rid of the Lottery orders (which still lye without the least hope that I can see of being sold). But I am now alarmd and vex'd again, on hearing of the prodigious and unexpected rise on Saturday night, not many hours after I gave my Commission. I have sent to my man . . . and can't tell yet whether he has sold it, or not, but am very uneasy about it.

(*P. Corr.* II, p. 39)

If Pope's orders to sell were too promptly carried out, he must have regretted it, for on 21 March stock opened at 187, and by the end of the week had reached 300 (*P. Corr.* II, p. 39, n. 2). By failing to ensure that the ratio of South Sea stock to be exchanged for government annuities should be clearly fixed, Parliament had opened the way to continuing price-inflation, and in the midst of these transactions, we hear the poet who was later to construct the most comprehensive satirical condemnation of the new finances and the political culture they engendered ruefully explaining to Lord Caryll:

The question you ask about the fair lady's gains and my own, is not easily answered. There is no gain till the stock is sold, which neither theirs nor mine is. So that, instead of wallowing in money, we never wanted more for the uses of life, which is a pretty general case with most of the adventurers, each having put all the ready money into the stock.   (*P. Corr.* II, p. 42)

By June the Company was offering £100 of South Sea stock in return for £1,000 worth of government annuities, with the Company then selling the £900 worth of South Sea stock they had 'saved' in the process. Before the end of June stock was realising £745, and in high spirits Pope and Gay plan to invest in real estate some of their expected profits (*P. Corr.* II, p. 49); in July, the month during which Pope sold shares, the market peaked at over £1,000. London was caught in a fever of speculation as the historic novelty of its first social participation in a bull market entirely seduced public attention. In July, Robert Digby congratulates Pope as the 'richest man in the South-Sea' and provides further evidence of a shared sense of the unlimited effects of newly transforming powers in the City: 'The London language and conversation is I find quite changed since I left it, tho' it is not above three to four months ago. No violent change in the natural world ever astonished a Philosopher so much as this docs mc.' That London language was to become a matter of serious contest, but Digby is quite carried away by it all, optimistically looking forward to the end of political divisions in society and to the introduction of 'more humanity than has of late obtained in conversation'. Either in light-hearted irony, or showing some naivety about the temperament of his correspondent, he enthuses: 'All scandal will be laid aside, for there can be no such disease any more as spleen in this new golden age. I am pleased with the thoughts of seeing nothing but a general good humour when I come up to town; I rejoice in the universal riches I hear of, in the thought of their having this effect' (*P. Corr.* II, p. 48). Digby was also wrong if he thought that Pope had completely withdrawn from the markets. In the middle of August, shortly before the fourth 'Money Subscription' and the issue of one and a quarter million pounds worth of South Sea stock at a price of 1,000, Pope is in the thick of things again, confiding urgently to Lady Mary Wortley Montagu: 'I was made acquainted late last night, that I might depend upon it as a certain gain, to Buy the South Sea-Stock at the present price, which will certainly rise in some weeks, or less. I can be as sure of this, as the nature of any such thing will allow, from the first and best hands' (*P. Corr.* II, p. 52). Not the best hands at all as it transpired: Pope was giving Lady Mary bad advice, since at this time South Sea stock hovered briefly around 800 and then went into decline.

   The South Sea was not the only object of investors' attentions, and government attempts to preserve its pre-eminence were to prove fatal. As a result of the passing of the Bubble Act in June, a move designed to protect the South Sea Company's position by restricting the growth of other joint-stock companies bidding for investment funds, public confidence would begin to ebb. But this was not brought about until the Lords Justices actually applied the new law, and they did not do that until 18 August. Even so, although the break was not at first disastrous, from this date the price of South Sea stock began to fall (*FR*, p. 149). By mid-September the writing was on the wall, and in a letter to Atterbury on the 23rd of that month, its expression thoughtfully tailored to the Godly calling of its recipient, for London's first stock market crash Pope turns biblical cadence to the service of an image he was to use again:

The fate of the South-sea Scheme has much sooner than I expected verify'd what you told me. Most people thought it wou'd come, but no man prepar'd for it; no man consider'd it would come *like a Thief in the night*, exactly as it happens in the case of our death. Methinks God has punish'd the avaritious as he often punishes sinners, in their own way, in the very sin itself: the thirst of gain was their crime, that thirst continued became their punishment and ruin. As for the few who have the good fortune to remain with half of what they imagined they had, (among whom is your humble servant) I would have them sensible of their own felicity ... *They have dreamed out their dream, and awaking have found nothing in their hands* ... The universal deluge of the S. Sea, contrary to the old deluge, has drowned all except a few *unrighteous* men: but it is some comfort to me that I am not one of them, even tho' I were to survive and rule the world by it.   (*P. Corr.* II, pp. 53–4)

We can see some of the later poetry in the making in a letter like this, where the tone and mode was to prove fertile for his mature verse, though Pope continued to invest. Nine months or so before the first appearance of *The Dunciad*, he confides to the Earl of Oxford that he has withdrawn his 'little stake from the Turmoil of the Stocks: and out of suspitions which gave me disquiet. But the same inquietude pursues me upon a different account. What to do with it any other way? I am like a man that saves, and lays together, the planks of a broken Ship, or a falling House; but knows not how to rebuild out of them, either one, or the other' (*P. Corr.* II, p. 444). And as late as 1740 he is asking Ralph Allen to buy shares in the Sun Fire Insurance Company, of which Pope held 31 at the time of his death (*P. Corr.* IV, p. 340).

The evidence suggests a considerable record of investment experience and when we encounter Pope's formal reconstructions of events, a proper caution is called for. His acknowledgement of the part played by Secretary of State James Craggs the younger in Pope's acquisition of a block of South Sea stock is a case in point:

> South-sea Subscriptions take who please,
> Leave me but Liberty and Ease.
> 'Twas what I said to Craggs and Child,
> Who prais'd my Modesty and smil'd
> Give me, I cry'd, (enough for me)
> My Bread, and Independency!
> So bought an Annual Rent or two.
> And liv'd – just as you see I do;
> Near fifty, and without a Wife,
> I trust that sinking Fund, my Life.[31]

In March, 1720, Pope had something like £500 in South Sea stock which he did not sell, probably, as Sherburn surmises (*P. Corr.* II, p. 70), influenced by his friend and neighbour Secretary Craggs who was at that stage actively supporting the Bubble in the House of Commons. Between them, Craggs father and son invested a total of £17,000 in South Sea stock during 1720, valued at £153,000. Secretary Craggs died of smallpox at a moment when he as well as his father, the Postmaster-General, was deeply involved in South Sea scandal. Craggs Senior died on 16 March under circumstances suggesting suicide and his South Sea gains were subsequently confiscated. Craggs junior personally obtained stock to bribe the King's mistress (and her two daughters), in order to ease the passing of the Company's bill through Parliament. As a member of the government, he brought in a list for the third 'Money Subscription' in June, totalling £691,500, from which Pope was a beneficiary (*FR*, p. 126). All of which suggests an alternative context for Pope's remark to Caryll shortly after the younger Craggs's death: 'There never was a more worthy nature, a more disinterested mind, a more open and friendly temper, than Mr Craggs. A little time I doubt not will clear up a character which the world will

[31] John Butt, *The Poems of Alexander Pope: Vol. IV, Imitations of Horace* (London, 1939), p. 273. Subsequent quotations are given parenthetically in the text.

learn to value and admire, when it has none such remaining in it' (*P. Corr.* II, p. 21). Those who wished to resist investigation into the dubious procedures of the South Sea scheme and to 'skreen' members of the Court and Administration who might suffer from such an enquiry were led by Aislabie, Secretary Craggs and Walpole in the Commons, and Stanhope and Sunderland in the Lords. In July, 1721, an over-worked Committee of Lawsuits, while untangling the claims and counter-claims it was briefed to investigate as a result of the stock market crash, was also charged with coercing what were called 'bor-rowers on the loan'. It started by drawing up a list of thirteen persons claiming stock subscribed for in the names of third parties, where the latter were indebted to the company. Among these debtors was John Gay, under whose name 'Alexander Pope of Twittenham' claimed £1,000 in the third money subscription (*FR*, p. 195), which was the subscription for which Secretary Craggs had brought in his huge list.

'Pray, if it is possible to remember a mere word of course in such a place as Exchange Alley', Pope asked Fortescue during that hectic summer, 'remember me there to Gay, for any where else (I deem) you will not see him as yet' (*P. Corr.* II, p. 48). John Gay certainly stayed in play longer than he should have. By early October, South Sea stock was down to £290 and Gay, in a letter to the bookseller Jacob Tonson probably written in that month complains: 'I cannot think your letter consists of the utmost civility, in five lines to press me twice to make up my account just at a time when it is impracticable to sell out of the Stocks in which my fortune is engaged.' Whereas Digby had looked for an improvement in civility consequent upon a collective social enrich-ment, under the pressure of impending disaster Gay pushes politeness over the edge:

I own my note engages me to make the whole payment in the beginning of September, had it been in my power, I would not have given you occasion to send to me, for I can assure you I am as impatient & uneasy to pay the money I owe, as some men are to receive it, and tis no small mortification to refuse you so reasonable a request, which is, that I may no longer be obliged to you.[32]

Gay's *Poems* had been published in May and having invested in South Sea stock the £1,000 put into his hands by subscriptions for the volume, he had held on too long in the hope of increasing his fortune and ended by losing practically everything. The Bubble had exploded, and by early December the panic and popular fury against an evidently

[32] *The Letters of John Gay*, edited by C. F. Burgess (Oxford, 1966), pp. 37–8.

complicit Parliament had developed into a crisis of constitutional proportions; South Sea stock stood at 191, having lost nearly 600 points since September 1. As Aislabie later put it when contemplating with hindsight the whole astonishing rise and fall:

It became difficult to govern it; and let those gentlemen that opened the flood-gates wonder at the deluge that ensued as much as they please, it was not in one man's power, or in the power of the whole administration, to stop it, considering how the world was borne away by the torrent.   (*FR*, p. 102)

Gay's losses were not total, however, and in February, 1721 he was transferring dividends to repay loans arranged during the boom for stock purchases. Pope's calculated self-presentations make his own case less easy to determine, but it seems that his gains were not substantial. He writes at the end of 1720 asking Caryll for payment of a debt he is owed, 'being in more necessity for present money than I ever yet was' (*P. Corr*. II, p. 60), and Gay evidently believed that Pope was financially discomfited. Early in 1722 Gay is telling Swift that '[Pope] has engag'd to translate the Odyssey in three years, I believe out of a prospect of gain than inclination, for I am persuaded he bore his part in the loss of the Southsea' (p. 43). Pope was to market his own literary production successfully enough for him shortly to achieve the kind of independence that would enable him to share and defend on a more equal footing a notion of Virtue with a peer group he admired. Gay, who was never to achieve the independence he similarly promoted for others and sought for himself, continued to act as agent and courier for Swift's investments in the South Sea Company as well as other bonds, advising the Dean on his interest accruals and telling him whether and when he has bought and sold on his behalf, and at what price. Within a decade, once-novel modes of investment and payment have become familiar terms between them as Gay writes to Ireland:

The day before I left London I gave orders for buying two Southsea or India Bonds for you which carry four p cent & are as easily turn'd into ready money as Bank Bills; which by this time I suppose is done.[33]

But Gay never forgot his experience in the Bubble year, and continues to remind Swift of the uncertainty inherent in all investment folios:

I have not dispos'd of your S Sea Bonds; there is a years interest due at Lady Day. But if I were to dispose of 'em at present I should lose a great deal of the premium I pay'd for 'em; perhaps they may fall lower, but I cannot prevail

[33] Ibid., p. 108.

with myself to sell 'em. The Roguerys that have been discover'd in some other companys I believe makes 'em all have less credit.[34]

A month later he repeats his nervousness and confesses uncertainty as to the most profitable course of action since South Sea bonds had fallen to fifty shillings from the six pounds he had paid for them: 'I believe the Parliament next year intend to examine the Southsea Scheme. I do not know whether it will be prudent to trust our money there till that time.'[35]

Swift's response to Gay's handling of his folio is typically paradoxical; simultaneously asking him to manage his 'South-Sea estate' as if it were Gay's own, but then insisting upon a particular exception: 'I mean ... gaming with the public, that is buying or selling lottery tickets, as you once proposed to me from your own practice' (*S. Corr.* IV, p. 14). Swift, who had been harvesting the interest on his holdings in the South Sea Company from as early as 1714, is attracted to the idea of investment in property, since he could then 'borrow money on the land and pay it by degrees or pay the interest as I pleased'. (*S. Corr.* II, p. 31). He was a careful investor who kept an equally careful eye on political developments and was throughout his life a competent manager of sometimes complicated livings, as his correspondence and his account books show. Shrewd enough to increase his private holdings from £500 in 1700 to £7,500 in 1736, by the time of his death in 1745 Swift's investments amounted to nearly £11,000.[36] He purchases land to add to his Laracor glebe, negotiates detailed rents and payments, invests income to increase the value of church property, seeking to double its value, and generally plans the improved succession of holdings he did not personally own (*S. Corr.* II, pp. 218, 255). He liked to complain about these duties, and on one occasion tells Pope that he would prefer to lose 'two or three hundred pounds rather than plague myself with accompts: so that I am very well qualified to be a Lord, and put into Peter Walter's hands' (*S. Corr.* II, p. 452), referring to the corrupt moneylender and estate manager who became a constant target for Pope's satire during the 1730s. Nonetheless, what his biographer says of the earlier years of Swift's investment holds as true for later developments: in real life Swift acted the part of a 'moneyed' man, making loans on mortgages, investing in South Sea stock, and owning outright no land to speak of (*S. Life* II, p. 488). Gay remained depend-

[34] Ibid., p. 121.   [35] Ibid., p. 123.
[36] *The Account Books of Jonathan Swift*, edited by P. V. Thomson and D. J. Thomson (London, 1984), p. cxxvi.

ent upon aristocratic patronage all his life, and became in an informal way estate manager for Queensberry. Pope was disbarred from owning property by his religion, yet devoted a great deal of effort and expense to improving his house and garden at Twickenham, becoming an authority on architectural and landscape design. These three gather around Bolingbroke (himself a successful investor) in defence of England's landed aristocracy at a time when history is moving decisively against it. In each of their cases, personal circumstance and practice diverge from an espoused political ideology concisely expressed in Swift's pamphlet-letter of 1720:

I have ever abominated that scheme of politicks, (now about thirty years old) of setting up a money'd Interest in opposition to the landed. For I conceived there could not be a truer maxim in our government than this, That the possessors of the soil are the best judges of what is for the advantage of the kingdom: If others had thought the same, Funds of Credit and South-sea Projects would neither have been felt nor heard of. (*SP* IX, p. 32)

From his perspective in Ireland, Swift had good reason publicly to oppose the money markets. While it might plausibly be argued that within England's developing economy the South Sea experience did not so much destroy as redistribute wealth, the drain of funds out of Ireland's limited resources had a disastrous effect. 'It is hardly credible what sums of money have been sent out of the kingdom and drowned in [the South Sea Company]', Archbishop King wrote: 'Men mortgaged their estates, gave bonds and judgements and carried their ready money there, and if we believe some, in money and debts and contracts Ireland is engaged a full million, which I believe is near double the current cash of the kingdom' (*S. Life* III, p. 155). The London *Mercury* informed its readers that Irish investors:

went late into the stocks, bought dear, extracted all the foreign gold out of Ireland, which was the best part of their current-coin, to make those purchases, so that money is become extremely scarce, the want of which makes the country people backward to bring their corn to market, in hopes the times will mend; whereby provisions are near as dear again as hath been known in [Dublin] for many years. (*S. Life* III, p. 155)

In a 1720 pamphlet, 'The Wonderful Wonder of Wonders', Swift constructs an image of the way credit works in the form of a character who is 'a sort of *Dependant* upon our family, and *almost* of the same *Age*; although I cannot directly say I have ever *seen* him. He is a Native of this Country, and hath lived long among us; but what appears wonderful, and hardly credible, was never seen *before*, by any Mortal' (*SP* IX, p.

281). But together with this profitable invisibility goes a sustained excremental metaphor which relates each textual event to the workings of this character's bowels: Swift is developing a pattern of image and association that will, in *Gulliver's Travels*, contaminate in pungent and decisive ways the Yahoos' passion for unlimited accumulation.[37]

When, also during the Bubble year, Swift laconically tells Richard Ford that he cannot understand the 'South-Sea Mystery', and adds that: 'perhaps the Frolick may go round, and every Nation (except this [Ireland] which is no Nation) have its Mississippi' (*S. Corr.* II, p. 342), he may not have known of plans to establish an Irish National Bank. The project received royal approval in July, 1721, and in September a sardonic Swift warns Archbishop King that since bankrupts are always for setting up banks, there could be little hope that Irish politicians would turn down the proposal (*S. Corr.* III, p. 101). But both Houses of the Irish Parliament threw the idea out in December and Swift was delighted to sing their praises: 'Your Hand alone from Gold abstains, / Which drags the slavish World in Chains.'[38] The victory was celebrated in more rollicking style in a ballad called 'The BANK Thrown Down' where promises of paper wealth are caustically treated:

> This BANK is to make us a New Paper Mill,
> This Paper they say, by the Help of a Quill,
> The whole Nations Pockets with Money will fill.   (p. 285)

The ballad opens up concerns with writing in the legal process of sanctioning dubious and delusory transformations of wealth, and plays upon fears not only that land values are jeopardised by the proposed new methods of accountancy and payment, but that lawyers are taking full advantage of their opportunities:

> In a *Chancery Bill* your Attorney engages,
> For so many Six-pences, so many *Pages*,
> But Six-pence a *Letter* is monstrous high Wages:
> Those that dropt in the *South-Sea* discover'd this *Plank*,
> By which they might Swimmingly *land* on a BANK.

> But the *Squire* he was cunning and found what they meant,
> That a Pack of sly Knaves should get fifty per Cent,
> While his Tenants in *Paper* must pay him his Rent:
> So for their *Quack-Bills* he knows whom to thank,
> For those are but *Quacks*, who mount on a BANK.

[37] See also 'The Riddle on the Posteriors', in *The Poems of Jonathan Swift*, edited by Harold Williams, 3 vols. (Oxford, 1958), I, p. 243.
[38] *Poems*, III, pp. 917–18.

Swift on several occasions exploits the figure of the mountebank to condemn the imaginary expectations conjured by investment in money markets: his pamphlet 'The Wonder of all the Wonders, that ever the World Wondered At' consists of nothing more than a string of unnatural and impossible tricks and deeds to advertise the coming to town of a magician (*SP* IX, pp. 285–6). Notwithstanding his remark to Ford, Swift understood well enough the lure of the market, and in their play with metaphoric transformations of capital liquidity, the opening stanzas of 'The Run upon the Bankers', written in 1720 but published in the same year as 'The BANK Thrown Down', show him playing upon fears that for many became all too real during the calamity of South Sea year:

> The bold Encroachers on the Deep,
> Gain by Degrees huge Tracts of Land,
> 'Till Neptune with a Gen'ral Sweep
> Turns all again to barren Strand.
>
> The Multitude's Capricious Pranks
> Are said to represent the Seas,
> Breaking the Bankers and the Banks,
> Resume their own when e'er they please.[39]

Chimerical expectations evaporate when real property is signed away in paper forms, and using an image that Pope was to adapt, Swift explores in more detail the role of writing in such easily managed transferrals of wealth:

> Riches, the Wisest Monarch sings,
> Make Pinions for themselves to fly,
> They fly like Bats, on Parchment Wings,
> And Geese their silver Plumes supply
>
> No Money left for squandering Heirs!
> Bills turn the Lenders into debters,
> The Wish of Nero now is Theirs,
> That, they had never known their Letters.[40]

Goose-quill pens provide the banker or his scrivener with the tools by which goods and property can be easily assigned from one person to another, suggesting simultaneously a more contemporary and destabilising resonance to Solomon's proverb (xxiii, 5): 'For riches certainly make themselves wings; they fly away as an eagle to heaven.' The

[39] Ibid., I, p. 239.   [40] Ibid., I, pp. 239–40

young Nero, about to sign someone's death warrant is said to have
remarked: 'How I wish I were illiterate.'[41] A movement from Solomon
to Nero debases Judaeo-Christian notions of justice: a shift into witchcraft imagery further condemns the immorality of paper-money transactions: 'Thus bankers o'er their Bills and Bags / Sit squeezing Images
of Wax.'

When the poem invites us to 'Conceive the whole Enchantment
broke' Swift asks his reader to consider what happens when the magical
bubble of confidence, of the belief or credit upon which banking
depends is pricked. In the resulting run upon the banks a double
transferral of agency takes place, from the human believers, or creditors, to inanimate bills of exchange, and then back again to motivate
human reaction. Given the sarcastic reference to banker's bills, we
should remember that the paper money of the time, issued by goldsmiths, banks and the Exchequer, was promissory notes, payable in coin
on demand:

> So Pow'rful are a Banker's Bills
> When Creditors demand their Due;
> They break up Counters, Doors, and Tills,
> And leave his emty Chests in View.[42]

The verse is concerned to leave gaping the actual losses incurred, as
opposed to the promissory paper exchanged. After comparing a banker
in these straits to Pluto, 'God of Gold and Hell', cowering in the
underworld at the prospect of resistance to nefarious practice, the poem
moves into mock-heroic simile, conjuring Faust's contracted exchange
of his soul for promised futures of property enhancement in ways that
look forward to Pope's Sir Balaam:

> As when a Conj'rer takes a Lease
> From Satan for a Term of Years,
> The Tenant's in a Dismal Case
> When e'er the bloody Bond appears.
>
> A baited Banker thus desponds,
> From his own Hand foresees his Fall,
> They have his Soul who have his Bonds,
> 'Tis like the Writing on the Wall.   (pp. 240–1)

The writing of fictions and evanescent wealth-creation are brought
together in unsettling ways, and when the ultimate run upon confidence 'At the last Trumpet' comes to pass, Swift complicates a

[41] Ibid., I, p. 240, n. 27.   [42] Ibid., p. 240

metaphor he uses more straightforwardly in his ballad. Now, the lines produce a slippage of signifier over signified for 'mountebank' ('a charlatan who appealed to his audience by means of stories, tricks, juggling and the like', *OED*), to shimmer in magical conjunction beyond its textual reversal and dismemberment: 'For in that Universal Call / Few Bankers will to Heav'n be Mounters.' Finally, and as part of its strategic recourse to the securities of biblical phrase and saying which traditionally draw to themselves forms of belief that had guaranteed a moral economy for centuries, the closing lines echo the Book of Daniel (v. 27):

> When Other Hands the Scales shall hold,
> And They in Men and Angels Sight
> Produc'd with all their Bills and Gold,
> Weigh'd in the Ballance, and found Light.   (p. 241)

Two of the banks found light in 1720, Martin's and Atwill's, are named in John Gay's treatment of a theme related to Swift's, but for Gay's mode of specifying his concerns, his full title provides appropriate contexts:

> A Panegyrical Epistle
> To Mr. Thomas Snow,
> Goldsmith, near *temple-Barr*:
> Occasion'd by his Buying and Selling the Third
> South Sea Subscriptions, taken in by the
> Directors At A Thousand *per cent.*[43]

When the poem was first published in February 1721, Gay still held South Sea stock, but had by then suffered his reversal of fortune. The 'third subscription' mentioned in the title was the company's third sale in June, 1720 of a block of its stock, called subscriptions because buyers paid for the stock in advance of issue; in this case putting 10 per cent down and contracting to pay the balance in instalments. But there was an interval of just over a year before the first of nine half-yearly payments fell due, during which time two interest payments would accrue to the buyers, and, it was assumed by them, the market value would rise. This third issue was fully subscribed in a single day, and those who did not manage to subscribe then were subsequently willing to buy the instalment contracts at a premium. While Thomas Snow of the banking firm Warner and Snow was successfully retailing these

---

[43] *John Gay: Poetry and Prose*, edited by V. A. Dearing and C. E. Beckwith, 2 vols. (Oxford, 1974), I, pp. 280–2. Subsequent quotations are given parenthetically in the text.

contracts, Gay was operating a subscription scheme of his own, taking money for his *Poems* before they were published. Part of this income he would in due course have to pay to his publisher, Jacob Tonson, but in the interim he invested it, putting down £1,000 in the third South Sea subscription. Since his stock contract bound him to buy shares to the value of £9,000, his original purchase was clearly speculative, and he was doomed to watch the market plummet after its spectacular rise.[44] Like Swift and Pope, Gay knew the slippage from classical credo to monetary credit, and circumstantial pressure made it possible for Gay to conceive of himself and the banker as engaging in comparable forms of profit-motivated enterprise where signifying boundaries between imaginative and imaginary productions become indeterminate.

If all that is needed is pen and paper for a 'creditable' dealer to retail contracts in a series of secondary transactions at rising prices, then one transaction becomes several through paper forms each of which is assumed to have valid contract status. 'A Panegyric Epistle' also mutates: while the pentameter form of the poem's own contract of engagement with the reader remains constant, shifts occur in the literary name given to it at different moments in its utterance. The poem's initial Horatian derivation involves an ironic invocation to Snow which then gestures at the close of the first stanza – with 'attend my Lay' – towards a kind of writing that had already evolved from an original signification of short lyric or narrative poem to become synonymous with *conte*. As the 'song' which then occupies lines 9 to 39 subsequently becomes 'this Moral Tale' about a banker and a poet in an insane asylum, Gay traces nominal shifts and changes in an unfolding continuity of narrative. But his address to the banker opens a further concern with the wealth of imaginative construction and the construction of imaginary wealth: as in Swift's verses, when fantasy takes hold the security of solid property is abolished:

> Why did *'Change-Alley* waste thy precious Hours,
> Among the Fools who gap'd for golden Show'rs?
> No wonder, if we found some *Poets* there,
> Who live on Fancy, and can feed on Air;
> No wonder, *they* were caught by *South-Sea* schemes,
> Who ne'er enjoyed a Guinea but in Dreams;
> No wonder, *they* their Third Subscriptions sold,
> For Millions of imaginary Gold:
> No wonder, that *their* Fancies wild could frame
> Strange Reasons, that a Thing is still the same,

44 Ibid., II, p. 608.

Though chang'd throughout in substance and in Name.
But *you* (whose Judgement scorns poetick Flights)
With Contracts furnish boys for Paper Kites.   (lines 17–29)

Gay knew whereof he spoke, and again those 'golden Show'rs' prefigure
the 'abundant show'r of cent per cent' that was to possess the soul of
Pope's Sir Balaam. Literary fancy merges with profit-motivated expectations that also stimulate the imagination, so while a hard-nosed
financier abjures 'poetick flights', as a stock-trader he nonetheless deals
in 'ideal Debts' (line 33), and what catches our attention is the mock-
eucharistic transubstantiation conjured by 'a Thing' being 'still the
same, / Though chang'd throughout in Substance and in Name'. The
terms of theological belief relating to a sacred transferral that divides
instead of unifying Christians are complicated by their secular association with substance changing from the material to the imaginary
world. Credit-notes, meanwhile, signify a promissory contract upon a
future where imagined wealth might transform into actuality. Since
'Madmen alone their empty Dreams pursue, / And still believe the
fleeting Vision true' (lines 34–5), the activities of poet and banker
coalesce. In the Bedlam asylum where the 'tale' is set, banker and poet
do fevered business together:

> There in full Opulence a *Banker* dwelt,
> Who all the Joys and Pangs of Riches felt:
> His Side-board glitter'd with imagin'd Plate;
> And his proud Fancy held a vast Estate.
>
> As on a Time he pass'd the vacant Hours,
> In raising Piles of Straw and twisted Bowers;
> A *Poet* enter'd of the neighb'ring Cell,
> And with fix'd Eye observ'd the Structure well.
> A sharpen'd Skewer cross his bare Shoulders bound
> A tatter'd Rug, which dragg'd upon the Ground.   (lines 44–53)

Fanciful structure contextualises frameless fancy, and when the
banker offers to sell the fantastic products of his overheated imagination, including 'Statues, Gardens, Fountains, and Canals; / With Land
of twenty thousand Acres round', the lunatic poet readily 'sign[s] the
Contract (as ordains the Law)'. Subsequently, when the banker in a
cooler moment seeks to retrieve something at least from his hectic deal –
'Give me a Penny, and thy Contract's void' – the poet promises to pay in
full, but using a precursor method to credit-notes:

> The startled Bard with Eye indignant frown'd.
> 'Shall I, ye gods, (he cries) my Debts compound!'

> So saying, from his Rug the Skewer he takes,
> And on the Stick Ten equal Notches makes:
> With just Resentment flings it on the Ground;
> 'There, take my Tally of Ten Thousand Pound.'   (lines 66–71)

Since tallies were sticks of hazel split and notched with one half given to a depositor and the other retained by the Exchequer to signify a specific amount paid or due, Gay's joke reverts to a method of receipt for payment that long pre-dates paper-currency. But other imaginative transubstantiations here suggest levels of uncertainty beyond the comic absurdities of the poem's surface narrative. 'Rug', in the sense of a coarse woollen mantle, also meant 'a torn-off portion, a catch or acquisition' (*OED*) and could thus be used to signify a share in something. Pope was to use the term[45] in its gambling sense of safe or secure and since to invest, of course, originally meant to clothe, to cover with a garment, Gay's joke detonates at different levels. Part of his implication is that security of linguistic representation is itself undermined by speculative transactions, and that when optimistic fancy is submerged in fantasy then boundaries between hitherto accepted signifying systems must also and inevitably be brought into question. As inevitably, then, representations of reality become a matter of personal belief and opinion.

In Ireland, meanwhile, Swift was vigorously publicising his own opinions. On 15 December 1720 he posted to London a poem called 'The Bubble' (later revised and called 'The *South-Sea*. 1721'), in which he tackled problems of perception and interpretation that were to be more fully explored in *Gulliver's Travels*. Deploying again the figure of a mountebank and, centrally, the image of land and real property in jeopardy, 'The Bubble' tracks a chimerical expansion of wealth associated with a southern ocean possessing the power magically to transform the dimensions of material substance:

> Ye wise Philosophers explain
> What Magick makes our Money rise
> When dropt into the Southern Main,
> Or do these Juglers cheat our Eyes?[46]

Once dipped in this 'liquid medium' the occult inflation of money-values 'cheats your sight' as the poem continues its conjuring metaphor:

[45] 'The Fourth Satire of Dr John Donne, Versifyed', in John Butt, ed. *The Poems of Imitations of Horace*, p. 37
[46] *Poems*, I, p. 250.

'behold, / Here's ev'ry Piece as big as ten. / . . . It rises both in Bulk and
Height, / Behold it mounting . . . / Behold it swelling'. Keeping in play
the image of solid coin magnified by water, whether a shilling in a basin
or a guinea in a bath, 'The Bubble' combines it with repeated misapprehensions of a water-reflected moon to remind the reader:

> So cast it in the *Southern* Seas,
> And view it through a *Jobber's* Bill,
> 'Put on what Spectacles You please,
> Your Guinnea's but a Guinnea still.'   (p. 255)

In *Gulliver's Travels*, Swift is to play with the contrast in the size of coins
between a Lilliputian *Sprug*, 'about the Bigness of a Spangle,'[47] and the
coins Gulliver offers to the farmer in Brobdingnag who 'wet the Tip of
his little Finger upon his Tongue, and [took] up one of my largest
Pieces, and then another; but he seemed to be wholly ignorant what
they were' (p. 68): a Brobdingnagian piece of gold is 'about the Bigness
of eight Hundred Moydores' (p. 80). But relationships between the two
texts amount to more than locally shared detail. Written as the South
Sea Company was so comprehensively crashing, 'The Bubble' presents
us with the figure of a 'deluded Bankrupt' still fantasising property-
acquisition based on paper wealth:

> In Stock three hundred thousand Pounds;
> I have in view a Lord's Estate,
> My Mannors all contig'ous round,
> A Coach and Six, and serv'd in Plate.   (p. 255)

In a scripted performance where magic and witchcraft merge with
classical image and biblical cadence, absurd apocalypse and comic
fraud combine unreal fantasy in Southern Seas with a fantastic reality
in London's money markets, while fictive and material worlds become
as uncertainly discriminated as they will for Gulliver and his readers.
So on his final voyage, Gulliver's apprehensions are not without precedent when he confounds paragons of reason with techniques of deception, considering that the Houyhnhnms 'must needs be Magicians, who
had thus metamorphosed themselves upon some Design' (p. 195).
Shortly afterwards he 'absolutely concluded that all these appearances
could be nothing else but Necromancy and Magick' (p. 198). Swift
called his own investment folio his 'South Sea estate', and in 'The

---

[47] Jonathan Swift, *Gulliver's Travels*, edited by R. A. Greenberg (New York, 1970), p. 45.
   Subsequent citations are given by both chapter and page parenthetically in the text.

Bubble' we watch castle-building in the air crossing terrestrial boundaries to sink in deep waters:

> While some build Castles in the Air,
> Directors build 'em in the Seas;
> Subscribers plainly see 'um there,
> For Fools will see as Wise men please.   (p. 257)

Women are busy too: figured as disappointed witches, 'the Female
Troops' gather at the gaming tables, 'their Losses to retrieve', and
contemporary newspaper accounts give us a flavour of the frantic
pursuit of enrichment Swift is satirising: 'Our South Sea ladies buy
South Sea jewels, hire South Sea maids, and take new country South
Sea Houses; the gentlemen set up South Sea Coaches and buy South
Sea estates'. When another journalist attempted stricter computation
he lost his own sense of moral discrimination in the process:

We are informed that since the hurly-burly of stock-jobbing there has appeared
in London 200 new Coaches and Chariots, besides as many more now on the
Stocks in the Coach-makers' yards; above 4,000 embroider'd coats; about 3,000
gold watches at the sides of whores and wives.[48]

Actual and imaginary significations of wealth shimmer from text to
context to text in an intoxicating circulation, as senses of connection
surface and submerge in a multiplying mirage of possibility and expectation, while the poem's voyager out into the extravaganza of South
Sea hallucinations bears at times an uncanny resemblance to Swift's
Lemuel. When Gulliver reports on his voyage to Houyhnhnmland (p.
191) that several sailors 'died in my ship of Calentures', a tropical fever
accompanied by delirium which caused sailors to leap into the sea, we
are carried back to the world of the poem:

> So, by a Calenture misled,
> The Mariner with Rapture sees
> On the smooth Ocean's azure Bed
> Enamell'd Fields, and Verdant Trees;
>
> With eager Hast he longs to rove
> In that fantastick Scene, and thinks
> It must be some enchanted Grove,
> And in he leaps, and down he sinks.   (pp. 251–2)

---

[48] Cited in Virginia Cowles, *The Great Swindle: The Story of the South Sea Bubble* (London, 1960),
p. 137.

Such metamorphoses are then differently deployed in a flight of fantasy specifically related to speculative ambitions and self-deceptions so that the poem can 'from a Fable form a Truth' about expanding and shrinking possibilities and failures, aspirations and decline. While the fall of Icarus was a familiar humanist symbol of the reward for high-flying ambition and folly, here it is related to paper-credit optimism:

> On *Paper* Wings he takes his Flight,
> With *Wax* the *Father* bound them fast,
> The *Wax* is melted by the Height,
> And down the towring Boy is cast.   (p. 252)

When Gulliver first sets out on the Antelope, he sails 'to the *South-Sea* ... and our Voyage at first was very prosperous' (p. 4), though later violent storms overtake them. The storm which threatens his subsequent trip to Brobdingnag arises from 'a Southern Wind, called the Southern *Monsoon*' (p. 63), and on his final voyage he tells us that when he puts in for replacements at Barbados and the Leeward Islands following 'the Direction of the Merchants who employed me ... and my Orders were, that I should trade with the *Indians* in the *South-Sea*, and make what discoveries I could' (p. 191). Swift encloses the imaginary geography of Gulliver's adventures within these stock market metaphors, to include all the visionary escapades, fantasies, concoctions and figments which make up the *Travels*, and Gulliver's dimensions rise and fall as do stock market expectations.

Gulliver's Travels gives indelible shape to the transfiguring of human possibilities during the early eighteenth century, and a brief detour into Bernard Mandeville's writing might suggest one possible context and butt for Swift's satirical repudiations. When Gulliver in Glubbdubdribb is depressed at learning that crime does indeed pay and that human behaviour is deteriorating, he goes counter to Mandeville's approaches to a similar society. And Mandeville's attitudes and priorities are reversed in Luggnagg where harsh legislation against the immortal Struldbrugs is justified because: 'Otherwise, as Avarice is the necessary Consequent of old Age, those Immortals would in time become Proprietors of the whole Nation, and Engross the Civil Power; which, for want of Abilities to manage, must end in the Ruin of the Publick' (p. 185). The Struldbrugs satirise a perception that whoever dies with most wealth has won the game, an aspiration that Mandeville would accept as appropriate for a market morality. When Gulliver, en route from Laputa, leaves Japan for Amsterdam, the wanton malice attributed to Dutch Christians ('Nominal Christianity' was the description Swift used elsewhere (*SP* II, p. 28)) may also include a stroke at the Dutch-man who was relatively uninterested in religion as such. 'Religion is one thing and Trade is another', Mandeville asserted, and trade is 'the greatest Friend to the Society'.[49] More fundamentally, by using its terms to describe an altered world of credit-based commerce and to celebrate its mobile opportunities, Mandeville assiduously undermined classical cognitions of wisdom, justice, courage and temperance. In pursuit of his notion that rather than the conquering of human passions it is their unbridled indulgence that is conducive to the common good, Mandeville traces in his 'Enquiry into the Origin of Moral Virtue' the evolution of moral codes and practices imposed by 'Lawgivers and other wise Men' upon a developing society. We glimpse Houyhnhnms and Yahoos when Mandeville's 'wise men', having discovered that flattery is the most powerful argument that can be used on human creatures, 'began to instruct them in the Notions of Honour and Shame'. They then seek to promote a spirit of emulation among men by dividing the whole species into two classes. One group consisted of abject, low-minded people, incapable of self-denial, enslaved to volup-tuousness and habitually yielding to every gross desire in order to heighten their sensual pleasure:

These vile grov'ling Wretches, they said, were the Dross of their Kind, and having only the shape of Men, differ'd from Brutes in nothing but their outward Figure. But the other Class was made up of lofty high-spirited Creatures, that ... opposed by the Help of Reason their most violent Incli-nations; and making a continual War with themselves to promote the Peace of others, aim'd at no less than the Publick Welfare and the Conquest of their own Passion.   (I, 43–4)

Mandeville's 'Enquiry' was first published in the expanded, 1714 edition of the *Fable of the Bees*. In 1723, when Swift was leaving his 'country of the Horses' (*S. Corr.* III, p. 5) to explore the lunacies of Laputa, Mandeville's book was reissued, was vociferously attacked, and was presented by the Grand Jury of Middlesex as a public nuisance. Nor was the Grand Jury entirely perverse in its assessment that the *Fable* recommended 'Luxury, Avarice, Pride and all kinds of Vices, as being necessary to Public Welfare' while portraying 'Religion and Virtue as prejudicial to Society, and detrimental to the State' (I, 385). This was excellent publicity and two further editions appeared in 1724 and 1725. Mandeville had produced a generational best-seller and his arguments and attitudes were anathema to Swift, who would nonethe-

---

[49] Mandeville, *Fable of the Bees*, I, p. 356.

less recognise both the force and the relevance of his analysis to contemporary London. If Laputa satirises a world of projecting initiative gone mad, the Houyhnhnms and the Yahoos of Gulliver's fourth voyage represent in part Swift's opposition to Mandeville's central and at the time shocking thesis that because the passionate indulgence of acquisitive and consuming egos contributes to increased economic activity and thus general prosperity, it could be said that private vices constituted public virtues. Swift could only have been horrified by Mandeville's thorough-going identification of economic prosperity with the public good, which effectively emancipated economics from generally received codes of morality.[50] By centring its analysis upon consumption, *The Fable* places civic ethics at the service of profitability as it rigorously subjectivises morality to project an economic system where each individual defines his conduct only by reference to his own interest. In such a scheme, society becomes no more than the mechanism – the invisible hand – by which these individuals harmonise.[51] If Mandeville's variety of Whiggism would hardly make him an attractive figure for Swift's preferences and predilections, his economic amoralism would certainly make him contemptible.[52] Practically everything that happened to England had already happened in one form or another in the Netherlands, as Swift had learned from his one-time patron William Temple, so there might also have been for Swift an uncomfortable self-perception in the moral to 'The Grumbling Hive': 'Fools only strive / To make a Great an honest Hive.'

Mandeville watches people mingling in society and rationalises their behaviour as market-led. He makes clear that he has in view 'a large and stirring Nation' in 'a trading country' (I, 104) with a flourishing capital city (I, 248), and grounds his perceptions in the processes of exchange. Since markets make people meet and relate in ways that require strategic adaptations of personal behaviour, Mandeville's concern is with the social psychology of 'commerce between well-bred people', who will cultivate 'well-bred concealment' from each other as they manoeuvre for profitable advantage (I, 77–8). To explain his poem's allegation that in certain respects the knave and the industrious

---

[50] Louis Dumont, *From Mandeville to Marx: The Genesis and Triumph of Economic Ideology* (London, 1977), p. 61.

[51] Ibid., p. 75.

[52] For Mandeville's political attitudes see H. T. Dickinson, 'The Politics of Bernard Mandeville', in *Mandeville Studies*, ed. Primer, pp. 80–97. Also, M. M. Goldsmith, *Private Vices, Public Benefits: Bernard Mandeville's Social and Political Thought* (Cambridge, 1985), pp. 120–59.

citizen are indistinguishable, Mandeville cites an example of futures trading in West Indian sugar, where two wealthy merchants engage in a drama of the biter bit by each in turn acting on information unknown by, and kept concealed from, the other. Wheeling and dealing find sociable forms as polite hospitality is conscripted in the service of confidence-trickery and mutual deception (I, 61–3). Decio and Alcander, both gentlemen in the eyes of society, do nothing illegal but rather what is typical and expected of them and without any involvement of what might be recognised as traditionally 'noble' virtues. Reflecting in his 1732 essay 'A Search into the Nature of Society', Mandeville is open about his fascination with market morality: 'To me it is a great Pleasure, when I look on the Affairs of human Life, to behold into what various and often strangely opposite Forms the hope of Gain and thoughts of Lucre shape Men, according to the different Employments they are of, and Stations they are in' (I, 349). The cash-nexus is recurrently a main focus, with Mandeville frequently selecting his examples from the world of buying and selling. His account of a young lady being duped by a draper emphasises the polite conversational and social intimacies permitted within the arena of exchange, to show how they are manipulated for profit. The draper's advantage in this transaction is never in doubt since 'the most material part of the Commerce between them, the debate about the Price, ... he knows to a farthing, and she is wholly Ignorant of' (I, 351).

Now that money has become 'the Cement of civil Society' (II, 350), the monetarisation of motive and response repeatedly focuses Mandeville's attempt to discover systems and rules which might account for trading practice. Everywhere, a developing capitalism engages his attention: 'As there is no living without Money, so those that are unprovided, and have no body to give them any, are oblig'd to do some Service or other to the society before they can come at it' (I, 101), and because the rules he speaks of 'consist in a dextrous Management of our selves' in which concealment and deception become determining attributes (I, 68), he engages in a social psychology for economic individualism: 'Every Individual is a little World by itself, and all Creatures, as far as their Understanding and Abilities will let them, endeavour to make that Self happy: This in all of them is the continuall Labour, and seems to be the whole design of Life.' It is the pursuit and consumption of purchasable commodities that Mandeville is concerned with and in a world where 'Man centres everything in himself, and neither loves nor hates, but for his own Sake' (II, 178), he describes the self-seeking sensibility thus called into operation. He foregrounds 'the Consumption

of things' (I, 86) in order to find the 'chain of causes' in a social
economy of traded goods and services: 'The short-sighted Vulgar in the
Chain of Causes seldom see further than one Link; but those who can
enlarge their View, and will give themselves the Leisure of gazing on
the Prospect of concatenated Events, may, in a hundred Places see *good*
spring up and pullulate from *Evil*, as naturally as Chickens do from
Eggs (I, 91). As economic egoism pursues its path towards a redefinition
of social norms, in Mandeville's view of concatenated events that norm
is already found in the relation between persons and things, in contra-
distinction to the traditional norms and valorisations of a landed
society's moral economy, which habitually bore on the relationship
between person and person.[53]

While the original verses of 'The Grumbling Hive' expose the partisan nature of a legal system operating ferociously against the poor and
benignly for the wealthy, Mandeville nonetheless affirms that when
vice turns into crime then punishment is due. A legal framework is
essential for the harmonious operation of a society of competitive
egoism:

> So Vice is beneficial found,
> When it's by Justice lopt and bound.   (I, 37)

Remark L in *The Fable* also makes clear the necessity of a contractual
protection for property-rights: 'The *Meum* and the *Tuum* must be
secured, crimes punish'd, and all other Laws concerning the Administration of Justice, wisely contriv'd, and strictly executed' (I, 116).
Mandeville derives examples from the marriage-bed to show that what
is lust at one moment becomes commendable vigour when passionate
indulgence is legally sanctioned by contract, and from the gaming-
tables to discern and describe the manipulated display of feelings and
attitudes (I, 77–8, 82). As provocatively, and even outrageously, but
with an eye to the realities of things, he will look for the economic
rationale for human behaviour in a commercial society by examining
the wholesale and retail market in gin as examples of general good
arising from individual vice,[54] and will also suggest that the brothel and
harlot trade shows 'a great deal of Prudence and Oeconomy' in the
'Markets of Love' (I, 96–7). For Mandeville the end of increased
circulation of money, goods and services is all, justifying the means

---

[53] Dumont, *Mandeville to Marx*, p. 77.
[54] Mandeville may have remembered that in 1700, the Duke of Lorraine had established 500
official brandy distilleries with the express intention of restoring a war-ravaged economy
(*FR*, p. 5).

which traditional moralists found intolerable: 'As long as the Nation has its own back again, we ought not to quarrel with the manner in which the Plunder is repay'd' (I, 104). On such grounds, his comparison of 'the Body Politick' to a bowl of punch adapts the terms of conventional moral categories to the consumption ethic being promoted, where in separation the several ingredients might be thought unlikely to 'make any tolerable Liquor':

Avarice should be the Souring and Prodigality the Sweetning of it. The water I would call the Ignorance, Folly and Credulity of the floating insipid Multitude; while Wisdom, Honour, Fortitude and the rest of the sublime Qualities of Men, which separated by Art from the Dregs of Nature the fire of Glory has exalted and refin'd into a Spiritual Essence, should be an Equivalent to Brandy.   (I, 105)

If civic discourse had 'by art' traditionally excluded ordinary people from the virtuous terms of commendation it articulated for the glory of a reigning aristocracy, Mandeville will have fun reconstructing them for a new and mobile world. He knew Amsterdam, and found the codes and conventions of England's emergent market morality interesting and intriguing enough for him to promote the shopkeeper as ideal citizen, both for the psychological perspicacity his trade requires (I, 351), and for the self-denying lengths to which he goes in service of others for his own ultimate advantage (II, 52). Certainly Mandeville found no overpowering reason to locate in landed individuals the kinds of profitable energy and industry he was keen to detect and describe. In his verses landed aristocrats figure as 'The Lazy Ones' who 'Indulg'd their Ease, with all the Graces / Of health and Plenty in their Faces' (I, 21), and when he constructed an ideal aristocrat of 'immense estate', it was to involve him in the commercialisation of moral assessment by discovering in him motives and desires comparable with those obtaining among shopkeepers and merchants. Given the social and economic power that landed wealth still exercised, the prominence which the Second Dialogue gives to its landlord is of some significance. During the seventeenth century, civic humanist discourse had been developing a system of moral hierarchy and social classification around this personality of landed integrity, and Mandeville is differently concerned to valorise citizenship in a post-revolutionary world where luxury, pride, envy and vanity are 'Ministers of Industry', and money the motor and cohesive element in a market economy. In *The Fable*, a world of different appearances displaces a previously accepted morality of fact and valuation. Social mobility in expanding markets brings into prominence fashionable self-presentation as a basis for public estimation of individual worth, where for those with money to indulge them, personal choice and preference create a 'Fickleness, / In Diet, Furniture and Dress' which in turn becomes 'The Very Wheel that turn[s] the Trade'. Mandeville traces the attractions of upward mobility through fashionable emulation: 'We all look above our selves, and, as fast as we can, strive to imitate those, that some way or other are superior to us.' That 'some way or other' would have been an outrage to those who still assumed a divine right of succession for their landed morality and one effect of a changing ethics that the *Fable* discloses is a partial levelling in certain sectors of society, at least as far as appearances are concerned. Because shopkeepers like mercers and drapers find no difference between themselves and larger-scale merchants, they 'therefore dress and live like them', while another net effect is the continuing stimulation of the garment industry and consequent employment for the poor: 'after so many various Shiftings and Changing of Modes, in trumping up new ones and renewing of old ones, there is still a *plus ultra* left for the ingenious' (I, 129).

In such transforming contexts, legal valorisations and social codes of practice shift and change in an evolving process:

> Their Laws and Clothes were equally
> Objects of Mutability;
> For what was well done for a time,
> In half a Year became a Crime;
> Yet while they alter'd thus their Laws,
> Still finding and correcting Flaws,
> They mended by Inconstancy
> Faults which no Prudence could foresee.
> Thus Vice nurs'd Ingenuity.   (I, 25–6)

In these formulations, civil society and the moral codes it finds congenial advance through a haphazard process of makeshift amendments in trials and errors without any predetermined end in view other than material well-being. When purchasable appearance becomes a decisive factor in social and personal systems of valuation, then the classical *politea* based upon freehold property of determinable tenure is significantly reshaped. Mandeville's repeated emphasis upon self-presentation and the deceptions and self-deceptions it often entailed composes a sustained opposition to neo-classical standards of moral value, and particularly to its promotion of any single correct standard. Insofar as classicism at the time sought to mediate the inherited notion that standards of taste and moral worth were the same for a self-identifying landed élite as they had been for Romans and Greeks, Mandeville's rejection of such defining standards as well as his denial of any single hierarchy of values makes him a spokesman for England's developing society as much as an opponent of its precursor forms and of those who sought their continuance. When any shopkeeper can self-interestedly assume the guise of a 'Gentleman-like-man, that has every thing Clean and Fashionable about him' (II, 350), the trappings of a 'gentleman' become increasingly difficult to separate from earlier definitions of what constituted gentlemanly substance. There is, additionally, an element of self-fulfilling prophecy in Mandeville's preliminary urban sociology, since anyone ambitious to make a mark in the world will 'wear Clothes above his Rank, especially in large and populous Cities, where obscure Men may hourly meet with fifty Strangers to one Acquaintance, and consequently have the Pleasure of being esteem'd by a vast Majority, not as what they are, but what they appear to be' (I, 128).

In a society of competing egos, fashionable appearance helps to drive the economy in a circular and mutually validating process. Praise feeds fashionable vanity, and virtue then becomes a fashionable commodity. When once-classical cognitions of public moral virtue are thus effectively privatised, it becomes increasingly difficult to determine the relationships between outward signs and inward graces, so that the social applause which functions as a kind of invisible wage paid to men of sense and judicious fancy, has a much greater spectrum to choose from (II, 17). Nor can the landed aristocrat, presented in such purity of conduct in the Second Dialogue that even Horatio, himself a prospective peer of the realm, cries out: 'Where is there such a Landlord in the World?' (II, 74), escape from the egoism that prevalently defines and organises the world he inhabits. Horatio remembers that Cleomenes has used the words 'seems' and 'appears' (II, 72) to describe his figure of landed propriety whose professed morality, it soon becomes apparent, also arises from self-deceiving fictions. As social attitudes change, we witness in Mandeville's landlord a contradiction between moralistic self-projection and a behaviour oriented towards the same kinds of material advantage and worldly satisfaction enjoyed by people whose wealth derives from money. Traditional moral discourse and the self-evaluations it promotes come into conflict with developing commercial practice, and in exploring these conflicts Mandeville suggests a fundamental unreality to the systems of personal accreditation by which status was acknowledged and behaviour customarily praised or condemned. A perceivable world, that is to say, contrasts with and diverges from the springs of motive and intention as an older discourse had presented them. As a result, the apparent self-justifications of Mandeville's landed gentleman co-ordinate unsettlingly with a newly prevalent identification of will and purpose through a social market of competing egos, so that what is brought into focus is the conflict between traditional forms of civic personality grounded in real property and endowed with an ethic of classical virtue, and market-oriented perceptions of individuality where passion and fantasy constantly fluctuate. Similar considerations lie behind Mandeville's assault upon then-conventional conceptions of honour, which he describes as 'a Chimera without Truth or Being, an Invention of Moralists and Politicians' (I, 198) designed to preserve particular structures of social power and their morality of landed self-presentation where, 'like the gout', honour is 'generally counted Hereditary, ... all Lords Children are born with it' (I, 199). It has been pointed out that courage was also considered to be a virtue peculiarly appropriate to landed gentlemen, and formed part of their ideological armoury against the idea of a standing army: 'The militia was an organisation officered and controlled by landed gentlemen. Being a gentleman entitled one to bear arms; the very dress of a gentleman included a visible weapon. Gentlemen were a military class and courage is a military virtue. The ideological counterpart of the small sword was "honour".' [55] Mandeville's treatment of the concept co-ordinates with his portrayal of a morally self-deluding aristocrat, and what Pope would idealise as 'eternal' values are presented as socially oppressive and increasingly redundant.

But Mandeville's analysis reaches beyond the pride of landed self-representation. More generally, the stability of the ego is itself compromised when what was once a classically derived and coherent moral structure based on *terra firma* is called into question by new forms of capital liquidity increasingly held and passed in paper pledges of credit that were by definition and practice uncertain and socially unstable. Since self-hood and personality were now increasingly identified through the tactics and strategies of exchange, while stock markets encouraged fantastic self-projections that for some visibly materialised in the insignia of wealth, all things were aflowing in ways never dreamed of by Heracleitus. Like Swift's, though in the service of an opposing ideology and practice, Mandeville's text exposes how 'a most beautiful superstructure may be raised upon a rotten and despicable

[55] Goldsmith, *Private Vices, Public Benefits*, p. 151.

Foundation' (II, 64). In his own way, Mandeville was as aware as Swift of the gap between the surfaces that individuals were presenting to each other socially and the motivating realities of their passions and interests. But Mandeville considered that he had effectively demonstrated 'how necessary our Appetites and Passions are for the welfare of all Trades and Handicrafts', openly acknowledging that such appetites and passions 'are our bad Qualities, or at least produce them' (I, 344). If, in *Gulliver's Travels*, Swift tears away at the civilised pretence of society to expose the Yahoo within, then Mandeville shows how the Yahoo within creates the only civilisation we know.[56] A society that Pope, Swift and Gay sought to avoid, deflect or moderate by directing against it their formidable satirical energies is disclosed in *The Fable of the Bees* as the necessary and undeniable here and now of everyday existence. But Swift inscribes an uncompromising antagonism to the hypocrisy that now appeared to be socially necessary, and given the prevalent imagery of conspicuous consumption in *The Fable*, there is some point in reading Swift's 'A Modest Proposal' as the ultimate response to any and all reasonably articulated projects designed to enrich or otherwise satisfy those with money to spend. 'A Modest Proposal' carefully maintains its facade of pseudo-dispassionate calculations of profit and loss in a prospectus of gain for the few amid general impoverishment. Deriving from his experience of colonial actualities in Ireland, the intensity of Swift's predatory scheme demolishes exploitative consumption with a chilling audacity that damns many of Mandeville's grounding assumptions. David Hume justified his inclusion of Mandeville among the 'late philosophers in *England*, who have begun to put the science of man on a new footing, and have engaged the attention, and excited the curiosity of the public', as evidence of an improvement in reason and philosophy he attributed to 'a land of toleration and liberty'.[57] Swift took a different view, and in *Gulliver's Travels* confronts a world made textually manifest in *The Fable of the Bees*.

[56] Philip Pinkus, 'Mandeville's Paradox', in *Mandeville Studies*, ed. Primer, p. 200.
[57] David Hume, *A Treatise of Human Nature* (1739), edited by L. A. Selby-Bigge, 2nd ed., rev. by P. H. Nidditch (Oxford, 1978), p. xvii and n.

3

'Some very bad effects': the strange case of *Gulliver's Travels*

As to what is called a Revolution-principle, my opinion was this; that, whenever those evils which usually attend and follow violent change of government, were not in probability so pernicious as the grievances we suffer under a present power, then the publick good will justify such a Revolution; and this I took to be the Case in the Prince of Orange's expedition, although in the consequences it produced some very bad effects, which are likely to stick long enough by us.

(*S. Corr.* II, p. 372)

The two-way telescoping of perceptions in *Gulliver's Travels* radically defamiliarises the proliferating objects of Belinda's universe. In the first two voyages, not only are the satiric glasses alternately convex and concave, they are also subject to the distortions of Gulliver's own lenses,[1] so that the reader encounters a calculated disordering of perception and participation that effectively destabilises any secure sense of the world of the book. In Brobdingnag, the construction and furnishing of a miniaturised box-apartment is presented in the same tones of pride and wonder Gulliver uses to describe his 'entire set of Silver Dishes and Plates, and other Necessaries, which in Proportion to those of the Queen, were not much bigger than what I have seen in a *London* Toy-shop, for the Furniture of a Baby-house'.[2] After his rescue he displays to Captain Wilcocks his 'small Collection of Rarities':

There was the Comb I had contrived out of the Stumps of the King's Beard; and another of the same Materials, but fixed into a paring of her Majesty's Thumb-nail, which served for the Back. There was a Collection of Needles and Pins from a Foot to half a Yard long. Four Wasp-Stings, like Joyner's Tacks: Some Combings of the Queen's Hair: a Gold Ring which one Day she made me

---

[1] J. A. Downie, *Jonathan Swift: Political Writer* (London, 1984), p. 273.
[2] *Gulliver's Travels*, ed. Greenberg, p. 84. Subsequent references are given by book, chapter and page parenthetically in the text.

Figure 2   'The Bublers Mirrour: or England's Folley', 1720

a present of in the most obliging Manner, taking it from her little Finger, and throwing it over my Head like a Collar . . . I shewed [the captain] a Corn that I had cut off with my own hand from a Maid of Honour's Toe; it was about the Bigness of a *Kentish* Pippin, and grown so hard, that when I returned to

England, I got it hollowed into a Cup and set in Silver. Lastly, I desired him to see the Breeches I had then on, which were made of a mouse's skin.

(II, vii, 121)

One immediate contrast is with Gulliver in Lilliput where the largest trees become a table and chair and two hundred sempstresses fashion his clothes; all of which is a far cry and then perhaps not so distant from Belinda's dressing-table and her 'rich Brocade'. Swift is developing unique ways of satirising a world of appearance and fashionable self-presentation, and Gulliver naturally assumes an estranged perspective on his fourth voyage to explain to his Master Houyhnhnm that in England 'those of my kind covered their Bodies with the Hairs of certain Animals prepared by Art, as well for Decency, as to avoid Inclemencies of Air both hot and cold' (IV, iii, 204–5): similarly his shoes become a 'Covering made from the Skin of some other Brute' (IV, iv, 210). Over the four books a comic use of wide-eyed naivety combines with an often corrosive irony as, in a series of strategic disorientations which now allies the reader with Gulliver and now sets us at variance, things once again are and are not quite what they seem. Disproportion plays with expectation in ways that repeatedly subject the reader to echo and memory from book to book and from text to social context. The Lilliputian hogshead that Gulliver drinks off at a draught (I, i, 7) prefigures the golden cup from which the Queen of Brobdingnag drank 'above a Hogshead at a Draught' (II, iii, 84), and the decorum of Pope's Belinda at her dressing-table is shattered when the Queen's maids of honour do not 'at all scruple while [Gulliver] was by, to discharge what they had drunk, to the Quantity of a least two hogsheads, in a Vessel that held above three Tuns' (II, v, 95). Also unlike Belinda, whose devotion to her mirror-image merges subjectivity in appearance, masking her self-estrangement, Gulliver after Brobdingnag is more radically displaced from any sustaining sense of self: 'I could never endure to look in a Glass after my Eyes had been accustomed to such prodigious Objects; because the Comparison gave me so despicable a Conceit of my self' (II, viii, 122). After spending time in Houyhnhnmland, his self-estrangement is so complete that: 'When I happened to behold the Reflection of my own Form in a Lake or a Fountain, I turned away my Face in Horror and detestation of my self' (IV, x, 243). *Gulliver's Travels* confounds the integrity of its protagonist's personality much as it undermines the security of the narrative which presents him. Only a steady determination 'to behold my Figure often in a Glass, and thus if possible habituate my self by time to tolerate the Sight of a human creature' (IV,

xii, 259), might conquer Gulliver's self-aversion. Among the Brobding-
nagians Gulliver is reduced to the doll-like status of an '*English Manni-
kin*' (II, ii, 74) and someone else's possession, before acquiring a specific
market-value when displayed 'for Money as a publick Spectacle' (II, ii,
76). Once his new master realises 'how profitable I was like to be' (II, ii,
78), Gulliver's price becomes an index of his shame when a thousand
pieces of gold is demanded for his sale to the Brobdingnagian Queen.
Reinforced by the ridiculous pride in grovelling he constantly maintains, Gulliver blandly narrates his incorporation into the processes of
commodity-exchange – he is reified as a clock-work mechanism and
taught 'a Sett of Words to make me sell at a higher price' (II, iii, 81) –
which produces in turn a generally induced conviction of his own
comparative insignificance: 'So that I really began to imagine my self
dwindled many Degrees below my usual size' (II, iii, 85).

The invented worlds a sea-borne Gulliver encounters are partially
designed to distract us from his grounding participation in a trading
society centred upon acquisition and exchange. While the adventures of
his fictive contemporary Robinson Crusoe are customarily read as
constituting a paradigm of individualist initiative separated from
market forces, Gulliver's originary status and nature as economic man
has not always received the attention it deserves. Although Crusoe is a
slave-owner and slave-trader before his shipwreck, his subsequent
record of a life of gain, technical security, adventure and everyday
ingenuity is uncomplicated by the processes of exchange and in that
sense does not engage directly in the trading experiences of its time, so
the suggestion that *Gulliver's Travels* begins where *Robinson Crusoe* ends;
enquiring and reflecting where the other rests content to act and
possess, is to the point.[3] The *Travels* involves market valuations and
Gulliver, too, is keen to possess. Beginning as a ship's surgeon, he 'got
some addition to his Fortune' from his earliest voyages. As he prepares
to leave home for his second adventure, he arranges his affairs with
entrepreneurial familiarity: 'My remaining Stock I carried with me,
Part in Money, and Part in Goods, in hopes to improve my Fortunes.
My eldest Uncle, *John*, had left me an Estate in Land, near *Epping*, of
about Thirty Pounds a Year; and I had a long Lease of the *Black-Bull* in
Fetter Lane, which yielded me as much more' (I, viii, 59). Details of this
kind confirm Gulliver's active participation in market forces that are
redefining the political personality and redirecting social priorities. His

---

[3] Nigel Dennis, *Jonathan Swift: A Short Character* (London, 1964), pp. 131–2.

first instinct when he is discovered by the farmer in Brobdingnag is, absurdly, to offer him money, but on his way to Laputa he is sufficiently at ease with procedures of commercial transaction to be given command of a sloop with the power to 'traffick' independently (III, i, 128). Gulliver is a trading projector who participates unselfconsciously in the commercial relations of economic individualism that were reordering political hierarchies and establishing markets domestically and overseas. Yet in an equally disconcerting breakthrough into the realities of colonial market-making, after leaving Houyhnhnmland he shows himself to be fully alert to the brute actualities a brave new world of marine initiative entailed:

For instance, a Crew of Pyrates are driven by a Storm they know not whither; at length a Boy discovers Land from the Top-mast; they go on shore to rob and plunder; they see an harmless People, are entertained with kindness, they give the Country a new Name, they take formal Possession of it for the King, they set up a rotten Plank or a Stone for a Memorial, they murder two or three Dozen of the Natives, bring away a Couple more by Force for a Sample, return home, and get their Pardon. Here commences a new Dominion acquired with a Title by a *Divine Right*. Ships are sent with the first Opportunity; the Natives driven out or destroyed, their Princes tortured to discover their Gold; a free Licence given to all Acts of Inhumanity and Lust; the Earth reeking with the Blood of its Inhabitants: And this execrable Crew of Butchers employed in so pious an Expedition, is a *modern Colony* sent to convert and civilise an idolatrous and barbarous People.   (IV, xii, 258)

As a merchant-adventurer Gulliver is already compromised in a text that roundly condemns the overseas effects of his business, while its domestic effects are dealt with in considerable detail. When a 'Company of *English* Lords and Ladies in their Finery and Birth-day Cloaths, acting their several Parts in the most courtly Manner of Strutting, and Bowing and Prating' (II, iii, 85) is produced for a discomfitingly diminished Gulliver in Brobdingnag to establish equivalences with his own society, the foregrounding of conspicuous display reminds us that the *Travels* repeatedly satirises a festival of consumption, as often as not figured literally. Five pages into the account of his first voyage Gulliver is enjoying 'Baskets full of Meat':

There were Shoulders, Legs, and Loins shaped like those of Mutton, and very well dressed, but smaller than the wings of a Lark. I eat them by two or three at a Mouthful; and took three Loaves at a time, about the bigness of Musket Bullets. They supplied me as fast as they could, shewing a thousand Marks of Wonder and Astonishment at my Bulk and Appetite. I then made another Sign that I wanted Drink.   (I, i, 7)

This seemingly gargantuan process is neatly reprogrammed when a pet monkey in Brobdingnag forces food from its own cheek-pouches into an unwilling Gulliver: 'I was almost choaked with the filthy Stuff the monkey had crammed down my Throat; but, my dear little Nurse picked it out of my Mouth with a small Needle; and then I fell a vomiting, which gave me great Relief' (II, v, 99). We find ourselves tracking forward to that moment in Book IV where Gulliver's horse-master confirms imperial trading as a corruption of virtuous appetite:

Nothing ... rendered the *Yahoos* more odious, than their undistinguished Appetite to devour every thing that came in their Way ... And it was peculiar in their Temper, that they were fonder of what they could get by Rapine or Stealth at a greater Distance, than much better Food provided for them at home. If their Prey held out, they would eat till they were ready to burst, after which Nature had pointed out to them a certain *Root* that gave them a general Evacuation.   (IV, vii, 227–8)

While his experience in Ireland sharpens Swift's perception of colonial practice, it is not until the fourth book that Gulliver's account of England examines the domestic role of money in an economy of expropriation and subordination enabling conspicuous consumption by the few at the expense of the many. In a series of disconsolate self-recognitions, Gulliver describes how only when a London Yahoo has accumulated a great store of a 'precious substance' can he purchase anything he chooses, including 'the finest Cloathes, the noblest Houses, great tracts of Land, the most costly Meats and Drinks; and have his Choice of the most beautiful Females'. Because '*Money* alone was able to perform these feats' its unlimited accumulation becomes the chief aim of all Yahoos, and Gulliver is then left to describe a different kind of spectacular disproportion since 'the rich Man enjoyed the fruits of the poor Man's Labour, and the latter were a Thousand to One in Proportion to the former'. He goes on to tell his master that in England 'the Bulk of our People was forced to live miserably, by labouring every Day for small Wages to make a few live plentifully' (IV, vi, 218).

When he is pushed to explain to his master 'what these costly Meats were, and how any of us happened to want them' Gulliver discloses the global dimensions of domestic consumption:

Whereupon I enumerated as many Sorts as came into my Head, with the various Methods of dressing them, which could not be done without sending Vessels by Sea to every Part of the World, as well for Liquors to drink, as for Sauces, and innumerable other Conveniences. I assured him, that this whole Globe of Earth must be at least three Times gone round, before one of our better Female *Yahoos* could get her Breakfast, or a Cup to put it in.

                                                           (IV, vi, 218–19)

The figure of woman as indulged and indulgent consumer is nothing new in male writing at this time, but an echo of Charles Davenant's attitude towards commerce is heard when Gulliver goes on to say that: 'In order to feed the Luxury and Intemperance of the Males, and the Vanity of the Females, we sent away the greatest Part of our necessary Things to other Countries, from whence in Return we brought the materials of Disease, Folly, and Vice, to spend among ourselves.' Gulliver's unselfconscious reflection produces a sense of developing social interdependence as it mingles with characteristic male responses a recognition of the developing division of labour: 'For instance, when I am at home and dressed as I ought to be, I carry on my Body the Workmanship of an hundred Tradesmen; the Building and Furniture of my House employ as many more; and Five Times the Number to adorn my Wife' (IV, vi, 219–20). Among its many concerns, *Gulliver's Travels* mounts a paradoxical critique of imperial commerce itself as leading inevitably to a degradation of the body politic; a critique which opens out the debate concerning the corruption of traditional landed virtue by unlicensed profit-seeking, and introduces ambiguities involving both Gulliver and his creator. Here is Davenant:

Trade, without doubt, is in its nature a pernicious thing; it brings in that wealth which introduces luxury; it gives a rise to fraud and avarice, and extinguishes virtue and simplicity of manners; it depraves a people, and makes way for that corruption which never fails to end in slavery, foreign or domestic. Lycurgus, in the most perfect model of government that was ever framed, did banish it from his commonwealth. But, the posture and condition of other countries considered, it is become with us a necessary evil ... However, if trade cannot be made subservient to the nation's safety, it ought to be no more encouraged here than it was in Sparta.[4]

Swift's political 'bad effects' correlate with Davenant's economic 'necessary evil' as, in reply to an earlier question from his Houyhnhnm master about the causes of war, Gulliver allows that 'sometimes our neighbours *want* the *Things* which we *have*, or *have* the *Things* which we want; and we both fight, till they take ours or give us theirs' (IV, vi, 213). Trade wars are related to the rising expectations of consumption Gulliver then goes on to elaborate. Beyond whatever the suppressed inclinations of Swift's psychology may have contributed to their textual intensification, a context for the repeated abuse to which the human body is subjected is a suspicion of commercial processes that were erasing traditional perceptions. Or, as Gulliver is made to realise by his

[4] Charles Davenant, *An Essay upon the Probable Methods of Making a People Gainers in the Balance of Trade* (London, 1699), pp. 154–5.

Houyhnhnm master: 'We disarmed ourselves of the few Abilities
[Nature] had bestowed; had been very successful in multiplying our
original Wants, and seemed to spend our whole Lives in vain Endeavours to supply them by our own invention' (IV, vii, 225). Yet in the
divided kingdom of the fourth book, the only way for Houyhnhnm
virtue to survive uncontaminated is at the expense of any developed
civil society among them. They 'have not the least Idea of Books or
Literature' (IV, iii, 203), 'their Knowledge is all traditional', being
'wholly governed by Reason, and cut off from all commerce with other
nations' (IV, ix, 238). In a further twist, if the Houyhnhnms are
without culture and choice, then the English citizens to whom Gulliver
returns are merely more civilised versions of Yahoos, and he is unable to
strike the balance his text momentarily signals. Elsewhere, connections
between projects of self-advancement, commercial expansion and
colonial subordination work their wonderful effects, as Gulliver learns
in Laputa, the book which was composed after the fourth but precedes
it in Swift's artistic ordering.

Gulliver's account of Lagado's Academy of Projectors produces ironised versions of his England, ranging from the zanily absurd to the
socially specific, with several of them, like the School of Languages,
contriving to be both at once. Swift's desire to be clearly understood is
well-known, to the extent that he would read work to servants to make
sure that his language was effective, and the mad projectors of the
Academy draw his fire in a treatment where plain style and idiocy
collide. Gulliver's unadorned delivery is also an ironic–naive narration
and the combination stimulates less immediate but more satirically
pungent effects. The School's first project, 'to shorten Discourse by
cutting Polysyllables into one, and leaving out Verbs and Participles;
because in Reality all things imaginable are but Nouns' (III, v, 158), is
an entertaining spoof on Bishop Sprat's advocacy of plainness as the
preferred style of the Royal Society. Unconcerned by the ideological
tyranny implicit in his call (in 1667, the year of Swift's birth) for 'a fixt,
and *Impartial Court of Eloquence*; according to whose Censure, all Books,
or Authors should either stand or fall', Sprat was intent upon reinforcing the Society's 'constant Resolution, to reject all the amplifications,
digressions, and swellings of style; to return back to the primitive
purity, and shortness, when men deliver'd so many *things*, almost in an
equal number of *words*'.[5] Gulliver's commitment to the ideals outlined

---

[5] Thomas Sprat, *History of the Royal Society*, edited by J. I. Cope and H. W. Jones (London, 1959), pp. 43, 113.

by Sprat is a continuing source of amusement. But no one matches Swift's ability to manipulate the plain style into such a variety of responses, to the extent that *Gulliver's Travels* as a whole can be read as an extended parody of the Royal Society's procedural codes and preferences. So it seems hardly credible that Swift's satire should rest content with simply mocking whatever it is the good professors themselves claim to be doing. His own concerns across four books entail significant extensions of 'things imaginable', and what first seems a skit at the Royal Society's expense soon develops into something more.

For the express purpose of extending human life, the School of Language's second project offers the expedient that 'since Words are only names for *Things*, it would be more convenient for all Men to carry about them, such *Things* as were necessary to express the particular Business they are to discourse on'. Women ('in Conjunction with the Vulgar and Illiterate') offer rebellion to this threatened infringement of their liberty and are thus ironically raised into alliance with the Ancients of tradition, while the learned and the wise of Laputa 'adhere to the new Scheme of expressing themselves by *Things*'. Transmitted through the exchange of items carried on their backs, speech thus becomes an objectivated commerce between individuals, another traded display of portable property: 'like Pedlars among us, who when they met in the Streets, would lay down their Loads, open their Sacks, and hold Conversation for an Hour together; then put up their Implements, help each other to resume their Burthens, and take their Leave' (III, v, 158). In parodic transformation a culture of commodities produces a reified discourse. As money moves from being the medium of exchange between commodities to becoming itself a sought-after and traded commodity, things become the stuff of communication between people. Then, as money comes to signify a universal equivalence, a language of barter may become a bartered language, to the profit of international commerce:

Another great Advantage proposed by this Invention, was, that it would serve as an universal Language to be understood in all civilised Nations, whose Goods and Utensils are generally of the same Kind, or nearly resembling, so that their Uses might easily be comprehended. And thus, Embassadors would be qualified to treat with foreign Princes or Ministers of State, to whose Tongues they were utter strangers.   (III, v, 159)

Other visionary schemes that Gulliver encounters in Book III correlate in hilarious ways with contemporary manifestations of stock market activity, enabling the argument to be put that Exchange Alley would be the appropriate neighbourhood for siting Lagado because the cultural matrix of *Gulliver's Travels* was the projecting society Swift knew.[6] Arthur Case, on the other hand, long ago suggested that on architectural evidence and given the emphasis placed upon the Academy's school of political projectors, it is not impossible that the description should be applied to the rapidly expanding government buildings on both sides of Whitehall.[7] Swift is satirising an entire political economy so both locations are imaginatively appropriate. *Gulliver* was being written at a time when problems associated with new financial procedures of investment and revenue-raising had been brought to a spectacular head in the South Sea Bubble, for many contemporaries an abiding symbol of London's projecting mania. And what seems now beyond dispute is the contextual centrality to the book generally and to the Voyage to Laputa in particular, of the South Sea Company's progress and demise, as well as the whole projecting and speculating mania of the period. The pent-up wealth and initiative which burst their banks in England after the Revolution Settlement are metamorphosed into the Academy's crazed misdirection of effort.

Defoe's acknowledgement that despite many abortive failures the projecting age did also manage to produce 'new Contrivances, Engines, and Projects to get money, never before thought of',[8] is satirised, amongst other things, by a contrivance in Lagado for the mechanical composition of books to give the world a complete body of arts and sciences if only 'the Publick would raise a Fund for making and employing five Hundred such Frames ... and oblige the Managers to contribute in common their several Collections' (III, v, 156). Gulliver has just come from another room 'where the Walls and Ceiling were all hung around with Cobwebs, except a narrow Passage for the Artist to go in and out' (III, v, 154), and Defoe's defense of credit-based projecting inventiveness is again subverted:

On the other hand, Multitudes of Mushrooms have obtain'd upon the World, whose Birth was the Produce of meer Vapour and Exhalation; who, as they sprung up in the dark Midnight Moments of Trade, when her Eyes were shut, and when she was as it were doz'd with Dreams and hagrid with wandering Ghosts of *Trade Whymsies*; so they were born to evaporate by Time, and dye in the handling, that by the Nature of them were destin'd to dissolve like a cloud, and spin out their own bowels like the Spider; that had nothing material in them, but being merely imaginary in their Substance, must of Course be lost in

[6] P. Rogers, 'Gulliver and the Engineers', *Modern Language Review*, 70 (1975), pp. 260–70.
[7] A. E. Case, *Four Essays on Gulliver's Travels* (Gloucester, MA, 1958), p. 89.
[8] Daniel Defoe, *An Essay Upon Projects* (London, 1697), p. 4.

the handing up and down, and leave nothing but Cobweb, and a tangled Husk of Emptyness in the Fingers of those Fools that were deceiv'd with the Appearance.[9]

Only imaginary emptinesses survive in Swift's imagined world, and against such craziness, and connecting with Swift's *Examiner* assaults upon wealth without landed foundation, traditionally virtuous conduct is promoted in the aristocratic opinions and experience of Lord Munodi whose estates Gulliver visits on his way to the Lagado Academy. Munodi's benevolent paternalism stands in a wasteland of perverse fantasy as a paradigm of right conduct based upon land-ownership and productive cultivation:

A most beautiful Country; Farmers Houses at small Distances, the Fields enclosed, containing Vineyards, Corn-grounds and meadows ... We came at last to the House, which was indeed a noble Structure, built according to the best Rules of ancient Architecture. The Fountains, Gardens, Walks, Avenues, and Groves were all disposed with Exact Judgment and Taste.

(III, iv, 150)

In transparent embodiment of Swift's gentler ironies, Munodi explains that for his own part:

being not of an Enterprising Spirit, he was content to go on in the old Forms; to live in the Houses his Ancestors had built, and act as they did in every part of Life without Innovation. That, some few other Persons of Quality and Gentry had done the same; but were looked on with an Eye of Contempt and ill Will, as Enemies to Art, ignorant, and ill Commonwealthsmen, preferring their own Ease and Sloth before the general Improvement of their Country.

(III, iv, 151)

Ill commonwealthsmen all, Swift's Laputan projectors are a queer bunch by anybody's reckoning, with whom the ironies of subsequent history have dealt equally oddly. Their discovery of the satellites of Mars had to wait until the nineteenth century for verification[10] and we do, as Bonamy Dobrée reminded us some years ago, now 'extract sunshine from cucumbers, though we put it into globules and call it Vitamin C', as well as make fruits ripen at all seasons of the year.[11] Capital investment makes things happen, often in unforeseen ways, but

9 Defoe, *Review*, III, no. 126, p. 503 (facsimile book 8).
10 See Marjorie Nicolson and Nora M. Mohler, 'The Scientific Background of Swift's "Voyage to Laputa"', for a detailed examination of Swift's satirical use of contemporary scientific experiments; rpt. in *Fair Liberty Was All His Cry: A Tercentenary Tribute to Jonathan Swift (1667–1745)* (London, 1967), edited by A. N. Jeffares, pp. 226–69.
11 Bonamy Dobrée, *English Literature in the Early Eighteenth Century* (Oxford, 1959), p. 455.

the grotesque comedy of Gulliver's third book presents a cavalcade of perversely misdirected capacities for which the suggestion that Laputa derives from the Spanish word for whore – also a commercial use of bodily energies – is not without plausibility. A frantic descent into nonsense does, anyway, derive purpose and place from contemporary England's feverish addiction to weird and wonderful ideas (and dupes) for raising (and expropriating) money by imposing on a public every bit as gullible as Gulliver. The projectors of Lagado, like their counterparts in London is Swift's clear implication, have threatened their country with want and with ruin.[12] Among the fraudulent and lunatic flotations in London at the time there were projects for a wheel of perpetual motion and for importing a number of large jackasses from Spain 'to improve the breed of British mules'. There were companies for the planting of mulberry trees and breeding of silk-worms in Chelsea Park and for insuring 'all masters and mistresses [against] whatever loss they may sustain by theft from any servant that is ticketed and registered with this society'. There was even a company 'for assuring the proprietors of the tickets in the government lotteries'. Of the numerous advertisements for overseas trading companies, one that addressed the growing plight of England's weavers and that may have caught Swift's eye was a project to sell '10,000 pieces of woollen cloth and the other woollen manufactures and preserve our countrymen from being carried into slavery'. There was also, and perhaps inevitably, 'a joint-stock for the immediate, expeditious and cleanly manner of emptying necessary houses throughout England, whereby very great advantages will accrue to the company in general by making large quantities of saltpetre, besides other conveniences for the benefit of the projectors'. Finally, and bringing with it a sense of fatal predestination, there was 'a company for buying and selling South Sea stock and all other public stocks'.[13]

In the South Sea Bubble and the financial systems that made it possible, where for Opposition writers nationwide speculation became indistinguishable from state peculation, Swift and his friends perceived in archetypal form the corruption introduced into the commonwealth by the moneyed interest. What Swift viewed with alarm and suspicion was the interdependence of government revenue and large-scale gambling, and he expressed a life-long public hostility to these new

[12] J. M. Treadwell, 'Jonathan Swift: The Satirist as Projector', *Texas Studies in Literature and Language*, 17 (1975–6), p. 455.
[13] W. R. Scott, *The Constitution of English, Scottish and Irish Joint-Stock Companies to 1720*, 3 vols. (Cambridge, 1910–12), III, pp. 445–58.

methods of revenue-raising. For those with cash to risk, a wholesale involvement in the South Sea Company indicated a society deeply penetrated by the craze for instant enrichment, and in the fictive worlds Swift constructs it seems that all value-systems are at question. It then becomes of some significance in the education of Gulliver from wide-eyed naivety to a creature who can barely tolerate human company that we watch a careful and detailed construction of his political education 'from a Court Whig, not into a Tory so much as into a Country Whig'.[14]

Clearly, the capitalist system struggling waywardly into existence far transcended the significance of even its most astute pilots and managers, but J. H. Plumb's description of *Gulliver's Travels* as one of the most remarkable and virulent satires ever to be written against Walpole remains accurate as far as it goes.[15] Walpole was canny enough to get out of the South Sea market before disaster struck, and the bursting of the Bubble was the making of his political career, marking the beginning of his twenty years of supremacy in British political life. Both his financial acumen in arranging for the rescue of the South Sea Company by the Bank of England, and his parliamentary finesse in limiting the scope of official enquiries called in response to popular outrage over the discovery of massive fraud and deception assured his unchallengeable right to superintendency of the nation's affairs. There was something awesome in the scale of corruption in which Walpole engaged and inevitably his success made him a symbol and figurehead of everything Opposition writers feared. In the aftermath of the Bubble a number of embarrassing disclosures rumbled on through the 1720s, including the impeachment in 1725 of Lord Chancellor Macclesfield (who was Bernard Mandeville's patron) over charges relating to the embezzlement of more than £100,000, and the expulsion of John Ward from the Commons two years later for fraudulent practices involving the forfeited estates of the former directors of the South Sea Company. So it becomes entirely probable that such an otherwise throwaway remark as 'human Creatures are observed to be more Savage and cruel in Proportion to their Bulk' (II, i, 66) might have been taken to refer to Walpole's extreme corpulence. It is anyway evident throughout the *Travels* that Walpole is effectively pilloried as the leading political architect of a despised new order, with much of the animus of this

---

[14] W. A. Speck, *Society and Literature in England, 1700–1760* (Dublin, 1983), p. 27. Speck shows how Swift constructs Gulliver as a Whig foil, to satirise the values of the Court Whigs (pp. 67 ff.).

[15] Plumb, *Sir Robert Walpole*, p. 104.

aspect of Swift's satire personally and passionately directed. But if he came to stand for everything Swift loathed in political life, then a satirical portrait of England's first minister should appropriately assemble a paradigm of corruption transcending individual contours; the particular generating the archetype. A constant Opposition theme stressed Walpole's responsibility for a contemporary worship of luxury made possible by monetary wealth, and although he may not always have been directly implicated in the dubious financial practices which came to light during his administration, Walpole's political methods led to him being directly associated with falling standards of public morality.[16] Since corruption on such a scale was only possible, according to the Opposition, because as well as the Crown's patronage Walpole could exploit his links with the moneyed interest, it becomes in turn understandable that the financial institutions and their system of public credit and paper money were regarded as the real sources of corruption.

Among those holding developed opposing ideologies, Walpole's political methods and the forces he represented were considered to be a powerful threat to the balanced constitution held to have been secured by the Revolution Settlement. Sometimes known as the 'Gothic' constitution, its Polybian balance comprised monarchic, aristocratic and democratic elements, with Crown, Lords, and Commons together guaranteeing stability and liberty. Powers were not separate but mixed, although each had a particular function: the sovereign being head of the executive, the House of Lords being the supreme court of justice, and the Commons controlling the voting of supplies. Working together harmoniously while retaining their independent privileges, these three elements were taken to ensure the survival of the constitution, and when we read such considerations back into Gulliver's experience of monarchs, different interpretative possibilities open up. Swift has great fun contrasting the delicacy and finesse of the rulers Gulliver meets with the boorish George I. But evidence from Lilliput that 'this Prince lives chiefly upon his own Demesnes; seldom, except upon great Occasions raising any Subsidies upon his Subjects' (I, ii, 16) implicates more specifically a monarch who spent much of his time in Hanover, and was there during part of the time that the South Sea Bubble was blowing. Then, when Gulliver hears that 'a Year or two before my Arrival, *Flimnap* would have infallibly broke his Neck, if one of the *King's*

---

[16] I rely for parts of this and the following paragraph on H. T. Dickinson, *Walpole and the Whig Supremacy* (London, 1973), pp. 143ff.

Cushions, that accidently lay on the Ground, had not weakened the force of his Fall' (I, iii, 21–2), the King's cushion has been read as signifying the King's mistress helping Walpole back to office. There were certainly good reasons for her offering assistance to Walpole: the King's mistress was one of those notables to whom the South Sea Directors had issued entirely fictitious stocks to sell when the price rose and thus to derive profit from nothing. The King, meanwhile, was the Governor of the South Sea Company. For a Whig administration, the less dishonourable these proceedings could be made to appear as far as any public was concerned, the better for their monarch's good name; and Walpole's screening abilities earned him the soubriquet he was to carry for years afterwards. 'Joining in the hue and cry against the guilty ministers would have made Walpole popular with the backbenchers in the Commons, but it would not have endeared him to the King, whose closest friends and mistresses were involved in the shady transactions under investigation.'[17] We are left wondering how plangently the irony must have resonated for Swift's earliest readers when after a mathematically precise description of how Gulliver's provisioning was calculated in Lilliput, the third chapter concludes: 'By which, the Reader may conceive an Idea of the Ingenuity of that People, as well as the prudent and exact Oeconomy of so great a Prince' (I, iii, 27).

It becomes possible then, to locate the ironic force of Gulliver's account of Lilliputian laws and customs:

They look upon Fraud as a greater Crime than Theft, and therefore seldom fail to punish it with death: For they alledge, that Care and Vigilance, with a very common Understanding, may preserve a Man's Goods from Thieves; but Honesty hath no Fence against superior Cunning: And since it is necessary that there should be a perpetual Intercourse of buying and selling, and dealing upon Credit; where Fraud is permitted or connived at, or hath no Law to punish it, the honest Dealer is undone, and the Knave gets the Advantage.

(I, vi, 39)

One part of the debate here involves Mandeville's rival perception that: 'Where Trade is considerable, Fraud will intrude ... and ... while Man advances in Knowledge, and his manners are polish'd, we must expect at the same time to see his desires enlarg'd, his appetites refin'd and his Vices increased.'[18] Swift did not wish to see such knowledge advanced and Walpole did, so Swift insists (but in Lilliputian mode) that traditional ways should be preserved because: 'Mistakes committed by

[17] W. A. Speck, *Stability and Strife: England 1714–1760* (London, 1977), p. 199.
[18] *Fable of the Bees*, I, p.185.

Ignorance in a virtuous Disposition, would never be of such fatal Consequence to the Publick Weal, as the Practices of a Man, whose Inclinations led him to be corrupt, and had great Abilities to manage, to multiply, and defend his Corruptions' (I, vi, 40–1). That Walpole had the Hanoverians eating out of his hand is suggested when the secret information Gulliver receives about 'a private intrigue' at court which threatened him with impeachment and the loss of his eyes is ironically mitigated by the opinion that 'it would be sufficient for you to see by the Eyes of the Ministers, since the greatest Princes do no more' (I, vii, 50). But it is also entirely characteristic of the narrative procedures of the *Travels* to loop its ironic perspectives back upon its readers as it does when, looking clearly through his own eyes, the King of Brobdingnag – 'a Prince of excellent Understanding' – wants to hear 'as exact an Account of the Government of *England* as Gulliver can provide'. Gulliver mentions 'the prudent Management of our Treasury', prompting the King's enquiry into the self-sacrificing public-spiritedness of members of the House of Commons. Over 450 members of both Houses of Parliament had gambled in South Sea stock and many had taken advantage of the preferential terms offered to them by the directors; which lends a certain piquancy to the King's curiosity as to 'whether such zealous Gentlemen could have any Views of refunding themselves for the Charges and Troubles they were at, by sacrificing the publick Good to the Designs of a weak and vicious Prince, in Conjunction with a corrupted Ministry' (II, vi, 105–6). By the time of the fourth book, the sustained attack on a '*First* or *Chief Minister of State*' (IV, vi, 221–2) is as comprehensive and explicit a denunciation of political malpractice as anything Swift wrote, and as we trace the topical barbs which an ironic naivety produces, Swift's elaborate concern to protect his anonymity as author of the *Travels* upon its first appearance becomes all the more understandable. Even the less personally directed elements of his critique of the new worlds Gulliver discovers share in the overwhelming discrediting of an entire social order, with the King of Brobdingnag's bemusement proving an excellent foil as a plain squire's incomprehension of the National Debt: 'he was still at a Loss how a Kingdom could run out of its Estate like a private Person. He asked me, who were our Creditors? and, where we found Money to pay them?' (II, vi, 106).

Among the diversions currently popular with the English nobility and gentry Gulliver had mentioned gambling to the King:

He desired to know at what Age this Entertainment was usually taken up, and when it was laid down. How much of their Time it employed; whether it ever went so high as to affect their Fortunes. Whether mean vicious People, by their

Dexterity in that Art, might not arrive at great Riches, and sometimes keep our very Nobles in Dependence, as well as habituate them to vile Companions; wholly take them from the Improvement of their Minds, and force them by the Losses they received, to learn and practice that infamous Dexterity upon others.

(II, vi, 107)

The corruption of England's aristocracy is again foregrounded, while to many of London's other early investors any difference between what they were doing themselves and what went on in any of the fashionable gaming clubs springing up across London must have seemed notional at best. The most judicious historian of the South Sea Bubble refers at one point to 'the game of poker now begun' (*FR*, p. 100), so behind Swift's irony lies a more fundamental kind of worry about the changing nature of politics and of the political skills newly requisite in a mobile universe of credit.

The real and more difficult targets of Swift's denunciation were the huge impersonal machinery of state which the financial revolution called into being, and its attendant and necessary (and for Swift corrupting) assault upon previous practice and upon established perceptions, priorities and codes of valuation. So when his biographer suggests that unlike most of Swift's works *Gulliver's Travels* does not finally stand within a specific context of public events he may well be right as far as allusion to precise event or personality is concerned. But Ehrenpreis's subsequent notion that the most profound and essential ingredients of the fantasy detach themselves from time and place is in danger of leaving Swift's masterpiece floating in some empyrean beyond culture and history (*S. Life* II, pp. 452, 454). The European movement into economic modernity revolutionised England after the Netherlands, and its impact upon selfhood and personality were profound enough to call for responses as complex as those assembled in *Gulliver*. For traditionalists the mortgaging of future generations' revenues brought into being a world morally less stable than the one preceding it. Investment morality speedily displaced hitherto normative constructions of ethics, and harmonies derived from inherited power-structures were comprehensively jeopardised by social and political behaviour increasingly based upon opinion concerning the future rather than on the myths and memories of a past.

As far as political topicality is concerned the signifying practices of the *Travels* have been exhaustively scrutinised. Since Sir Charles Firth's British Academy lecture in 1919,[19] Arthur Case has argued for a more

---

[19] C. H. Firth, 'The Political Significance of *Gulliver's Travels*,' *Proceedings of the British Academy* (1919–20), pp. 237–59.

consistently allegorical reading and a more or less strict pattern of political identification: Irvin Ehrenpreis has developed the idea that part I of the *Travels* is largely an allegory of English political history from 1708 to 1715, in which Gulliver stands largely for Bolingbroke, Secretary of State from 1710 to 1714. Ehrenpreis goes on to suggest further possible identifications and locations, including the relevance of a ravaged Ireland to the wasteland created for the subject peoples of Laputa. Ehrenpreis's subsequent attachment to Bolingbroke of ideas expressed by the Houyhnhnms shows how Swift's hidden history of his times inserts and commingles events and relationships across more than two decades. When Gulliver tells his master about: 'the *Revolution* under the Prince of *Orange*; the long war with *France* entered into by the said Prince, and renewed by his successor the present Queen' (IV, v, 212), he makes it easier to accept that Swift created much of *Gulliver* out of his own memories and experiences of and reflection upon an extended historical moment. So a rage for systematically precise correlations sometimes conflicts with the book's design and is explicitly not Ehrenpreis's intention. Subsequent research has shown how inaccurate some of Arthur Case's earlier conclusions are and how unhistorical his methods of reading,[20] and even the generally accepted identification of Flimnap with Walpole has been called into question.[21] As more and more details of political topicality are brought to light, the more apparent it becomes that *Gulliver's Travels* is teasing the reader by merging character and event into fictional contours and by constantly shifting its ground to create serial and overlapping senses of fleeting recognition and partial apprehension. As it comes to us now, *Gulliver*'s structured intentions disclose narrative occasions and events that should and should not relate to any determining picture of actuality. Its sometimes quasi-allegorical, sometimes more loosely allusive and referential confusions of one possible political identification with another relate more provocatively to Swift's perception of a dissolving classically conceived autonomous personality founded upon a solid base of landed integrity. As this personality translates into new kinds of dependent individuality seeking appropriate definition in a relativised world of mobile value, *Gulliver's Travels* develops answerable narrative strategies.

Throughout the book, Gulliver and those who read him are sub-

---

20 J. A. Downie, 'Political Characterisation in *Gulliver's Travels*', *The Yearbook of English Studies*, 7 (1977), pp. 108–20.

21 By F. P. Lock, in *The Politics of 'Gulliver's Travels'* (Oxford, 1980), pp. 86–7, 115–16.

jected to discomfiting permutations of perception and construction, so
that the threat to individual integrity and self-knowledge which corruption had always implied and which was reinforced by the rise of
forms of property seeming to rest on fantasy and false consciousness
becomes both a central topic and a structural principle of the writing.
In a mischievously deceptive organisation of narratorial subjectivity,
the illusion of verisimilitude[22] for which the writing strives plays an
equally destabilising role. Gulliver's unreliability is notorious – witness
his claim to have swum across the channel between Lilliput and
Blefuscu pulling fifty nine-foot-long Lilliputian battleships. But the
uncertainties his text insinuates are of various kinds, physical and
mental. While it is a function of Gulliver's naivety repeatedly to expose
how 'ill a judge of Things' he is (I, vii, 52), we rarely see him putting on
the spectacles which he tells us he needs because of 'the weakness of
[his] eyes' (I, ii, 20). So we should be on our guard when he describes
for us the 'exact proportion' of Lilliputian creatures (I, vi, 38):

The tallest Horses and Oxen are between four and five Inches in Height, the
Sheep an Inch and a half, more or less; their Geese about the Bigness of
Sparrow.

These are, J. A. Downie remarks, either tiny sheep, or enormous
geese,[23] and their disproportion forms part of a systematic strategy to
undermine both the credibility of our narrator and the security of the
discourse which presents him. Swift further impresses upon us Gulliver's difficulties with language and speech, with truth, fiction and lying.
If Gulliver were to repeat back in England what he had seen, 'every
Body would believe that I *said the Thing which was not*: that I invented
the Story out of my own Head' (IV, iii, 206), which of course Swift is
partly doing. And whereas the Houyhnhnms possess a language that
'expressed the Passions very well' (IV, i, 90), Gulliver is 'put ... to the
Pains of many Circumlocutions to give my Master a right Idea of what
I spoke; for their Language doth not abound in Variety of Words,
because their Wants and Passions are fewer than among us' (IV, iv,
209). Similarly, the Houyhnhnm insists that: 'the Use of Speech was to
make us understand one another', while in the absence of proper
communication he is 'led to believe a Thing *Black* when it is *White*' (IV,
iv, 207); which shades unsettlingly into Gulliver's subsequent description of the role of money in purchasing arguments from lawyers who

---

[22] See Frank Brady, 'Vexations and Diversions: Three Problems in *Gulliver's Travels*', *Modern Philology*, 75 (1978), pp. 346–67.
[23] Downie, *Swift: Political Writer*, p. 271.

are: 'bred up from their Youth in the Art of proving by Words that *White* is *Black*, and *Black* is *White*. To this Society all the rest of the People are Slaves' (IV, v, 215). Gulliver's horse-master can have no comprehension of the effects wrought by a speculating society trading upon the confidence inspired by Credit, and laughs at the idea 'that a Creature pretending to *Reason*, should value itself upon the Knowledge of other Peoples Conjectures' (IV, viii, 234). Since in the new order of things the proprieties of classically defined value no longer supply either public polity or private personality with a language in which to invest a coherent moral structure, Gulliver's misprisions and misapprehensions mirror the reader's in a disconsolate if comic circularity.

'I have got Materials for a Treatis proving the falsity of that Definition *animal rationale*', Swift wrote to Pope, 'and to show it should be only *rationis capax*'. He went to explain that the 'whole building of my Travells is erected ... Upon this great foundation of Misanthropy' (*S. Corr.* III, p. 103). While the shift in definition from man as reasoning animal to man as only possessing the capacity but not always the will or strength to reason is a crucial distinction, it is also a major concession to transforming forces in the world Swift addresses. His misanthropy is historically contextualised in a book which directs much of its antagonism against the corruption of a classically grounded and reasonable personal integrity by the passions of acquisition and accumulation in a market society based upon credit and paper-money circulation. In that sense his country of the horses represents a doomed culture. It is a central principle of the Houyhnhnms 'to cultivate *Reason*, and to be wholly governed by it' (IV, viii, 233), and in many respects they encode an ideal rational existence. But nothing is straightforward in the *Travels*: the Houyhnhnms lead an emotionally restricted life. Personal love, joy or regret have virtually no meaning for them: 'They have no Fondness for their Colts or Foles', Gulliver notices (IV, viii, 234); friends and relations express neither joy nor grief when one of them dies, 'nor does the dying Person discover the least Regret that he is leaving the World' (IV, viii, 239). They relate more to the Stoics of antiquity than to anyone else: quadruped figurations of a philosophy Swift criticised in his *Thoughts on Various Subjects*. There, in Louis Landa's words: 'The Stoic rationalistic ideal, the man without passion, is exposed as being in sharp contrast to the Christian ideal which, however much it condemned the bad passions, still stressed the compassionate nature of man' (*SP* 1, p. 244). Not only does the Houyhnhnm ideal go against Christianity, it is manifest that the horses

stand against most of the rest of sociable practice as Gulliver presents
and represents it: as with so much else in the *Travels*, we are unable to
find anchoring perspectives. Gulliver mediates for us in disconcertingly
ambiguous ways as the book repeatedly suggests, preventing us from
any secure identification with his textual positioning. While Gulliver's
own proximate identification as a Yahoo is made evident when he strips
to bathe in a stream and is subject to the sexual advances of a female of
the species (IV, viii, 232–3), he acknowledges to an unhappy Master
that back in London, Houyhnhnms possess 'not the least Tincture of
Reason' (IV, iv, 209). Gulliver's horse-master can only look upon him
and his kind as 'a Sort of Animals to [whom] ... some small Pittance of
Reason had fallen, whereof we made no other Use than by its Assistance
to aggravate our *natural* Corruptions, and to acquire new ones which
Nature had not given us' (IV, vii, 225). Meanwhile, Gulliver has been
'as much astonished to see the *Houyhnhnms* act like rational Beings, as
[his Master] or his friends could be in finding some Marks of Reason in
a Creature he was pleased to call a Yahoo' (IV, iii, 206). Gulliver is
divided within himself long before he becomes divided from his fellow
Londoners at the close of his adventures and in that sense he functions
as a metaphor for our own encounters with the tales he tells. Stable
definitions and determinations of virtuous and vicious behaviour begin
to crumble as the frontiers of subjectivity between Houyhnhnm and
Yahoo fracture and discursive boundaries between Reason and Passion
intersect. Swift is negotiating the gap which now separated social and
personal morality and he presents us with the formation of a cultural
identity no longer containable within classical formulations being composed, rather, out of an array of oppositions and negatives.

As well as the Houyhnhnms, much of what Swift considered valuable
in a preceding social order and the political personality it promoted
and sustained is given clear voice by the King of Brobdingnag, while its
passing into different valorisations is conveyed through a pervasive
textual construction of uncertainty. A world that Swift's earliest readers
might have thought they could retrieve from his satirical modulations,
turns out to be a world that some of them are losing while others may be
gaining. A referential world which we in turn may think we can
reconstruct with some clarity turns out to be not so easily grasped.
Swift's literary technique invokes a lost integrity of discourse to produce
an anxiety of orientation, a dislocating indeterminacy to which Gulliver and his first readers are subjected much as we are. Added to the
constant puzzle as to whether or not at any given point an author is
satirising a narrator is the complicating factor of an irony that fre-

quently deconstructs perceptions from within, leaving the reader repeatedly at a stretch to know with any security which interpretative position might be valid and for how long. There are times when a precise political identification of figures and events in the *Travels* may seem of determining use, but there is a more persuasive relevance in the kind of symbolic topicality it characteristically shapes to reach more subversively from his text to his society and then to us. In the financial and political reconstruction that Walpole supervised after the Bubble, fraud and corruption became a matter of government policy: if the new financial instruments had brought panic to the country and disaster to many investors, they had also created equally spectacular enrichment, and trade continued to expand. As more people shouldered their way into inheriting a larger portion of the earth than might otherwise have come their way, they were changing themselves as they changed both actual structures of power and in consequence the ways in which political rule was still traditionally perceived and manipulated. The political complexion of a parliamentary succession was permanently affected and its institutional continuity would henceforth move within the altered frameworks now in place, passing its innovative arrangements on to succeeding generations. While a relatively stable world of real property gave way to one of less certain determinations, a political generation had been instructed in the hysterical volatility of money markets, so that it could no longer be a matter of idle surmise but of widely shared experience that opinion, fantasy and egotistical passion could and did visibly affect the conduct of the state. 'I remember', Gulliver tells us, 'it was with extreme Difficulty that I could bring my Master to understand the Meaning of the Word *Opinion*, or how a Point could be disputable; because *Reason* taught us to affirm or deny only where we are certain; and beyond our knowledge we cannot do either' (IV, viii, 233). It was a fundamental principle of Exchange Alley that investors *did* speculate optimistically beyond their knowledge: fantasy fuelled by passionately desired future acquisition was displacing 'reasonable' procedure, and the notion that a traditionally conceived Polybian balance still obtained in the ruling of the country had received a terminal shock.

   The Lilliputian prince who wisely lives upon his own 'demesnes'; the Brobdingnagian king who asks 'whether a private Man's house might not better be defended by himself, his Children, and Family' (II, vi, 107); the Lord Munodi who seeks to do no more than that (III, iv, 151); even the Gulliver in Houyhnhnmland who begins a description of his domestic management with the claim that he 'had settled [his] little

Oeconomy to [his] own Heart's Content' (IV, x, 241): each of these articulates a version of Aristotelian self-sufficiency and autonomy. Each represents a traditional preference for political and social relations based upon territorial possession as an alternative to the engrossing of civil power by the men of money and their new instruments of finance. Each of them looks back to an era when independence could be differently defined and when notions of regional or otherwise localised paternalism could be proposed as justifying prevailing dispositions of power. But equally, each of them was inevitably being displaced by a modernising and progressive establishment of financial and agrarian capitalism and a new political state. The '*Sextumvirate*' conjured by Gulliver in Glubbdubdrib, 'to which all the Ages of the World cannot add a Seventh' (III, vii, 167), identifies a public virtue so conspicuously lacking in the society which made the book a best-seller. That public virtue survives in the Houyhnhnms who can be as complete patriots as were the citizens of the Roman republic because they comprise one self-identifying community. The price they pay for their virtuous integrity is confinement within the political economy of their own territory: in their austere and agricultural society, the Houyhnhnms have no use for money, drive no trade and build no ships.[24] Harking back as it does to Bishop Berkeley's 1721 essay *Towards Preventing the Ruin of Great Britain*, there is both poignancy and irony in the final vision Gulliver calls up in Glubbdubdrib:

I descended so low as to desire that some *English* Yeomen of the old Stamp, might be summoned to appear; once so famous for the simplicity of their Manners, Dyet and Dress; for Justice in their dealings; for their true Spirit of Liberty; for their Valour and Love of their Country. Neither could I be wholly unmoved after comparing the Living with the Dead, when I considered how all these pure native Virtues were prostituted for a Piece of Money by their Grand-children.   (III, viii, 173)

Commerce and its enabling systems of credit were here to stay though, and these attempted reconstructions of a golden past were being decisively influenced by forces and priorities powerful enough, it would seem, to corrupt even the torch-bearers of the new order. It is not true, Edward Thompson claims, that Walpole's system of brutally imposing Whig interests on every branch of public service, including the purchase and intimidation of electors and the diversion of public money into private pockets, was identical with that of twenty or fifty years before, even if it is true that the system was to be inherited, with

24 M. M. Kelsall, '*Iterum* Houyhnhnm: Swift's Sextumvirate and the Horses', *Essays in Criticism*, 19 (1969), pp. 37–8.

little modification, by George III and the Tories. 'Somewhere between the Puritan gentry and officers of the Commonwealth and the great Whig managers of the 1720s some lapse had taken place.'[25] Whether or not that is the case, *Gulliver's Travels* traces a decline in English republican discourse, so when Edward Said maintains that one of the most consistent themes in Swift's work is loss, and that even above its lithe power his writing frequently sets out to communicate a literal sense of loss,[26] the vanishing of a preferred political world forms a part of the rationale for these communicated attitudes.

But Swift is difficult. The Gulliver who cherishes his domestic economy in Houyhnhnmland is the Gulliver who repeatedly abandons his family for the lure of travel and adventure. The author who made money available to the needy on humane terms and who gave a third of his income to charity while saving half of what was left to leave a fortune to charity; who remained a devout Christian, praying in secret and going to church early so as not to be seen, was the author whose journalistic polemic was repeatedly indifferent to truth. His biographer records Swift's propensity for 'specious insinuations', 'slanderous innuendo', and 'invidious vituperation' (*S. Life* II, pp. 493, 531, 705): nor does it always seem sufficient to accept this as legitimate tactics for political street-fighting in print. Additionally, the man who created one of the most durably effective assaults upon pride in the English language is the man who was driven by a consuming ambition: 'All my endeavours, from a boy, to distinguish myself, were only for want of a great Title and Fortune, that I might be used like a Lord by those who have an opinion of my parts; whether right or wrong, it is no great matter' (*S. Corr.* III, pp. 330–1). Moreover, the writer celebrated in a tercentenary tribute of essays called *Fair Liberty Was All His Cry* (1967), is the writer whose rage against the journalists who had published attacks against either himself or the ministry he served was such that in 1711 he begged the Secretary of State to make a lesson of them. As it happens, neither the policy of the administration nor the practice of the courts of law supplied the remedy Swift sought and those who were arrested could only be threatened and released.[27] Gulliver's contempt for the 'Discoverers, Witnesses, Informers, Accusers, Prosecutors, Evi-

---

[25] Thompson, *Whigs and Hunters*, p. 216.

[26] Edward Said, 'Swift as Intellectual', in *The World, the Text, and the Critic* (London, 1984), p. 75.

[27] In *Swift: The Man* (II, p. 517) Ehrenpreis remarks that the episode lingered in Swift's imagination to become at last one of Gulliver's adventures in Lilliput [i.e. the punishment of the 'ringleaders'].

dences, Swearers' in the anagrammatic kingdom of Walpole's Tribnia (III, vi, p.162), consorts uneasily with the fact that it was Bolingbroke, the Secretary of State to whom Swift turned for repressive action, who passed a Stamp Act in 1712, creating such a climate of political intimidation that Walpole had to set up a clandestine press in his own home because no printer would dare handle one of his pamphlets. Swift cut his journalistic teeth as a propagandist on behalf of Lord Oxford of whom it has been claimed that in the area of intelligence, propaganda and counter-propaganda, he was at least the equal of Walpole, whose Robinocracy owed a tremendous amount to this Tory predecessor.[28] In *The Conduct of the Allies*, Swift presented a full-blown conspiracy thesis in which the Tory country gentlemen wished to believe,[29] while anyone reading *Some Free Thoughts upon the Present State of Affairs*, Swift's 1714 tract in favour of the Church of England's ruling preservation of all its rights, powers and privileges, cannot help but reflect that the only surviving freedom it allows is the expression of a desire for tyrannical control over every aspect of political life in order to eradicate all opposition to a single ecclesiastical regime. In the *Examiner* (no. 34) he defended the Qualification Act, intended to exclude all but landed proprietors from the Commons, and it has even been suggested that one of the reasons that Swift so often satirised Walpole and his men of money in monstrous and bestial terms is that they had committed the sin of tampering with divinely ordained relationships.[30] Swift is stubbornly resistant to any attempt to incorporate him into a preferred ideology, then or now, and the ambivalences of his life are read as disconcertingly across the four books of *Gulliver*. Perhaps it is true that by 1724 Swift had changed; that his connection to the Tories had lost any ideological force apart from a deep attachment to the church, and that while his intimates included a number of would-be Jacobites, he was now more libertarian and anti-monarchical than the ruling party (*S. Life* III, p. 287). It is certainly an attractive proposition: but the image that troubled George Orwell also reminds us that that for most of his life Swift allied himself with the reactionary values of a great landed aristocracy, an established church and an imperial monarchy, whose combined political programme, had it been successful, would have heralded the triumph of bigotry, hierarchy, authority and legitimacy in early eighteenth-century England.

The final image of the Houyhnhnms is still troubling. A Gulliver

[28] Downie, *Robert Harley*, p. 183.   [29] Ibid., p. 148.
[30] Kramnick, *Bolingbroke and his Circle*, pp. 212, 217.

'safely' back in England denies his rulers the option of colonial rule over his beloved horses, praising instead a sociable community 'civilised' by them. But the text then kicks backwards to produce one of the most horrific images of the four voyages:

Imagine Twenty Thousand of them breaking into the Midst of an *European* Army, confounding the Ranks, overturning the carriages, battering the Warriors Faces into Mummy, by terrible Yerks from their hinder Hoofs.

(IV, xii, 258)

The book's convincingly cruel hoax on a society's claim to possess a civilising mission is largely generated through a calculated disordering of perception which here presents hitherto reasonable and benevolent figures doing murderous violence. As elsewhere, Swift's writing produces a bewildering array of responses, including in this case the recognition of a ruined ideal, a recognition from which Gulliver turns away, preferring the Houyhnhnms as magisterial dispensers of classical humanist cognitions of value: 'the first Principles of Honour, Justice, Truth, Temperance, publick Spirit, Fortitude, Chastity, Friendship, Benevolence, and Fidelity' – which are now retained 'in name only'. *Gulliver's Travels* involves a compelling if often confounding struggle for the content and continued applicability of these codes and categories and it is a measure of its complexity that while the abuse of each of these virtues is subject to parody, contempt and a sometimes ferocious satire, in our last image of the horse-community that best represents them, they have blood on their hooves. It seems that Swift well knew the difficult truths of Walter Benjamin's thesis that there is no document of civilisation which is not at the same time a document of barbarism. More than that: 'just as such a document is not free from barbarism, barbarism also taints the manner in which it was transmitted from one owner to another'.[31] Whether or not any direct attempt is made to read the life from the book, a pattern of ironic reversal and opposition that operates intratextually as well as intertextually keeps the reader gingerly ill-at-ease, and although it may at first seem anachronistic, Michel Foucault's suggestion that the frontiers of a book are never clear-cut comes to impress its relevance: 'beyond the title, the first lines and the last full stop, beyond its internal configuration and its autonomous form, it is caught up in a system of references to other books, other texts, other sentences: it is a node within a network'.[32]

[31] Walter Benjamin, *Illuminations: Essays and Reflections*, edited by Hannah Arendt (New York, 1968, rpt. 1985), p. 356.
[32] Michel Foucault, *The Archaeology of Knowledge* (New York, 1972), p. 23.

The network of encounter and response which now enshrines *Gulliver* in the English literary canon also records a pattern of division and repudiation every bit as fractious as Swift's own opinions. If he witnessed the making of the English middle classes in a phase of unprecedented expansion and incorporation and did not like all that he saw, some of their representatives have at times reacted in a spirit of equal contestation. While we may wish to leave out of account Francis Jeffrey's politically motivated animus and Thackeray's obsequious moralising, it is perhaps useful to remember that La Bruyère laid against Rabelais, whom he accused of 'scattering so much filth in his writing', many of the charges subsequently levelled at his great pupil:

Rabelais above all is incomprehensible: his book is a mystery, a mere chimera ... It is a monstrous jumble of delicate and ingenious morality and of filthy depravation. Where it is bad, it excels by far the worst, and is fit only to delight the rabble; and when it is good, it is exquisite and excellent, and may entertain the most 'delicate'.[33]

This comment is relevant for reasons to which we shall return, but it is interesting that in the present century a leading voice, and for years in British university departments of English Literature *the* leading voice of dissenting noncomformity expressed a kind of division in his reaction to Swift that is in turn traceable back to the *Travels*:

A great writer – yes; that account still imposes itself as fitting, though his greatness is no matter of moral grandeur or human centrality; our sense of it is merely a sense of great force. And this force, as we feel it, is conditioned by frustration and constriction; the channels of life have been blocked and perverted.[34]

Leavis rightly dismisses moralist and idealist readings of Swift, but then goes on to say that there is no reason to lay emphasis on intellect in Swift: 'He is distinguished by the intensity of his feelings, not by insight into them, and he certainly does not impress us as a mind in possession of its experience.' Just over thirty years later, and in a different spirit of radicalism, Edward Said took up the cudgels on behalf of 'Swift as Intellectual' to examine George Orwell's remarks about the durability of *Gulliver*, and to suggest that with the force of belief behind it: 'a world-view which only just passes the test of sanity is sufficient to

---

[33] Quoted in Mikhail Bakhtin, *Rabelais and his World*, translated by Helene Iswolsky (Bloomington, IN, 1984), p. 108.
[34] F. R. Leavis, *The Common Pursuit* (London, 1953), pp. 86–7.

produce a great work of art'.[35] Swift saw just such a 'world-view'
producing great effects in society, and while Said identifies his local
activism, his pamphleteering and his work as a columnist and a carica-
turist as underestimated sources of energy and intensity that deliver 'the
active content of Swift's mind as we are able to grasp it in its essential
resistance to any fixed boundaries',[36] that active, resisting mind as well
as the disintegrating boundaries it produced are everywhere apparent
in *Gulliver's Travels*.

We can usefully take the idea of an anarchic resistance back to
someone Pope also identified as a precursor of *Gulliver*'s savage comedy.
Swift's indebtedness to Rabelais becomes available to us in newly
illuminating ways through Mikhail Bakhtin's researches into the carni-
valesque, and in highly appropriate ways too, since Bakhtin's work is
motivated and informed by a powerful antagonism to an oppressive and
corrupt regime. Referring to the formalisation that takes place when
the grotesque loses its living tie with folk culture and becomes a literary
genre, Bakhtin acknowledges that 'the contents of the carnival-grotesque element, its artistic, heuristic, and unifying forces were preserved
... in the work of Swift'.[37] He goes on to describe the main function of
the carnival-grotesque as being to consecrate inventive freedom, to
permit the combination of a variety of different elements and their
rapprochement, to liberate from the prevailing point of view of the
world, from conventions and established truths, from clichés, from all
that is humdrum and universally accepted. Both Swift and Rabelais
deploy a style of grotesque realism; both recognise that the essential
principle of grotesque realism is degradation and in both, images of the
human body with its food, drink and defecation, play a predominant
role. To read Bakhtin on the defining characteristics of carnival is also
to acknowledge a series of conjunctions in Swift's text: the language of
the market-place; such popular-festive forms as the king's uncrowning;
banquet imagery; the grotesque usage of the body and in particular its
lower stratum, or what Bakhtin calls 'the mighty thrust downwards into
the bowels of the earth, into the depths of the human body',[38] each of
these has an equivalent mode in Swift and when Bakhtin quotes

[35] George Orwell, *In Front of Your Nose, 1945–1950*, edited by Sonia Orwell and Ian Angus, vol.
IV of *The Collected Essays, Journalism and Letters of George Orwell*, 4 vols. (New York, 1968),
pp. 222–3.
[36] *The World, the Text, and the Critic*, p. 55. Said develops R. P. Blackmur's recognition (in, *A
Primer of Ignorance* (New York, 1967), p. 13), that 'true anarchy of spirit should always show
(or always *has* showed) a tory flavour'.
[37] Bakhtin, *Rabelais*, p. 34.   [38] Ibid., p. 370.

Pinsky's definition of the grotesque, *Gulliver's Travels* might be the text in view:

In the grotesque, life passes through all the degrees, from the lowest, inert and primitive, to the highest, most mobile and spiritualised; this garland of various forms bears witness to their oneness, brings together that which is removed, combines elements which exclude each other, contradicts all current conceptions.[39]

But as always with Swift difference is all: notions of unity are repeatedly called in question and whereas for Rabelais the exaggerations of grotesque realism have a positive, assertive character, in *Gulliver* the laughter is as often as not edged with pessimism and negativity. Two remarks by Bakhtin suggest why this might be so; the first being that 'the material bodily principle [the source of much grotesque vitality] is not contained in the bourgeois ego',[40] and the second that 'images of the grotesque are contrary to the classic images of the finished, completed man, cleansed, as it were, of the scoriae of birth and development'.[41] Given the socio-economic events during the years of *Gulliver*'s composition, there were pressing reasons for Swift so savagely to represent the demise of classic images of self-hood, but self-recognitions seem also to have been influential. He could hardly have been unaware that the political preferences he argued for, and the ideology that gave them coherence and credibility, were part of a historical rearguard action with no hope of survival. This suggests that ironies of presentation which frequently deconstruct preferred and foregrounded ethical values must relate in part to his alertness, sharpened by his interest in the writing of history, to processes of change that were making classic humanist ideals increasingly untenable. Yet within this complicated matrix of tensions and oppositions, the more his formidable energies come into conflict with governing principles, and the more his fictive form interrogates traditional categories that were changing as investment expectations changed the ordering of social life, the more he comes to us as a product of the liberalising society he comprehensively satirises. The inventive freedoms his text consecrates, and the varieties of different elements it permits and organises correlate discursively with the expanding processes of exchange, substitution, transference and equivalence of a market society and its credit-based paper-money machinery of circulation. In this remarkable transition to the fully fledged novel not even the plain style remains the constant it

[39] Ibid., p. 32, n. 12.   [40] Ibid., p. 19.   [41] Ibid., p. 25.

at first appears, but functions instead as an ensnaring system to betray us in deeper consequence. Within its destabilising conventions everything else transmutes, vacillates, crosses discursive boundaries; and Swift's text appears suspended between the stability of landed integrity and the strife of entrepreneurial innovation. As long as the *oikos* of antiquity could be made to relate to a network of socially, culturally and ideologically self-contained and self-sufficient units, each estate could make sense in its own terms, and England was small enough to lend national contours to an insular system of propertied independence. But market-led commercialisation necessarily destroys the isolation of these landed entities, breaking down the ideological self-sufficiency of what had been more-or-less enclosed local spheres of influence, so that while they had not, in Swift's time, lost their sense of an individual profile, they were rapidly ceasing to be self-sufficient. Capitalism, Bakhtin suggests in another context, jolted these worlds and wove them into its own complicatedly evolving unity: 'Every atom of life trembled with this contradictory unity of the capitalist world and capitalist consciousness, permitting nothing to rest easily in isolation, but at the same time resolving nothing.'[42] Bakhtin finds the true spirit of what he calls 'this world-in-the-state-of-becoming' elsewhere, but it becomes reasonable to suggest that we can trace some of its origins in the textual tergiversations of *Gulliver's Travels*.

Because Swift sought to influence the directions being taken by the language of civic humanism, a reading of *Gulliver's Travels* as one of the last explicit statements in the famous quarrel between the Ancients and the Moderns implies further reasons why classic images of 'finished man' should have been particularly attractive to Swift in their terminal purchase on a 'real' world. But if it is true that *Gulliver* keeps alive the classical vision at a time when not only the importance of the quarrel but even the use of the classical viewpoint is being crucially reformulated, then ambivalences in Swift's treatment will relate to his recognition of a cherished ideology swamped by history while rival forms of inventive freedom gain purchase. Within these tensions, techniques of the grotesque become instruments of revenge against a modernity that was assaulting and reconstructing hitherto integrating definitions. Since the only way in which Gulliver feels he can preserve virtue after leaving Houyhnhnmland is by a repudiation of the mores, and even a rejection of the company of his own kind, that virtue is by definition no

---

[42] Bakhtin, *Problems of Dostoevsky's Poetics*, edited and translated by C. Emerson (Manchester, 1984), p. 19.

longer civic: his morality is unhealthily privatised. The sources of
Gulliver's psychosis are complex, but perhaps in revenge for what they
were doing, his narrative turns the material bodily principle central to
Rabelaisian carnival against the possessive egoism of an ascendant
bourgeoisie concerned to obliterate its own origins, a revenge from
which few of us can escape. It has become a commonplace in Swift
criticism that any implied solidarity with the reader, no matter how
provisional, is itself an ironic entrapment designed to leave us beleaguered. One of his favoured techniques is to attack what he imperso-
nates, becoming the thing he satirically targets, so that the space
between satirist and satirised virtually disappears. Additionally,
because *Gulliver* enters the sphere of science fiction, floating between
worlds, it raises problems of generic, as well as ontological and ethical
categorisation. The uncertainty of orientation it develops and maintains encodes a way of exploring problems of ideology and of individuality arising from the emergence of new forms of property and
political economy. An irresistible restructuring of social and economic
practice necessarily involves a discursive reappraisal and reordering of
the constitution of the self and of its limits and possibilities. Notions of
personality hitherto associated with real property and with the autonomy thereby sustained, enter a period of reconstitution for which
Swift's text provides uneasy co-ordinates. The opposing worlds of
Gulliver do not achieve a harmonious balance, and are not designed to
do so since a radical anxiety is being expressed about the inevitability of
participation in altered practices and changed perceptions. The text
discloses its eighteenth-century obsession with Reason and the Passions
as forces in the conflict between landed and moneyed interests, and not
only in its stark contrast between the Yahoos of passion and the
Houyhnhnms of reason, though perhaps most strikingly there.

It is as though shifts in the logic and forms of social process bring
attendant realisations that actions, events and consequences may no
longer relate directly to individual control. Despite its hero's several
rescues, *Gulliver's Travels* contrives to cast doubt upon the possibility of
escape from the worlds it conjures, including the possibility of escape
from the savagery of its own satire and even to the extent of participating in the very inhumanity it exposes. As it shadows forth inversions,
alterities and reversals, an increasing sense of entanglement is conveyed. But at the same time there is an expanding sense of expressive
freedom so that we domesticate the book too conveniently if we read it
as a static exploration of opposed possibilities coming to an expository
climax in the fourth book with, say, Hobbes's view of man in a state of

mutual antagonism and fear of violence on one side of the equation, Locke's vision of a reasonable society harmoniously and benevolently co-ordinated for the common good on the other, and with Gulliver somehow in between. The strength of feeling in Book Four might be more usefully understood as part of Swift's own bitterly resisted accommodation to a historical shift from a Hobbesian to a Lockean state; a shift that was reconstituting the patriarchally secured local economies several times favoured in his book. Swift's attempt to bring together radically opposing forces, and join global inversions of perception, whether through the medium of the carnival-grotesque or through the sometimes corrosive solvent of his irony comes, finally, to signify a powerful conflict within a changing society. Caught between the admired virtue of a patriarchal ideal already attached to a passing ideology and the monetarised state of a present and future society, he is dealing with heterogeneities that when yoked together only split apart more extremely, as the schizophrenic condition of his protagonist at the book's close suggests. In a bifurcation of experience that would later be theorised as an alienation from history, economic developments drive a wedge into inherited systems of value where prior foundations of civic personality in landed property give way to new and less stable definitions. The communicated strength of feeling in *Gulliver's Travels* significantly derives from Swift's unwilling recognition that in England after the Revolution Settlement, the mainsprings of both motivation and perception were, in the lexicon of the time, pride and passion which we can locate in a complicated cross-weave of fantasy and self-interest. Unlike Mandeville, what Swift and like-minded contemporaries found difficult to grasp was how individual pursuits of private interest could possibly develop any sustaining sense of the common good. So perhaps a surviving comic spirit is the necessary safety valve for Swift's beleaguered preferences. In a sequence of narratives where Gulliver repeatedly leaves *terra firma* for the sea we read multiply ironic and compromised meditations on the historical transition from a morality founded on real property to one founded on capital liquidity, mobile property and the shifting vanities and fantasies of a new possessing class. If Swift's dark laughter is therapeutic, it is also prognostic.

4

'Bilk'd of virtue': *The Beggar's Opera*

Lockit. Mr Peachum, – This is the first time my Honour was ever called in
   Question.
Peachum. Business is at an end – if once we act dishonourably.
Lockit. Who accuses me?
Peachum. You are warm, Brother.
Lockit. He that attacks my Honour, attacks my Livelyhood – and this
   Usage – Sir – is not to be borne.
Peachum. Since you provoke me to speak – I must tell you too, that Mrs
   Coaxer charges you with defrauding her of her Information Money,
   for the apprehending of curl-pated *Hugh*. Indeed, Brother, we must
   punctually pay our Spies, or we shall have no Information.[1]

In *The Beggar's Opera* honour is the word every bit as much as self-
interest is the motive, and money is now blatantly the solvent of all
relationships. Denounced as demoralising by both the Archbishop of
Canterbury and Daniel Defoe, *The Opera* took London, then the
provinces, by storm when John Rich was persuaded to accept it for his
little theatre in Lincoln's Inn Fields after Colley Cibber refused to stage
it at Drury Lane. It ran for a record-breaking sixty-two nights in the
first season, and went on to be staged somewhere in England in nearly
every year for more than a century and a half.[2] After the riot of satirical
treatment to which it subjected him, and to which his only available
reponse on the play's first night had been to laugh with the rest of the
audience, Walpole banned *Polly*, the sequel Gay produced to capitalise
on his success. In consequence Gay made more from the printed copies
of the much inferior *Polly* than he did from the performances of *The
Opera*. Within a parody of currently fashionable Italian opera the

---

[1] John Gay, *The Beggar's Opera*, in *Dramatic Works*, edited by John Fuller, 2 vols. (Oxford,
1983), II. Further citations will be given by act, scene and line parenthetically in the text.
[2] W. E. Schultz, *Gay's 'Beggar's Opera': Its Content, History and Influence* (Yale Univ., CT, 1923),
p. xxi.

immediate joke, of course, lay in the projection of London as a den of thieves, with the political bite of the satire coming from the implicit and wholesale indictment of the Whig administration in general and of Walpole in particular. If we had no further evidence that the ascendant Hanoverian Whigs who rode to power on the back of the new finance and stayed there after the collapse of the South Sea Company appeared to some contemporaries as no more than a state banditry, then Gay's manipulation of the comic-opera would remain convincing testimony.

At some pains to construct as comprehensive a condemnation of Walpole as was possible within the framework of ironic burlesque, Gay is at times outrageously pointed. On the surface, repeated references to the 'great man' call the First Minister to mind since quite apart from his political power Walpole weighed over twenty stones and this was already a popular nick-name. '*Bluff Bob*' (I, iii, 26), suggesting Walpole's alleged lack of good manners as well as his political double-dealing also became a popular soubriquet, and '*Bob Booty*' carried the implication that Walpole plundered the public purse. 'Bob' itself was slang for a shoplifter's assistant, and Gay's first audiences would have been entertained by these innuendoes. But name-calling is the least of it. The quarrel between two characters not only complicit with criminals but running them in a business-like fashion and keeping stock-records and orderly accounts of stolen goods, was as direct. While Gay is careful to keep allusions and references to Walpole shifting from context to context, theatre-goers would similarly have recognised in the figures of Lockit and Peachum, the first a corrupt Newgate prison-keeper and the second a receiver of stolen goods and informer, representations of Walpole and his brother-in-law Lord Townshend, also a Minister of State: the firm of Townshend and Walpole, as the prime minister himself called it.[3] 'What of *Bob Booty*?' asks Mrs Peachum as her husband looks for a likely candidate for execution in time for the next Quarter Sessions, and in his reply Peachum refers to the fact that Booty 'spends his Life among Women' (I, iv, 1–5). It is one of several allusions to Walpole's love-life and towards the end of the same scene Peachum's insistence on the proper mode of conduct for Polly to follow is explicit: 'My Daughter to me should be, like a Court Lady to a Minister of State, a Key to the whole Gang' (I, iv, 82–3). With Captain MacHeath's relationship to Polly and Lucy forming a main strand in the plot, the libretto keeps Walpole's extra-marital relationship with Maria Skerret constantly in the audience's mind.

---

[3] Speck, *Stability and Strife*, p. 209.

By placing Walpole allusively, and personal and political chicanery directly at the centre of its web of connections the *Opera* achieves an unusual density of signification, one of the threads being the systematic equation of criminality with high society. Peachum's opening song sets the tone, and his placing of the lawyer on a par with his own dealings brings into operation the formal ordering of social relations that the play co-ordinates. Long before the Beggar himself draws a 'morality' into open statement, patterns of repetition infiltrate a competitive appropriation, deception and betrayal into all levels of society, with economic advantage the guiding motive. In defence of her daughter, Mrs Peachum remarks that 'she loves to imitate the fine Ladies, and she may only allow the Captain Liberties in the View of Interest' (I, iv, 93–4). For much of the 1720s Gay held the minor Court sinecure of Commissioner of the State Lotteries which may have sharpened his own perception of the suitability of cards and gambling as social metaphors, and again a question from Mrs Peachum triggers the appropriate associations: 'What business hath [MacHeath] to keep Company with Lords and Gentlemen? he should leave them to prey upon one another' (I, iv, 53–5). Given that 'handsome daughters' take 'as much pleasure in cheating a Father and Mother, as in cheating at Cards' (I, viii, 46–7), these parodied valorisations feed into domestic structures of relationship while Lockit's song generates a fitting sense of the intersections between codes of card-playing and a more general civic necessity of maintaining relations across competitive atomisation:

> *Thus Gamesters united in Friendship are found,*
> *Though they know that their Industry all is Cheat;*
> *They flock to their Prey at the Dice-Box's Sound,*
> *And join to promote one another's Deceit.*   (III, ii, 12–15)

When Peachum earlier agrees that 'in one respect indeed, our Employment may be reckoned dishonest, because, like Great Statesmen, we encourage those who betray their Friends' (II, x, 16–18), it sounds initially like a time-honoured and timeless political slur. But in the aftermath of the South Sea débacle the song that Lockit then sings suggests a shared and ruling complicity in corruption:

> *If you mention Vice or Bribe,*
> *'Tis so pat to all the Tribe;*
> *Each crys – That was levell'd at me.*   (II, x, 24–6)

The experience upon which every first-run audience of the play could draw was memory of the Bubble year, so although the meaning had been current for some time before 1720, the use of 'bubble' as both verb and noun meaning to delude or cheat and a dupe (at II, xiii, 55–6, and III, i, 42 respectively), is topically effective when projecting is individuated. 'You should never do anything', says Lockit to his daughter, 'but upon the foot of interest. Those that act otherwise are their own bubbles', and the song which follows is sung to a tune called 'South Sea Ballad'. Self-interest forms the spring of motive and action throughout as the libretto percolates economic gain into personal construction, and showing a marked ignorance of animal ecology but a corresponding knowledge of his own society, Lockit states openly what is everywhere inferred: 'Lions, wolves and Vulturs don't live together in Herds, Droves or Flocks. Of all animals of Prey, Man is the only sociable one. Every one of us preys upon his Neighbour, and yet we herd together' (III, ii, 4–7).

The pickpockets, footpads and highwaymen who prey upon their fellow citizens are in turn exploited and squeezed by Peachum and Lockit in a general system of more or less violent expropriation and betrayal, and the play has been read as an intervention in the debate between Hobbes and the several replies to him constructed by Shaftesbury. In Hobbes's sceptical view, man's predatory nature calls for the social imposition of powerful and vigorously applied law and authority to keep these self-interested instincts in check. Shaftesbury's more optimistic view argues that self-interest and social interest might be the same and that like the other passions, sociability was both instinctive and conducive to the common good. 'There is little doubt', one response concludes, 'that the Hobbesian view pervades *The Beggar's Opera*, but Gay's achievement is to throw up as an ironical alternative the sentimental Shaftesburian view of things, appearing, as it were, to weigh the two social theories judiciously in the balance, hinting that there *might* be exceptions to the general Hobbesian rule.'[4] Since Macheath and Polly were popular figures, audiences could identify with them in optimistic and high-spirited ways, so it might be useful to extend this reading to include John Locke, a writer who in some senses mediates between Hobbes and Shaftesbury, and who became interested in the moral code of highwaymen when he was considering whether any innate moral principles might be said to exist upon which civil society might be constructed:

Justice and keeping of contracts, is that which most men seem to agree in. This is a principle which is thought to extend itself to the dens of thieves, and the confederacies of the greatest villains . . . Justice and truth are the common ties of

[4] Ian Donaldson, ' "A Double Capacity": *The Beggar's Opera*', in *Modern Essays on Eighteenth-Century Literature*, edited by L. Damrosch Jr (Oxford, 1988), p. 154.

society; and therefore even outlaws and robbers, who break with all the world besides, must keep faith and rules of equity amongst themselves; or else they cannot hold together.[5]

Locke is the great apologist for the social market in its early English form, whereas Gay takes the force of monetarist morality to his own anarchic and comic-grotesque conclusions where even the sustaining notion of honour among thieves is undermined by Macheath's betrayal at the hands of a member of his own gang. Gay takes Hobbes's description of society as a 'war of all against all' into his representation of a London in the grip of competitive individualism where the power of egoism reigns alongside ever-increasing interdependence. In doing so he satirically ambiguates Hegel's subsequent determination that Hobbes's phrase describes a society that is contradictory and self-destructive: the *Opera* invents a plural form to complicate and assuage the oppositions it generates, effectively ironising what John Locke presented as a signal accomplishment. Whatever moved Locke to write the second *Treatise of Civil Government* (1690), there can be little doubt that he approved of the revolution and also of the form of government and social order he found in England:[6] insofar as Locke's theories were of service to the Whig state, there is something to be said for reading *The Beggar's Opera*, as a satirical rebuttal of some of their main premises and postulates.

Locke's justification of a monetary and commercial state as the natural human condition removed the moral disability with which unlimited appropriation had hitherto been handicapped. By further justifying as natural a class differential in rights and in rationality, Locke provided a positive moral basis for the accumulation of property beyond the limits of immediate use:[7]

God gave the World to Men ... for their benefit, and the greatest Conveniences of Life they were capable to draw from it ... He gave it to the use of the Industrious and Rational, (and *Labour* was to be *his Title* to it;) not to the Fancy or Covetousness of the Quarrelsom and Contentious.[8]

The structure of Gay's play already appears as a comic subversion of this emerging market morality, and other elements in Locke's theory are ironised in Gay's treatment. Locke also puts money at the heart of his

---

[5] Locke, *Concerning Human Understanding*, p. 66.

[6] John Plamenatz, *Man and Society: A Critical Examination of Some Important Social and Political Theories From Machiavelli to Marx* (London, 1963), p. 209.

[7] C. B. Macpherson, *The Political Theory of Possessive Individualism: Hobbes to Locke* (Oxford, 1962), pp. 194 ff.

[8] John Locke, *Two Treatises of Government*, edited by Peter Laslett (Cambridge, 1960, rpt. 1992), p. 309. All references to Locke's second *Treatise* are to this edition and are given parenthetically in the text.

system and by supposing an original contract between the individual and society, freely entered into for the protection of property, he provided the metaphor of an overarching legal framework which it becomes the business of *The Beggar's Opera* to satirise. For Locke it is the introduction of money into any territory which leads to the appropriation of all the land it contains, leaving some without any. Money makes it profitable for the individual to produce commodities for commercial exchange, 'to draw *Money* to him by the Sale of the Product', and so makes it advantageous to extend the possession of land 'beyond the use of his Family, and a plentiful supply to its Consumption' (p. 319). There is only one way for people to become full members of society: 'Nothing can make any Man so, but his actually entering into it by positive Engagement, and Express Promise and Compact. This is that, which I think, concerns the beginning of Political Societies, and that *Consent which makes any one a Member* of any Commonwealth' (p. 367). The structure of society is conceived as a business partnership contractually entered into for the preservation of property, with Locke envisaging market society as a freely contracted participation in a giant trading company; freely contracted, that is, by those with sufficient capital to invest. Those with only their labour to sell are subject to this state, but not business partners in it.

'Why are the Laws Levell'd at us?', jibes Jemmy Twitcher in a comic introduction of terms traditionally used to justify acquisition and possession: 'are we more dishonest than the rest of Mankind? What we win, Gentlemen, is our own by the Law of Arms, and the Right of Conquest' (II, i, 9–12). Aristocratic notions of honour and courage get a good ragging in the *Opera*, although there is no easy point of rest in Gay's text; it is Jemmy Twitcher who will betray Macheath. One of the play's characteristics is its refusal of any moral cover for the audience: no sooner is the possibility mooted of an escape from the interest-dominated individualist perspectives it everywhere discloses than the plot will turn to cut off the avenue of potential release. Matt of the Mint speaks ironically to Locke's determination that the advent of money as the means of circulation propelled individuals into the possession of more than was required for use and plentiful supply. 'This partage of things', says Locke, 'in an inequality of private possessions, men have made practicable out of the bounds of societie, and without compact, only by putting a value on gold and silver and tacitly agreeing in the use of Money' (p. 320). Money becomes a separate realm of co-ordination outwith society's discursive parameters, whereas: 'we are for a just Partition of the World', says Ben Budge, and Matt's rejoinder to the prevailing state of affairs is also not without a certain perverse conviction: 'We retrench the Superfluities of Mankind. The World is Avaritious, and I hate Avarice. A covetous fellow, like a Jack-daw, steals what he was never made to enjoy, for the sake of hiding it. These are the Robbers of Mankind, for Money was made for the Free-hearted and Generous, and where is the Injury of taking from another, what he hath not the Heart to make use of?' (II, i, 24–30). Such parodies of newly conventional assumptions multiply as *The Beggar's Opera* proceeds to take monetarist morality at those face values it was showing in contemporary London, and many of which are discernible in Locke. By the tropes he used when arguing for *The Reasonableness of Christianity*, Locke had already entangled Virtue in the terms and figures of a monetarised reasoning, opening the way for Gay's text to present itself as a high-spirited if unsettling exposition of the economic priorities underlying Locke's founding attempt to discover a rational justification for Christian moral behaviour:

The [ancient] philosophers, indeed, shewed the beauty of virtue; ... but leaving her unendowed, very few were willing to espouse her ... But now there being put into the scales on her side, 'an exceeding and immortal weight of glory'; interest is come about to her, and virtue now is visibly the most enriching purchase, and by much the best bargain ... The view of heaven and hell will cast a slight upon the short pleasures and pains of this present state, and give attraction and encouragements to virtue, which reason and interest, and the care of ourselves, cannot but allow and prefer. Upon this foundation, and upon this only, morality will stand firm, and may defy all competition.[9]

By making a virtue of success, Locke sang the new world of possibility. Self-promoting valuations become rhetorical figures decking virtue in her post-Revolutionary Settlement guise – as a goddess of profitable exchange. The scales of the shopkeeper displace those of justice and, figured as a virgin up for public auction, the attractions of virtue become a matter of looking for the best buy. This resolution of virtue into commodity-values becomes in turn the stuff and content of the world Gay depicts. 'Am I then bilk'd of my Virtue?', cries Lucy Lockit when confronting Macheath's incorrigible sexual duplicity, 'Can I have no Reparation?' (II, xiii, 21–2). By its seductive use of the language of social grace to present underworld criminality, the *Opera* satirically appropriates Locke's normative assumptions, and by systematically subjecting its characters and contexts to valorisations deriving from a money economy, the play puts every mode of relationship at

[9] John Locke, *The Reasonableness of Christianity*, edited by I. T. Ramsay (London, 1958), p. 70.

issue, from the personal and familial to the social and hierarchical. Meanwhile the formal pretexts and pretences of private and public morality are comically ransacked. As are those of Justice: time itself is formulated according to the operations of law-courts as corrupt as everything else, and Filch's servicing of female prisoners so that their pregnancies might keep them from the hangman shows us human procreation subjected to the self-interested demands of survival in a punitive legal system stripped of any validity other than the perpetuation of those norms of criminality that keep it in existence.

In this constructed world, then, penitence is feebleness of purpose (I, ii, 41–2); murder a matter of business priorities (I, iv, 25–9); moral scruple a sign of frailty made the more acceptable by its fashionable prevalence (I, iv, 30–4); and gratitude a plaything of profit (I, xi, 14). Love and marriage are similarly presented in ways diametrically opposed to the conventional (and convenient) dictates of Christian wisdom. It is typical of the 'double capacity' (I, i, 10) Gay makes his figures serve, that Peachum's reaction to the prospect of his daughter's marriage is expressed in trade and advantage-seeking terms as it brings to light the specific and actual subordination of woman in eighteenth-century marriage contracts: 'If the Wench does not know her own Profit, sure she knows her own Pleasure better than to make herself a Property!' (I, iv, 86–7). These contracts are anyway more honoured in the breach than the observance, as Mrs Peachum observes: 'All Men are Thieves in Love, and like a Woman the better for being another's Property' (I, v, 5–6). In a world that so sedulously relates ethics to the circulation of goods, sexual favours also become commodities to be traded like any other and Mrs Peachum sings marriage in monetary imagery; the wife being passed from partner to partner like coin of the realm:

> A Wife's like a Guinea in Gold,
> Stampt with the Name of her Spouse;
> Now here, now there; is bought, or is sold;
> And is current in every house.   (I, v, 11–14)

The equation of sexual desire with commercial exchange is ironised in different ways in Macheath's recognition that 'a man who loves Money, might as well be contented with one guinea as I with one woman' (II, iii, 2–4). Reducing desire to an all-encompassing cash-nexus makes prostitution an appropriately correlative system of personal encounter and helps to contextualise the play's repeated references to the oldest profession. Moll Flanders knew a thing or two about surviving in this society and when looked at through the opera-glasses Gay provides, Moll becomes an early example of a successful business-woman in the newly prevailing dispositions. Although Polly is not a prostitute, any inclination we may feel to exempt her from this general state of affairs is somewhat inhibited by her assessment of the qualities appropriate to a monetarised state: 'A Woman knows how to be mercenary, though she hath never been in a Court or at an Assembly. We have it in our Natures, Papa. If I allow Captain *Macheath* some trifling liberties, I have this watch and other visible Marks of his Favour to show for it' (I, vii, 2–6). A reconstruction of feelings as portable property enters the realm of intimacy with another card-playing metaphor when Polly continues: 'A girl who cannot grant some Things, and refuse what is most material, will make but a poor hand of her Beauty, and soon be thrown upon the Common' (I, vii, 6–9). And the power of money as universal solvent is further indicated when Peachum consoles his wife: 'But Money, Wife, is the true Fuller's Earth for Reputations, there is not a Spot or a Stain but what it can take out. A rich Rogue now-a-days is fit Company for any Gentleman; and the World, my Dear, hath not such a Contempt for Roguery as you imagine' (I, ix, 8–12).

Personal and social values are systematically displayed in monetarised forms, so that the commodity lists popular in journalism at the time for their socially flattering recognition of new riches becoming available for consumption, take on a different emphasis when they compose a record of thieving that will determine whether or not the culprit will hang: the longer the list of thefts the greater the security of life and liberty to the perpetrator. The acquisition and circulation of goods is differently and then not so differently perceived when it moves through a criminal fraternity where, in the commerce of sex, it is not youth or beauty but fashionable self-presentation that fixes the price 'from half a Crown to two Guineas'. For Mrs Trapes there is no difference between the running of a brothel and any other investment and management programme: 'What with Fees and other Expences, there are great Goings-out, and no Comings-in, and not a Farthing to pay for at least a Month's cloathing. – We run great Risques – great Risques indeed' (III, vi, 48–51). The manipulative powers the *Opera* inventively displays in all of its characters, conceals and then reveals their own manipulation by powers outside themselves, and to attribute this merely to avarice is to mystify what the play lays bare – that a developing social order, in its internal psychology as well as its external manifestations, is becoming subordinate to a system of motive that is in fact its moving spirit. Because everyone shifts for themselves in the

pursuit of money, the arrangement that presents itself, initially indicated by the plethoric incidence of the term 'money' itself, is a world
where money pursues everyone. As it reconstructs value in the play,
money translates previous valorisations into the commercial operations
of a banking system. Thus, *'Friendship for Interest is but a Loan, / Which they
let out for what they can get'* (III, iv, 8–9), and even *'Death is a Debt, / A
Debt on demand – So, take what I owe'* (III, xi, 76–7). Lockit and Peachum
consult their account-book to see how their equity in a still-living
Macheath might best be divided between them, and the object of their
attentions sings the true motive and worth of 'Court friends' in their
commodification of the human individual: *'They promise, they pity, / But
shift you for Money, from Friend to Friend'* (III, iv, 14–15). As money
triumphs over other forms of possession and relationship, subordinating
them to its own regime, so the human circulates in exchange for cash.
Subjectivity equates with objects ceaselessly changing places in a chain
of equivalences that courses through the *Opera*'s social formation. The
world that Gay constructs, a 'satire of a world where everything is for
sale',[10] simultaneously sets its characters at odds with one another and
unites them in a set of characteristic social relations. Many of these
equations have been described with wit and precision, making it a
pleasure, in considering further what they are, to pick up threads of
analysis woven into William Empson's celebrated essay of the 1930s.

'The stock device of the play', Empson writes, 'is a double irony like a
Seidlitz powder, piling a dramatic irony onto what was already an
irony. This forces one to read back a more complex irony into the first
one, and the composure of language of the characters makes us feel that
the speaker took the whole sense for granted ... The trick of style that
makes this plausible is Comic Primness, the double irony in the acceptance of a convention ... No sentence of the play is quite free from this
trick', and this double-irony method, out of which the jokes are
fashioned, is inherent in the whole movement of the story.[11] As Empson
picks his way through the play's satiric layering it becomes ever clearer
that things are never *quite* clear, and that we are constantly at a turn to
discover a stance towards the text that might enable a more detached
assessment of its ethical concerns. Double-meaning becomes a mode of
double-dealing, so that duplicity seems to include our own reactions.
When the point of the joke is so often that the villains are right, not that

[10] Maynard Mack, *The Augustans* (Princeton, NJ, 1961), pp. 17–18.
[11] William Empson, '*The Beggar's Opera*: Mock-Pastoral as the Cult of Independence', in
Versions of Pastoral, pp. 165–250, at pp. 170, 178.

they are wrong, Empson suggests that the only viable response is that
the root of the normal order of society is a mean injustice and while it
would be ludicrous to be complacent about this, one cannot conceive its
being otherwise. Gay's conclusion, therefore, is not that society should
be altered but that only the individual can be admired. Empson
demonstrates how so much of the play's zest stems from a cool application of the profit motive and its reasoning apparatus to a variety of
human relationships, and from an equally unassuming implication of a
whole society in the nefarious operations of London's underworld. 'I
know that if one would be agreeable to men of dignity', Gay wrote in a
letter where we see the idea of the *Opera* germinating, 'one must study to
imitate them, and know which way they get Money and places. I
cannot wonder that the talents requisite for a great Statesman are so
scarce in the world since so many of those who possess them are every
month cut off in the prime of their Age at the old-Baily.'[12] Accordingly:
'the thieves and whores parody the aristocratic ideal, the dishonest
prison-keeper and thief-taker and their families parody the bourgeois
ideal (though the divine Polly has a foot in both camps); these two
ideals are naturally at war, and the rise to power of the bourgeois had
made the war important. Their most obvious difference is in the form of
Independence that they idealise.'[13] Empson is writing in the nineteen-
thirties, when some of the connections between public corruption,
private wealth and political liberty in the eighteenth century were
beginning to be opened up. 'Bribery', says Namier, 'to be really
effective, has to be widespread and open; it has to be the custom of the
land and cease to dishonour the recipients, so that its prizes may be
attractive for the average self-respecting man.'[14] Since no one bribes
where he can bully, corruption becomes a mark of English freedom and
independence.[15] Gay subjects these processes to parody and satire, so
that when in Empson's argument 'independence' shades into 'individualism' the history of the times makes the reading he develops
persuasive in other ways. An earlier remark he makes opens the way to
a different emphasis of interpretation, where the nature of this individualism begins to find appropriate form. 'Clearly', says Empson, 'it is
important for a nation with a strong class-system to have an art-form
that not merely evades but breaks through it, that makes the classes feel
part of a larger unity or simply at home with each other ... the
half-conscious purpose behind the magical ideas of heroic and pastoral

---

[12] *Letters of John Gay*, ed. Burgess, p. 45.   [13] Empson, *Versions of Pastoral*, p. 217.
[14] Lewis Namier, *The Structure of Politics at the Accession of George III* (London, 1929), p. 219.
[15] Lewis Namier, *England in the Age of the American Revolution* (London, 1930), pp. 4–5.

was being finely secured by *The Beggar's Opera* when the mob roared its applause both against and with the applause of Walpole' (p. 162). We discover that Gay had in fact produced a remarkable exercise in artistic accommodation to his world, with the *Opera* comically incorporating many of the things Mandeville had to say about the same society, but in an ambiguous celebration and integration of the reconstructed values with which it makes such durable sport. Gay was laughing literate London into forms of self-recognition.

W. B. Piper's more recent reading of the play fully acknowledges its debt to Empson but wants to employ a metonymic/metaphoric distinction to overturn the conclusion that only the individual can be admired, by demonstrating that 'the Opera dissolves individuality in a metaphoric stew'.[16] In this approach, for the inhabitants of Gay's world the metonymic capacity – the capacity to separate and to distinguish between items and levels of experience – has weakened and the tendency to equate and to substitute – the metaphoric tendency – runs wild. Because a case can be made for the validity of both readings, Empson's and Piper's, it will be helpful to rehearse some of the latter's arguments. Even from its collocation of discourse and song, the fabric of *The Beggar's Opera* is decidedly metonymic. A system of 'expressive contiguities' keeps us alert to this aspect while a pervasive metonymic discrepancy between high and low society is revealed. But within this structure the dominant pattern is one of similitudes that sometimes surreptitiously but nonetheless consistently undermine difference and contiguity. Peachum's first song and statement is a tissue of such similitudes, and the details of Peachum's virtually universal equation, which includes 'each' neighbour and 'all' professions, echo and re-echo through the play. As pointedly, Peachum and Lockit are virtual mirror-images of each other, and beyond their particularised presentation, the identities of Polly and Lucy come together through the similarity of their figures of speech and the duets they sing:

> Polly.   *I'm bubbled.*
> Lucy.   *I'm bubbled.*
> Polly.   *Oh how I am troubled!*
> Lucy.   *Bambouzled, and bit!*
> Polly.   *My distresses are doubled.*
> Lucy.   *When you come to the Tree, should the Hangman refuse,*
>   *These fingers, with Pleasure, could fasten the noose.*
> Polly.   *I'm bubbled, &c.*   (II, xiii, 55–62)

---

16 W. B. Piper, 'Similitude as Satire in *The Beggar's Opera*', *Eighteenth Century Studies*, 21, no. 3 (1987–8), p. 342, n. 10.

As part of this comic hall of mirrors, the thieves stress their similarities with the nobility, and the play's tropic inventiveness repeatedly erodes professional and social difference. Money reduces the qualities Gay introduces to quantities and thus allows for what Piper terms 'the frightful material equation' of anything with anything and of anyone with anyone. All relationships in this world can be resolved into business arrangements, love into 'fees' and 'debts'; freedom into 'garnish' and 'perquisites'; thievery into a cure for 'avarice'; and marriage into a mesh of fortunes, pay, jointures, contracts. Not only are specified amounts of money substituted for actual persons but in a world where capital can rationalise any metaphor at all, 'the experiential, the natural tissue of lively identities and interesting differences has been cancelled'. The *Opera*'s most insistent pattern of repetition presents the illusion of personal individuality, of particularity in nature and action, only to undermine it, and although Macheath stands out as a character of some integrity, he too can be reduced to forty pounds; he equates women with one another and with money and so also suffers in the play's 'pathologically metaphoric atmosphere'.[17]

We are left wondering how a reading of the play as tending to promote egotism and independence can co-exist with one which sees in it the virtual obliteration of human beings in their particular natures. But Empson reminds us that the play uses credit both about business and about glory, an equation of some interest: that 'ruined' may mean either married or not married, and that one of the play's persistent complications is its demonstration that all human beings, because they are independent, arc forced to prey upon one another.[18] In the war of all against all, possessive individualism paradoxically dissolves into one-dimensional similitude: the all-pervasive metaphor of the transforming powers of money generates this most levelling equation of all, rendering the particular into the general and difference into sameness. Money erases every difference between commodities precisely because as the universal medium of exchange money is the equivalent form common to all of them. Locke had seen something of this in his 1691 pamphlet about the lowering of the interest rate, when he described how 'Money in its Circulation driving the several wheels of Trade' connects landowner, labourer, broker and shopkeeper:

Now Money is necessary to all these sorts of Men, as serving both for Counters and for Pledges, and so carrying with it even Reckoning and Security, that he,

[17] Ibid., pp. 342, 345.   [18] *Versions of Pastoral*, p. 192.

that receives it, shall have the same value for it again, of other things that he wants, whenever he pleases.[19]

Gay satirises this presentation and as structured in the *Opera*, his perceptions were honed on direct experience of an invading difference that allows individuals to exist, even in their self-perceptions, only according to the fluctuating values of a market economy where:

forms of property were seen to arise which conveyed the notion of inherent dependence: salaried office, reliance on private or political patronage, on public credit. For these the appropriate term in the republican lexicon was corruption – the substitution of private dependencies for public authority – and the threat to individual integrity and self-knowledge which corruption had always implied was reinforced by the rise of forms of property seeming to rest on fantasy and false consciousness. Once property was seen to have a symbolic value, expressed in coin or credit, the foundations of personality themselves appeared imaginary or at best consensual.[20]

'Every reference to money in the Opera', Empson suggests early in his essay, 'carries a satire on ... it no less complete than those of Timon of Athens which Marx analysed with so much pleasure',[21] and the young Marx on Shakespeare comes to sound like a time-travelling reviewer of *The Beggar's Opera*'s first night. 'If *money* is the bond which ties me to *human* life and society to me, which links me to nature and to man, is money not the bond of all *bonds*? Can it not bind and loose all bonds? It is the true *agent of separation* and the true *cementing agent*, it is the *chemical* power of society.'[22] As he reads Timon's speech on the power of gold in Act IV, scene iii, Marx observes Shakepeare bringing out two of its particular properties; that it is the visible divinity which transforms all human and natural qualities into their opposites, universally confusing and inverting things and bringing together impossibilities; and that it is 'the universal whore, the universal pimp of men and peoples' (p. 377). Marx's recognition that what he called 'the special difficulty in grasping money in its fully developed character as money'[23] lay in the fact that money transmutes a social relation between people into an external thing, shades back into Gay's text. The *Opera* parodies a process of exchange that is accomplished through two metamorphoses of opposite yet mutually complementary character – the conversion of

[19] John Locke, 'Some Considerations of the Consequences of the Lowering of Interest, and Raising the Value of Money', in *John Locke: Locke on Money*, edited by P.H. Kelly, 2 vols. (Oxford, 1991), I, p. 233.
[20] Pocock, *Machiavellian Moment*, p. 464.   [21] Empson, *Versions of Pastoral*, pp. 205–6.
[22] Marx, *Early Writings*, p. 377.   [23] Marx, *Grundrisse*, p. 239.

commodities into money, and the reconversion of money into commodities. By directly inserting the human as commodities in this process the libretto transforms its living subjects into traded objects and thus makes fine sport of its perception that the two moments of this metamorphosis are at once distinct transactions – selling, or the exchange of the commodity for money, and buying, or the exchange of money for the commodity – and one unified act: selling in order to buy. Marx had his own way of incorporating classical authority to negotiate these things and quotes Plutarch: 'As Heracleitus says, all things exchange for fire, and fire for all things, just as gold does for goods and goods for gold.'[24]

Living through the hectic early decades of the financial revolution, suffering badly from his failed investments in the South Sea Company and remaining active in the stock market until his death in 1732, Gay learned how the installation of credit money was transvaluing human relations into the ownership of things. The *Opera*'s system of metaphoric equivalences co-ordinates with a subsequent perception of money as the universal equivalent form. In his later life Marx described the circulation of money as 'the constant and monotonous repetition of the same process ... Nothing is immune from this alchemy ... Just as in money every qualitative difference between commodities is extinguished, so too for its part, as a radical leveller, it extinguishes all distinctions.'[25] He had already registered his perception that money is not exchanged for a particular quality, a particular thing, but for what he called 'the whole objective world of man and nature', so that seen from the standpoint of the person who possesses it: 'money exchanges every quality for every other quality and object, even if it is contradictory; it is the power which brings together impossibilities and forces contradictions to embrace'.[26] When it is characterised in this way, he suggests, money is 'the universal inversion of *individualities*'.[27] In high dudgeon at this, Marx is nonetheless astonished at the near-global expansion of human energies it was his project to describe, and his own metaphoric ingenuity betrays the sometimes bemused wonder with which he responded to modern economic practice: his moral opprobrium comes garlanded with an intoxicating richness of trope, and there are perceivable connections between the way he expresses himself and the linguistic transvaluations of identity in *The Beggar's Opera*. But down in Exchange Alley in the 1720s, where modern economics was a novel

---

[24] Marx, *Capital*, I, p. 200, n. 16.   [25] Ibid., pp. 210–11, 229.
[26] Marx, *Early Writings*, p. 379.
[27] Ibid., p. 378.

experience and its systems far from secure, things were not always seen as the *Opera* sees them.

Appearing first as 'promises of money' the new paper forms were becoming more and more difficult to distinguish from the 'real' thing. When the perspective then switches round and the new paper instruments are rapidly recognised as money itself, for a time the hierarchy of money forms and the limits of monetary capacity are blurred. In the years preceding and following the South Sea collapse such blurring was endemic, and became itself a technique of manipulation. 'People must not know what they do', John Blunt had said, 'the execution of the scheme is our business.'[28] The *Opera* acknowledges the function of money as a determining agency that generates substitutions and transformations apparently at will, and presents a calculated confusion of values and perceptions where the figure of money rules all things. Gay's anarchic wit then comes to seem entirely appropriate, with his play's formal ambivalences – now pastoral, now parody; now operatic, now popular song; now heroic, now satirically mocking – encoding formal correlatives for a wider social drama of entirely uncertain aims and ends. Heroic tragedy, Italian opera, pastoral, popular ballads and sentimental comedy merge bizarrely together, continually awakening ironical memories of other kinds of literary experience, yet nevertheless forming a whole which is in some ways curiously life-like.[29] Like *The Rape of the Lock* (and Dryden before that), we see in *The Beggar's Opera* hybrid forms developed to accommodate a new world visibly emerging from the chrysalis of the old, but still powerfully attached to inherited structures of perception. When, in the play's penultimate scene, the beggar is addressed as 'honest friend' by the player who persuades him to turn his back upon 'strict poetical justice', we witness a final ironic turn. Honesty comes at last into conflict with the writer's self-interest (which by pandering to 'the Taste of the Town' will ensure commercial success), and we re-enter Italianate operatic artifice for the sake of a happy ending. At least we think we do. Macheath's last statement stages deception through double-speak and his final song is a promissory note on temporarily deferred gratification. Tomorrow will bring another day; but it will be the same as all the rest. The only place to go is back to the beginning and enjoy it all again.

[28] Cited in *FR*, p. 170.   [29] Donaldson, 'Double Capacity', p. 144.

5

'Abusing the city's best good men': Pope's poetry of the 1730s

On 5 December 1726 Bolingbroke's newspaper, launched as a platform of opposition to Walpole's ministry, opened with a justification of its name. Because a nationwide degeneracy has 'put Virtue and Honesty almost quite out of countenance ... it is for this reason that I have entitled my paper the CRAFTSMAN; under which general character I design to lay open the frauds, abuses, and secret iniquities of all professions, not excepting those of my own, which is at present notoriously adulterated with pernicious mixtures of Craft and several scandalous Prostitutions.'[1] Its awareness of the employment of writing in this social process strikes a chord of recognition but *The Craftsman*'s sights were elsewhere, and it welcomed the new year by directly addressing 'the Great Man' for the first time, looking back to the English Renaissance to determine that:

The character of a *Great Man* was not to be acquired, in those Times, by understanding the paltry Business of a *Money-Scrivener*, or a *Stock-jobber*; by a skill in usury, brokage, and the tricks of *Exchange Alley*; or by colloguing with certain *great Bodies* of men, in order to defraud, bubble, and beggar the rest of the Nation; not by suborning false judgement; and hiring Men to prostitute their consciences for sordid lucer. (p. 73)

Thereafter, the 'Great Man' is repeatedly subjected to a variety of satirical treatment, with the phrase itself forming something of a threnody as issue after issue returned to the attack. The political patron of credit-based commerce is seen as having survived by corrupting the political process and Walpole is so effectively placed at the centre of the newspaper's concerns that his presence is felt whatever the particular corruption being exposed. When *The Craftsman* set out to acquaint its readers with 'the behaviour of a *favourite Director*; who is the DIRECTOR of *Directors*, and their SCREEN-MASTER GENERAL', it used a soubriquet

---

[1] *The Craftsman: Being a Critique of the Times*, edited by Caleb D'Anvers, 2 vols. (London, 1728), I, pp. 8–9. Subsequent citations are given parenthetically in the text.

that stuck to Walpole for the rest of his life. Memories of the South Sea Bubble could thus be focused in one person while signifying a general condition of abused financial power:

The rise and fall of these commodities do, in no small degree, affect every other kind of property in these kingdoms; as was to be seriously felt in the fatal year of 1720 ... It is well known *who* were the most busy *selling out* before and immediately after the *Hanover Treaty* was finished, in order to make their best market of that *artful rise* of the stocks.   (p. 125)

That artful rise is associated with the decline of art, and helping to shape an audience for the first *Dunciad*, the newspaper thundered against the 'great *Decay of Learning*' and pilloried those engaged in 'polite literature' who acted 'in defence of our Modern *Dulness* and *Stupidity*':

When the favours of *Great Men* are heaped only on themselves, their own Relations and immediate Dependants; when all Places of Truth, Honour, and Profit center in two or three Families at most; when pensions, presents, grants, patents and reversions are either sold or engrossed; and everything runs in the same *foul Channel of Corruption and Self-Interest*; then, I say, Men of Merit and Ability have just Reason to complain, remonstrate and protest; and it is ridiculous to expect that Art, Wit or Learning should flourish, in any degree, under such a rapacious, selfish and usurious Administration.   (p. 171)

The reign of Dulness is further suggested in a warning about 'the dangers of a POLITICAL LETHARGY, which lays all the noble faculties, generous passions, and social virtues, as it were by *Opium*, in a profound Trance, and thereby leaves publick Ministers at their discretion, and under a strong temptation to do whatever their ambition dictates, with impunity, and without observation' (p. 235). When John Gay was made informal steward to the Duke of Queensberry in 1730, Swift took the opportunity of praising the virtue of a poet serving in that office in equally explicit condemnation of Walpole's continuing stewardship of the nation's affairs after the death of George I:

> I knew a *brazen* Minister of State,
> Who bore for twice ten Years the publick Hate.
> In every Mouth the Question most in Vogue
> Was, *When will* THEY *turn out this odious Rogue?*
> A Juncture happen'd in his highest Pride:
> While he went robbing on; *old Master* dy'd.
> We thought, there now remain'd no room to doubt:
> *His Work is done, the Minister must out.*
> . . .

> But not a Soul his Office durst accept:
> The subtle Knave had all the Plunder swept.
> And, such was then the Temper of the Times,
> He ow'd his Preservation to his Crimes.
> The Candidates observ'd his dirty Paws,
> Nor found it difficult to guess the Cause:
> But when they smelt such foul Corruptions round him;
> Away they fled, and left him as they found him.[2]

Swift's poem 'To Mr. Gay' was not printed until 1735, by which time *The Craftsman* had published (in 1732) further uncompromising attacks which lead us into Pope's contributions to the campaign:

But if there should be any man amongst us, as I hope and believe there is not, who hath made it his constant endeavour, for many years past, to substitute a fantastical credulity in the room of Publick Credit, and to establish the vile traffick of stockjobbing on the ruins of Trade, Industry and Virtue; if he hath done all in his power to convert a great kingdom into a society of gamesters, and acquired a reputation for wisdom by his skill in picking pockets; if he hath ... likewise eminently distinguished himself as the patron of Stockjobbers, Projectors, and Bubblemongers, to whom they might always fly for protection against the ... cries of the injured; and if by these means, he hath raised up a powerful party and combination on his side, who will ever find it in their interest to obstruct all enquiries into these practices, and to prevent the redemption of our debts; ... He ought to be pointed out to the nation in the strongest colours, that the people may know and be convinced, to whom their calamities have been owing, and to whom their vengeance is due.

From the introduction of gold and gambling in its fifth line, Pope's *Epistle To Bathurst* (1733) mounts a sustained assault on the political economy inaugurated with the Revolution Settlement and assiduously nurtured and managed for over a decade prior to the poem's publication by the Prime Minister, whose shadowy figure hovers in the background of the entire text. The poem has been persuasively read as really an attack on Walpole, friend of Chartres and other villains in the poem, patron of Phryne, screener of the Directors of the South Sea Company, and proponent of the Excise Bill.[3] It also seems likely that for Pope's earliest readers the public image of Chartres could anyway be used as a surrogate figure for Walpole himself, and it is quite possible that publication of *Bathurst* in January was timed to coincide with a renewed attack by its addressee in the House of Lords calling on the

---

[2] *Swift's Poems*, II, p. 536.
[3] E. R. Wasserman, *Pope's 'Epistle to Bathurst': A Critical Reading with an Edition of the Manuscript* (Baltimore, 1960), p. 54.

Directors of the South Sea Company to account for the current state of affairs concerning former directors' forfeited estates.[4]

But the poem proceeds in complex ways, creating structural tensions by combining a repudiation of the new order and its representatives with a fascination for the subjects and objects of abomination: Pope's love-hate relationship with his commercial society was continuing in different ways. There was at any rate something about London's fashionable glitter that powerfully compelled his attention, and F. W. Bateson has remarked upon at least a superficial sympathy between his mind and that of Mandeville, despite Pope's theoretical disapproval (*TE* II, p. 82). In the *Bathurst* lines: 'Then careful Heav'n supply'd two sorts of Men, / To squander these, and those to hide agen' (13–14), a cosmic harmonising of spendthrift and miser relates to Mandeville's perception as expressed in *The Fable of the Bees*:

Was it not for Avarice, Spendthrifts would soon want Materials ... Was it not for Prodigality, nothing could make us amends for the Rapine and Extortion of Avarice in Power ... I look upon Avarice and Prodigality in the Society as I do upon two contrary Poisons in Physick, of which it is certain that the noxious Qualities being by mutual Mischief corrected in both, they may assist each other, and often make a good Medicine between them.[5]

The mingling of opposites was something Pope knew about and in the *Essay on Man* he would write that 'true SELF-LOVE and SOCIAL are the same' (*TE* III, i, p. 166). The epithet 'true' would be a crucial discrimination but there is an identifiable Mandevillean intertext here also. *Bathurst* reproduces the echo in the couplet: 'Extremes in Nature equal good produce, / Extremes in Man concur to gen'ral use' (163–5), showing Pope's familiarity with this structure of response as he develops his argument.[6] Like Mandeville, Pope is turning the passions to socially productive use, but he is additionally concerned to incorporate these personal and social tensions into a reasonable God within whose greater plan for good they harmonise. Balanced verse portraits of parsimony and of prodigality bid for artistic equilibrium, while the power of the writing is triggered by characters treated as contemptible and threatening: the figures of John Blunt as historical and Sir Balaam as fictive paradigm linger in the mind. Perhaps there was also an element of

---

[4] Vincent Carretta, 'Pope's "Epistle to Bathurst" and the South Sea Bubble', *Journal of English and Germanic Philology*, 77 (1978), pp. 213 ff.

[5] *The Fable of the Bees*, I, pp. 101, 103–4, 106.

[6] See P. J. Alpers, 'Pope's "To Bathurst" and the Mandevillian State', *English Literary History*, 25 (1958), pp. 23–42; rpt. in Mack, *Essential Articles*, pp. 438–59.

self-recognition in that Pope's neo-classical proprieties and his sometimes venomous satire represent seemingly opposed characteristics,
while his success in subordinating the passion of one to the reasonable
form of the other is a mark of his couplet mastery. In several ways he
forged a metre out of – and often against – genuine and complicated
antagonisms both private and public, and within these oppositions and
conjunctions a fierce satire threatens to unbalance an embedded ethical
programme designed to moderate the worst effects of corruption. Pope
had his share of savage indignation, and the harmony between 'Oeconomy' and 'Magnificence' which the poem claims to discover in Bathurst's own life-style is differently tuned by the expressive power of an
antagonism focused on widespread social abuse. Most unlike Mandeville also is Pope's response to the complete lack of discrimination that
money exhibits. In lines which sardonically appropriate the tropes of
militant protestantism he challenges terms of Dissenting discourse that
justified economic success, by implicating John Blunt's non-conformist
origins (a 'Baptist shoemaker's son and a man of the City if ever there
was one').[7] The poem insists that: 'Riches [are] in effect / No grace of
Heav'n or token of th'Elect', and cannot be, because they are patently
and evidently:

> Giv'n to the Fool, the Mad, the Vain, the Evil,
> To Ward, To Waters, Chartres, and the Devil.

Pope's moral vision is a social one and each of these characters represents wealth variously generated by fraud and by usury as well as by
gambling, and each is a product of their times in particular ways. The
subsequent introduction of 'the grave Sir Gilbert [Heathcote]' (103),
sometime governor of the Bank of England, establishes wider social and
financial parameters for the satire: the suggestion of Walpole's mistress
and second wife Maria Skerret in the figure of Phryne buying 'the
whole Auction' (121) against the rise in excise duty her lover was trying
to pilot through the House of Commons, implicates a parliament
corrupted by insider-dealing. Further evidence of a perceived ethical
decay across society comes with the appearance of Denis Bond (102), a
director of the Charitable Corporation set up to help the poor. Having
discovered that his own and his fellow-directors' personal enrichment
could be greatly advanced by investing their Corporation's subscribed
funds on the stock exchange, Bond did so crying 'Damn the poor, let us
go into the City, where we may get Money.' *Bathurst* composes a litany

---

[7] Erskine-Hill, 'Pope and the Financial Revolution', p. 205.

of moral transgressions arising from monetary egoism, and moves from socio-economic specificity in terms of named personality and event to paradigms and archetypes shaped as quasi-allegorical figures possessed by forces and driven by motivations which they are seemingly powerless to resist.

The poem is concerned to trace the suborning it documents to the advent and dissemination of paper forms of postponed money-payment which substituted a material insubstantiality for the dimensions of the commodities they thereby circulated. The process begins with 'commodious gold' circulating naturally but soon tempting criminality, and soon being corruptly dispensed:

> Trade it may help, Society extend;
> But Lures the Pyrate, and corrupts the Friend:
> It raises Armies in a Nation's aid,
> But bribes a Senate, and the Land's betray'd.   (31–4)

The most glaring recent instance of money bribing a senate and betraying the land may still have been the promotion of the South Sea scheme, though there are other applications. In a broader perspective, Pope's attempt to discriminate virtuous from corrupt uses of money connects with John Locke's, from which the excesses of *Bathurst* depart in comically distressing ways:

The Necessity of a certain Proportion of Money to Trade, (I conceive) lyes in this. That Money in its Circulation driving the several Wheels of Trade, whilst it keeps in that Channel ... is all shared between the Landholder, whose Land affords the Materials; the Labourer who works them; the Broker, (*i.e.*) Merchant and Shopkeeper, who distributes them to those that want them; And the Consumer who spends them.

In Locke's account, as long as money keeps in that proper channel of trade, transactions are subordinated to reason and reasonable need so that virtue and the acceptable use of money go hand in hand:

For Mankind, having consented to put an imaginary Value upon Gold and Silver by reason of their Durableness, Scarcity, and not being very liable to be Counterfeited, have made them by general consent the common Pledges, whereby Men are assured, in Exchange for them to receive equally valuable things to those they parted with for any *quantity* of these Metals.[8]

How sane it all sounds in contrast to Pope's construction where the shift from perdurable quantities of metal specie to the promissory note of paper money signifies a powerful threat to once-solid foundations for

[8] *Locke on Money*, I, p. 233.

trade and commerce. In *Bathurst*, the receipt of 'equally valuable
things' pledged in paper form constitutes a clear and present danger to
wealth-sustaining landed property and its associated virtue. In Pope's
imagery, the exchange of commodities via paper money subverts the
nation-state's integrity as much as it does the individual personality,
and his gambling metaphor mocks heroic proportion in a Hogarthian
carnival of gamblers astride cheeses riding to their moral dissolution,
and card-players making paper wagers (and giving or receiving paper
payment) for the substance of their property. Incredulous at this
behaviour, the poem ironically proposes an economy of barter as the
only way of forestalling a wholesale debauchery of personal and political estates in London's fashionable gambling clubs:

> His grace will game: to White's a Bull be led,
> With spurning heels and with a butting head.
> To White's be carried, as to ancient games,
> Fair Coursers, Vases, and alluring Dames.   (55–8)

Swift called White's 'the common Rendezvous of infamous Sharpers
and noble Cullies', and 'the Bane of half the *English Nobility*' (*SP* IX, p.
50), and Pope's verse-paragraph concludes by turning in mock-scorn
against its own exaggerated disbelief:

> Oh filthy check on all industrious skill,
> To spoil the nation's last great trade, Quadrille!   (63–4)

Gambling clubs were thriving in London, so such recognitions of a
widespread social addiction would have registered additionally for
anyone who had lived through the previous twenty years or so, while as
literary metaphor, card-playing repeatedly leads straight to the stock
market. It had become common practice for speculating stockjobbers to
buy up batches of tickets in government lotteries, and resell them by
dividing each ticket into shares, generating much wider participation in
state-sanctioned gambling schemes,[9] and lottery loans were by now a
well-established way of raising revenue. Defoe had condemned
attempts 'to Stock-jobb the Nation, Couzen the Parliament, ruffle the
Bank, run up and down the Stocks, and put the Dice upon the whole
Town',[10] and while the South Sea Bubble was blowing, Sir John Blunt's

---

[9] The Opposition use of Quadrille as symbol of the manoeuvring for political and trade
   advantage between European states during the 1720s and 1730s has been examined by
   Mack, *The Garden and the City*, p. 184, n. 5.
[10] Daniel Defoe, *The Anatomy of Exchange Alley* (London, 1719), pp. 37–8.

Figure 3 'A Monument Dedicated to Posterity in commemoration of ye incredible Folly transacted in the Year 1720'

vigorous pursuit of the South Sea Company's best interests left no doubt about the instincts to which he was appealing:

On all occasions he freely declared his opinion, without mincing the matter, that he was not for disposing the Company's money to traders and such other fair dealers; but to those who frequented [Exchange Alley]; and to Ladies and Gentlemen, who came from the other end of the town, with a spirit of gaming: for such, according to him, were the most likely to advance the price of the stock.[11]

The *Epistle to Bathurst* keeps the South Sea Company's activities closely in view as it constructs a vision of London society in thrall to the prospect of limitless enrichment. After pointing to the bulky unsuitability of gold for silent subversion (and thus comically enlisting its material substance as a check upon current forms of bribery), there follow the most celebrated lines in Pope's later writing, at least as far as the advent of a credit economy is concerned:

> Once, we confess, beneath the Patriot's cloak,
> From the crack'd bag the dropping Guinea spoke,
> And gingling down the back-stairs, told the crew,
> 'Old Cato is as great a rogue as you.'
> Blest Paper-credit! last and best supply!
> That lends Corruption lighter wings to fly!
> Gold imp'd by thee, can compass hardest things,
> Can pocket States, can fetch or carry Kings;
> A single leaf shall waft an Army o'er,
> Or ship off Senates to a distant Shore;
> A leaf, like Sybil's, scatter to and fro
> Our fates and fortunes, as the winds do blow:
> Pregnant with thousands flits the Scrap unseen,
> And silent sells a King or buys a Queen.   (69–82)

Highly polished versification forges a self-containment for lines dense with satirical reference. In the phrases 'fetch or carry' and 'ship off' and the activity of buying and selling we watch the values and practices of commerce unsettle prevailing dispositions, while Pope annotates details of the trade in crowned heads and kingdoms as if they were commodities circulating in the markets of Europe:

In our author's time, many Princes had been sent about the world, and were great changes of Kings projected in Europe. The partition-treaty [1700] had dispos'd of Spain; France had set up a King of England [1701], who was sent to

---

[11] Toland, 'The Secret History of the South-Sea Scheme', p. 410.

Scotland, and back again [1709 and 1733]; the Duke of Anjou was sent to
Spain [1700], and Don Carlos to Italy [1731].

(*TE* III, ii, pp. 90–1, n. 72)

Subsequent references to the spectacular enrichment of Joseph Gage in
the French stock market's Mississippi scheme which unfolded at the
same time as the South Sea affair,[12] and to Gage's attempted use of his
profits to bid for the crown of Poland, lend further shade and definition
to the notion of selling a king. Bringing in Peter Walter at lines 125–8,
to 'be what Rome's great Didius was before', takes us to the auctioning
of the Roman Empire by the Praetorians after the death of Pertinax
(AD 193), and its purchase by the Roman lawyer Didius Salvius
Julianus. Also implicated in these imperial and trans-national deals is
Walpole's domestic betrayal, as the Opposition saw it, of accepted uses
of the apparatus of power. When George II seemed at his accession in
1727 to be on the point of dispensing with Walpole's services, it
transpired that if the price were right this king, too, could be bought:

Walpole knew his duty. Never had a sovereign been more generously treated.
The King – £800,000 a year down and the surplus of all taxes appropriated to
the civil list, reckoned by Hervey at another £100,000: the Queen – £100,000 a
year. The rumour ran that Pulteney offered more. If so, his political ineptitude
was astounding. No one but Walpole could have hoped to get such grants
through the Commons ... a point which his Sovereign was not slow in
grasping.
 'Consider, Sir Robert,' said the King, purring with gratitude as his minister
set out for the Commons, 'what makes me easy in this matter will prove for your
ease too; it is for my life it is to be fixed and it is for your life.'[13]

Crowns and kingdoms were seemingly up for sale everywhere and
Pope develops the sense of money buying its way into power by
exploiting the fact that the government of British India was then
entrusted to a chartered company operating for profit.[14] The East India
Company had earlier incorporated into itself part of England's national
debt and was to return plunder to the home market on a scale that
would dwarf Roman precedent; all of which must have represented an
alluring structure of possibility for would-be investors. But by the same
token it would then take no great leap of the imagination to connect the

[12] For an account of the Mississippi adventure, in many ways a mirror-image of the South Sea
débacle, see Carswell, *The South Sea Bubble*, pp. 77–97.

[13] Plumb, *Walpole: The King's Minister*, pp. 168–9.

[14] Jacob Viner, 'Man's Economic Status', in *Man Versus Society in Eighteenth-Century Britain: Six
Points of View*, edited by J. L. Clifford (Cambridge, 1968), p. 24.

commercial arrangements by which London farmed its territories in India with the proposed engraftment of Britain's national debt wholesale into another privately managed chartered company. In the composite figure of Sir Balaam, Pope worries at this connection when the lines: 'Asleep and naked as an Indian lay, / An honest factor stole a gem away' draw our attention to the Indian *Nabob* Thomas Pitt's purchase, when he was governor of Fort St George in Madras, of what became known as the Pitt diamond. Typically, the allusion insinuates rather than states explicitly connections between a plundered Indian sub-continent and the auctioning of power at home to another great trading company. Typical too is Pope's cross-weaving into journalistic accounts to add to the force of his allegations. Some nine months before the publication of *Bathurst*, *The Craftsman* constructed an image of the Garden of Eden despoiled. The Tree of Knowledge is now a Tree of Corruption with a Walpole figure perched in its branches: '*a round portly Man*, of a swarthy Complexion ... He sate enthron'd ... and, plucking the *golden apples* on every Side, toss'd them down amongst the Croud beneath Him.' As the persona approaches more closely, he sees that the golden apples are inscribed with such words and phrases as '*Charitable Corporation*', and '*Bank Contract*': 'But there were two Inscriptions, which I could not thoroughly understand. The first was *East India*, ... The second was *South-Sea*.'[15] It was perfectly possible for Opposition writers to represent South Sea and associated manipulations as putting state revenues out to private tender, and entirely natural for them to exploit their fears for political purposes. As they witnessed an unprecedented expansion of enterprising initiative throughout society, sectors of Britain's ruling élite were unable to countenance with any equanimity the prospect of a privatised or semi-privatised state being bought over by new instruments of financial power. It was, after all, the landlords of England who had to pay a land-tax of four shillings in the pound to pay off the interest on the national debt to its public creditors. On behalf of this landed interest, Pope satirises an entire political economy.

As far as executive and policy-making responsibilities are concerned, *Bathurst* traces the displacement of monarchical power from the conduct of Britain's affairs by parliamentary forces demonstrably subordinated to the needs and demands of monetarised commercial priorities. Not that all monarchs were slow to react to these developing arrangements: 'shipping off senates' had been effectively accomplished when the French Regent banished the parliament of Paris because of its oppo-

---

15 *The Craftsman*, no. 297 (25 March 1732).

sition to Law's financial proposals, while a letter to Swift in 1729 detonates a political charge closer to home in the phrase 'or buys a Queen':

She [Queen Caroline] having just now received a much richer present from Mr Knight of the S. Sea; and you are sensible she cannot ever return it, to one in the condition of an outlaw.   (*P. Corr.* III, p. 80)

Robert Knight was the cashier of the South Sea Company who organised illicit stock transfers to Members of Parliament and others, and who fled to the Netherlands rather than face the House of Commons Committee of Secrecy investigation in 1721. 'Ministers must have been very glad [Knight] was out of the way. There is no reason to think he was exaggerating when he declared that "if he should disclose all he knew, it would open such a Scene as the World would be suprised at" ' (*FR*, p. 112). Wherever he can, Pope derives additional authority from classical allusion, and the *Bathurst* lines on paper-credit develop a continuity of image and emphasis from 'a leaf like Sybil's', priestess to Apollo, one of the gods revered by the Emperor Augustus. Apollo concerned himself not only with the arts, but with the establishment of cities, with constitutions, with codes of law and their interpretation, and Pope's lines invite us to compare an altered mode of cultural dominance seen as actively subverting his preferred presentations of power.[16]

Alien forces are felt to be assuming control, and classical allusion is repeatedly conscripted into a campaign of opposition to them. Pope's verse is pregnant with meaning in several ways as he places the consequences and effects of the financial revolution at the heart of his satire and expresses doubts about money travelling invisibly to accomplish its aims and objectives and thereby jeopardising territorial independence as well as individual integrity. Whatever the political language of the day continued to claim, the borders of the nation-state were to become increasingly irrelevant to profit-led movement of speculative funds as foreign participation in stock exchange dealings rapidly installed itself as an inevitable part of the process. Pope's comic apotheosis of paper-credit gives us an early perception of capital flexing its international wings: leaves most unlike Sybil's were flitting unseen all over Europe and beyond. Sybil, of course, has changed her allegiance, and now prophesies the rising and falling fortunes of powers that displaced Apollo's; powers then newly mobilising in the world's

---

[16] But see Howard Weinbrot, *Eighteenth-Century Satire: Essays on Text and Context from Dryden to Peter Pindar* (Cambridge, 1988), pp. 21–33.

expanding money markets, and the linkage between a classical *polis* and contemporary London is designed to register with a silent power as unsettling as that of share-dealing. By the time of Pope's death the financial practices which focused his satirical vision are already the natural environment to be inherited by succeeding generations, and his growing recognition of this may help to account for an ironic treatment that not only arraigns the South Sea Company's leading architect, but also works to vindicate him as being as much a creation as a creator of the new times. The moment also affords a prefiguring of the apocalyptic imagery that is to recur in the satires of the 1730s before bringing the final *Dunciad* to a close:

> Much injur'd Blunt! why bears he Britain's hate?
> A wizard told him in these words our fate:
> 'At length Corruption, like a gen'ral flood
> (So long by watchful Ministers withstood)
> Shall deluge all; and Av'rice creeping on,
> Spread like a low-born mist and blot the Sun;
> Statesman and Patriot ply alike the stocks,
> Peeress and Butler share alike the Box,
> And Judges job, and Bishops bite the town,
> And mighty Dukes pack cards for half a crown.
> See Britain sunk in lucre's sordid charms,
> And France revenged of ANNE's and EDWARD's arms!'
> 'Twas no Court-badge, great Scriv'ner! fir'd thy brain,
> Nor lordly Luxury, nor City Gain:
> No, 'twas thy righteous end, asham'd to see
> Senates degen'rate, Patriots disagree,
> And nobly wishing Party-rage to cease,
> To buy both sides, and give thy Country peace.   (136–52)

This is buying into society on a grand scale, and to match Blunt's ambition, Pope's melodramatic sarcasm moves beyond immediate personality to incorporate the socio-economic changes that made Blunt's story credible and his achievements possible. The implication of Walpole in the figure of the prophesying wizard re-establishes him as a manipulative presence within the poem and against whom 'watchful' Tory ministers were proving so ineffectual. An upwardly mobile 'low-born' mist rising through society catches nicely the tones of social superiority surprised and provoked by a monetary breach in tradition which allows bishops and butlers to sit next to each other in public, and reminds us that money was not simply lost by the market crash, but redistributed in often unforeseen ways. Although the process had not

gone very far by the 1730s, it seems reasonable to conclude that there
was a tendency for investment in both joint-stock companies and
long-term government debt to filter down from the 'mercantile bourgeoisie' to the citizenry as a whole.[17] 'How', Blunt was to recall, 'did
Persons of all Ranks and stations, lay aside all manner of distance, and
almost Decency, to become the humble Suitors for Subscriptions: not
only to the *Directors* of the South Sea Company, but also to the *meanest*
and *Vilest* of *People*.'[18] Since the law, religion and the aristocracy share
'alike' in the vices of a stockjobbing, cheating and gambling society,
Blunt becomes only a scapegoated representative of general practice.
And if the irony selects him as its focus, it also condemns members of the
'Patriot' opposition for succumbing to the stock market and consequently failing to mount an effective alternative to Whig rule. There
is anyway a more general contamination in that Blunt had some years
earlier been Secretary to the Sword Blade Bank, so his success at buying
both 'sides' of political society goes back additionally to the failed
fortunes of an earlier, Tory administration.[19] To construct a Tory
paradigm against these degraded figures, Pope finds his equivalent for
Gulliver's fictional Lord Munodi in the historical John Kyrle, the Man
of Ross, here developed into an ideal portrait of independent
squirearchy, paternalistically benevolent to the tenants of a rural community, and angelically guarded in the 'golden Mean' that the poem
proposes as an alternative ethics. Pope admitted to a 'small exagger-
ation' in his portrait (*TE* III, ii, p. 110, n. 250), but it seems that in all
significant details his picture is accurate: documentary verisimilitude is
not the problem in his account:

> Whose Cause-way parts the vale with shady rows?
> Whose Seats the weary Traveller repose?
> Who taught that heav'n-directed spire to rise?
> The MAN OF ROSS, each lisping babe replies.
> Behold the Market-place with poor o'erspread!
> The MAN OF ROSS divides the weekly bread:
> Behold yon Alms-house, neat, but void of state,
> Where Age and Want sit smiling at the gate:
> Him portion'd maids, apprentic'd orphans blest,
> The young who labour, and the old who rest.

[17] Peter Earle, *The Making of the English Middle Class: Business, Society and Family Life in London,
    1660–1730* (London, 1989), p. 151.
[18] John Blunt, *A True State of the South Sea Scheme* (London, 1722), p. 41.
[19] Howard Erskine-Hill's chapter on 'Much Injur'd Blunt' offers a useful summary of the
    South Sea scheme and Blunt's role in it; in *The Social Milieu of Alexander Pope: Lives, Example
    and the Poetic Response* (London, 1975), pp. 166–203.

> Is any sick? the MAN OF ROSS relieves,
> Prescribes, attends, the med'cine makes and gives.
> Is there a variance? enter but his door,
> Balk'd are the Courts, and contest is no more.
> Despairing Quacks with curses fled the place,
> And vile Attorneys now an useless race.   (259–74)

Not Walpole for a moment, but a Christ-like, compassionate figure hovers in the background of a market-place signifying a traditionally moral rather than an innovatively monetarised economy. Pope is at pains to promote his ideal patriarch as father, provider, law-giver and friend, actively engaged in the community of interests for which he is responsible. Yet different readers share a sense of discomfort at the awkward mechanism of the 'lisping babes' couplet here,[20] while the picture of an abstracted 'Age' and 'Want' smiling in expectation of the next hand-out raises other questions. It may well be the case that if there is a strain in the writing, it is that of a poet pushing consciously at limits out of a desire to celebrate genuine worth and to build a bridge between the heroic and the actual:[21] it is also possible that a strain in the writing relates to more specific tensions in the society the poem addresses. It is of some relevance that John Kyrle had died in 1724 at the age of ninety, which means that Pope's gearing of his verse to support Bolingbroke's attempted mobilisation of the lesser gentry against Walpole leads him back to a figure who belonged more rather than less to the preceding century. Images of a benign moral economy associated with the paternalist ethic will recur and are important for Pope's ideological predispositions; but given the profound changes then taking place, insofar as the Man of Ross portrait does idealise an English squirearchy, nostalgia and actuality come into discomfiting conflict.

Finding space in the market-place for the dependant poor is an assumed function of Pope's seigneurial ideal, and while his poetry also records the debauching of the landlords whose allegiance he sought, as far as tenure of real power was concerned Pope's moral order belonged to them in a poetic scheme of things as exclusive as it sought to be ethically inclusive, creating lacunae in his vision and setting limits to his political tolerance. Given the ways in which they complicatedly relate,

---

[20] See, for example, Rachel Trickett, *The Honest Muse: A Study in Augustan Verse* (Oxford, 1967), Erskine-Hill, *The Social Milieu*, and the review of Erskine-Hill's book by Anne Bowler in *Essays in Criticism*, 27 (January, 1977), pp. 70–7.

[21] Vincent Newey, 'Pope, Raymond Williams, and the Man of Ross', *Essays in Criticism*, 27 (January, 1977), p. 371.

it is of some interest that in John Locke's contract-society the exclusion
of the landless labouring poor also constitutes a potential threat:

The labourer's share [of the national income], being seldom more than a bare
subsistence, never allows that body of men, time, or opportunity to raise their
thoughts above that, or struggle with the richer for theirs (as one common
interest) unless when some common and great distress, uniting them in one
universal ferment, makes them forget respect, and emboldens them to carve to
their wants with armed force: and then sometimes they break in upon the rich,
and sweep all like a deluge. But this rarely happens but in the male-adminis-
tration of neglected, or mismanaged government.[22]

A central attraction in Pope's landed ideality was precisely its claim to
forestall this possibility by reconstituting a moral economy of interlock-
ing duties and responsibilities: in effect an idealised discursive restoration of the old order's benevolent management. If, though, we leave
Bathurst briefly and turn to the *Epistle to Burlington*, we soon recognise
that Pope's defence of spendthrift prodigality as a means whereby 'the
Poor are cloath'd, the Hungry fed',[23] echoes disconsolately in later
'trickle-down' theories of wealth-creation and expenditure. 'Health to
himself, and to his Infants bread / The Lab'rer bears', Pope continues,
since 'What [the spendthrift landlord's] hard Heart denies, / His
charitable Vanity supplies' (170–2). Leaving the labouring poor to the
mercies of a profligate landlord in the hope that egoism will prompt him
to benevolence seems as ethically destitute as consigning them to the
goodwill of figures *Bathurst* scathingly condemns:

> The grave Sir Gilbert holds it for a rule,
> That 'every man in want is knave or fool:'
> 'God cannot love' (says Blunt, with tearless eyes)
> 'the wretch he starves' – and piously denies:
> But the good Bishop, with a meeker air,
> Admits, and leaves them, Providence's care.   (103–8)

Mandeville was more candid:

To make ... Society happy and People easy under the meanest Circumstances,
it is necessary that great Numbers of them should be Ignorant as well as Poor
... Men who are to remain and end their Days in a Laborious, Tiresome and

---

[22] *Locke on Money*, 1, pp. 290–1.
[23] 'Epistle IV: To Richard Boyle, Earl of Burlington', in *Poems of Alexander Pope*, vol. III, ii
(London, 1951), edited by F. W. Bateson, p. 148. Subsequent citations are given by line
parenthetically in the text.

Painful Station of Life, the sooner they are put upon it, the more patiently they'll submit to it for ever after.[24]

Perhaps inevitably, then, for the *Burlington* epistle to construct its political image of 'chearful Tenants bless[ing] their yearly toil', it must postpone as a promissory note on the future any actual restoration of the terms and arrangements of patriarchal *noblesse oblige*:

> Another age shall see the golden Ear
> Imbrown the Slope, and nod on the Parterre,
> Deep Harvests bury all [that] pride has plann'd,
> And laughing Ceres re-assume the land.   (173–6)

In *Bathurst*, the evident contradictions between Pope's ethical priorities and the different paths being taken by England's programme of modernisation, drive him into interesting rhetorical figures:

> What Nature wants, commodious Gold bestows,
> 'Tis thus we eat the bread another sows:
> But how unequal it bestows, observe,
> 'Tis thus we riot, while who sow it, starve.   (21–4)

There is possibly a warning to profligate mismanagers here, but it comes in an extraordinary inversion which unsettles its own ironic stance. While a process of expropriation and distribution produces a riot of excess that pointedly excludes those producing the material to be consumed, Pope's lines as pointedly exclude any resistance the labouring poor might offer. Bread riots appear only in textually submerged form, in a peculiar transferral of agency from the dispossessed to those conspicuously consuming the fruits of their labour.

But far from passively suffering, the poor are rattling the bars of the couplet that denies them energy: they organised and 'rioted' in their own behalf. Edward Thompson's recent work helps to break the generalised historical silence of the rural poor in eighteenth-century England, and suggests that not all 'Want' was content to wait at the alms-house gate for the grace and favour either of engrossing landlords or of forestalling traders. It is as clear that food riots were recurrent in a sustained pattern of rural and urban resistance to high prices as it is apparent that Pope's lines testify to these outbreaks only in the textual act of expropriating their potentially disruptive energies. Thompson reproduces a piece of doggerel that was stuck to a church door in 1630

---

[24] *Fable of the Bees*, I, pp. 287–8.

and which raises necessary questions about the benevolence of traditional, aristocratically sanctioned land-management:

> The Corne is so dear
> I dout mani will starve this yeare
> If you see not to this
> Sum of you will speed amis.
> Our souls they are dear,
> For our bodys have sume ceare
> Before we arise
> Less will safise ...
> You that are set in place
> See that youre profesion you doe not disgrace ...[25]

By the very nature of things the record of the illiterate and inarticulate
is patchy and slanted, but larger-scale risings in 1740, 1756, 1766, 1795
and 1800 serve to outline a more or less hidden history of the time.
Spasmodic rises in food prices provoked keelmen on the Tyne to riot in
1709, and tin miners to plunder granaries at Falmouth in 1727.[26] When
an Exeter crowd demonstrated in the market for wheat at 10s. a bushel,
their arguments were described as being 'very cogent':

> give us whatever *quantity* the Stock in Hand will afford, & at a price by which
> we can attain it, & we shall be satisfied; we will not accept any Subscription
> from the Gentry because it enhances the Price, & is a hardship on them.[27]

If we now return to the Man of Ross dividing the weekly bread, we can
suggest that any strain in the writing derives in part from its nostalgic
restoration as living possibility of a structure of subordination and
acceptance which in the changing contexts of Pope's society stretches
the terms of civic humanism beyond their natural tolerance and credibility.

Pope's writing ignites when it dissects what have since been called the
restless and immoral energies of capitalist enterprise, particularly
because for Pope the inexorable advance of that system is accompanied
by an accelerating collapse among the ruling-classes, old and new, into
corrupt acquisitiveness.[28] In *Bathurst*, the engrossment of civic and
individual attention by rising and falling share-markets is indelibly
condemned in the rise and fall of Sir Balaam, a figure whose origins
suggest a Puritan background and whose subsequent damnation enlists
biblical phrase and cadence in the service of universalising allegory.

---

[25] E. P. Thompson, *Customs in Common* (London, 1991), p. 226.
[26] Charles Wilson, *England's Apprenticeship, 1603–1763* (London, 1965), p. 345.
[27] Quoted in Thompson, *Customs in Common*, p. 244.   [28] Newey, 'Pope', p. 372.

The portrait touches historic archetype otherwise, in that Clarendon had described bankers as 'a tribe that had risen and grown up in Cromwell's time, and were never heard of before the late troubles.'[29] The poem's secular wizard is now become a 'Satan ... wiser than of yore, / And tempts by making rich, not making poor', who as 'Prince of Air' sends shipwrecks to Sir Balaam's coastlands to produce for him an unkind start to his initially unwilling rise in society. But it was gambling on the stock exchange that really created the openings with a shower of unearned income, 'at which point the merchant degenerates into the moneyed man':[30]

> The Tempter saw his time; the work he ply'd;
> Stocks and Subscriptions pour on ev'ry side,
> 'Till all the Daemon makes his full descent,
> In one abundant show'r of Cent. per Cent.,
> Sinks deep within him, and possesses whole,
> Then dubs Director, and secures his soul.   (369–74)

We watch the rape of Danae by Zeus transformed to a shower of gold vying with a parody of the biblical Fall; and when rival narratives merge in this way, individual destiny transforms into archetype. Elevation from humble origins to the Board of the South Sea Company might seem sufficient, but contemporary circumstance enables a further rise, and when Sir Balaam receives his due from the wizard earlier mentioned: 'In Britain's Senate he a seat obtains, / And one more Pensioner St. Stephen gains', Walpole gains another placeman.

The 'Daemon' who descends upon Sir Balaam also visits a warped aesthetic upon Visto, representative of the *nouveaux riches* satirised in the *Epistle to Burlington*:

> What brought Sir Visto's ill got wealth to waste?
> Some Daemon whisper'd, 'Visto! have a Taste.'
> Heav'n visits with a Taste the wealthy fool,
> And needs no Rod but Ripley with a Rule.   (15–18)

Earlier versions of the lines had instead of 'Visto' a 'Shylock' commonly associated with Walpole who was spending vast sums on his Houghton seat at this time; and Ripley was Walpole's architect. So an attack upon vast expenditures of new wealth on private property carries specific political condemnation. The poem assembles further evidence that

[29] Quoted in Christopher Hill, *The Century of Revolution: 1603–1714* (London, 1961, rpt. 1983), p. 187.
[30] Peter Dixon, *The World of Pope's Satires* (London, 1968), p. 138.

money was buying into land in a considerable way and shifting balances of social power, and lays the charge that subsequent departures from classical decorum in property enhancement were a disfigurement of classical proportion. These things were of a piece in Pope's ethics, which he continued to promote in spite of prevalent deviations. His praise of a friend's landed virtue in 1722 carried a depressing corollary: 'When I have been describing [Digby's] agreeable seat, I cannot make the reflection I have often done upon contemplating the beautiful villas of other noble-men, raised upon the spoils of plundered nations, or aggrandized by the wealth of the public. I cannot ask myself the question, "What else has this man to be liked? What else has he cultivated or improved? What good, or what desirable thing appears of him, without these walls?" ' (*P. Corr.* II, p. 239). Out in the fields of England the *nouveaux riches* were paying their own pipers and in opposition to them, representatives of the civic virtue that Pope promoted were praised and complimented. It seems likely that in assigning the copyright of the 1729 *Dunciad* to the Whig landowner Burlington (together with the Earl of Oxford and Lord Bathurst), Burlington's promotion of a proper Roman style in architecture was important to Pope's relations with him, relations which developed as Burlington deserted Walpole to join the Opposition.[31] Read in this light, the poem (and particularly its final verse paragraph) composes a flattering invitation to its addressee to join the Patriot Opposition and engage in public works for the common good under the benevolent stewardship of a Patriot King. Aristocratic virtue and landed integrity combine in an investment morality of improvement within the established hierarchy of England's ancient order:

> Bid the broad Arch the dang'rous Flood contain,
> The Mole projected break the roaring Main;
> Back to his bounds the subject Sea command,
> And roll obedient Rivers thro' the Land;
> These Honours, Peace to happy Britain brings,
> These are Imperial Works, and worthy Kings.   (199–204)

But the common good was in other hands, and one of the more effective strokes of *The First Satire of the Second Book of Horace Imitated*, published a month after the *Epistle to Bathurst* and reading very much like a distressed meditation upon it, is its closing insinuation that the nature of Walpole's domination of the country's affairs is such that

---

[31] H. T. Dickinson, 'The Politics of Pope', in *Pope: Essays for the Tercentenary*, ed. Nicholson, p. 6.

without his approval nothing would stand much chance of making
headway, whereas with it success was assured:

> P. *Libels* and *Satires!* lawless Things indeed!
> But grave *Epistles*, bringing Vice to light,
> Such as a *King* might read, a *Bishop* write,
> Such as Sir *Robert* would approve – *F.* Indeed?
> The Case is alter'd – you may then proceed.
> In such a Cause the Plaintiff will be hiss'd,
> My Lords the Judges laugh, and you're dismiss'd.   (150–6)

Neither the King nor Walpole cared a jot for poetry and that is part of
the joke, though Walpole cared very much about what was said about
him; which is perhaps why Pope dramatises the dangers he courted and
the risks he ran in producing personalised satire. He is similarly concerned, in a world so visibly manipulated by politically motivated
money-payments, to identify himself as financially independent –
'Un-plac'd, un-pension'd, no Man's Heir, or Slave' (116) – and proud
of his ability to expose a ruling rapacity: to 'Bare the mean Heart that
lurks beneath a Star' (108).

Certainly condemnation is the scale of *The Fourth Satire of Dr. John
Donne, Versifyed*, where a return to the political artifice of courtly
performance foregrounds the stock market chatter of a corrupt court
butterfly and where moral seriousness stirs within gossipy acclimati-
sations. In the context of a degenerate court, Pope satirises the triumph
of deceptive style over morally destitute substance; and where fashionable appearance becomes thread-bare, the speech of self-presentation is
a babel of superficial skills from which the poet's desire to escape is itself
a marker of surviving virtue. George II's German accent (68), Aretiso's
lascivious sonnets and a social addiction to 'Harlequins and Operas'
signify together a decline in English cultural standards that help to
create a climate where self-display masks ethical bankruptcy in a
crucial departure from Donne's original:

> Who, having lost his Credit, pawn'd his Rent,
> Is therefore fit to have a *government*?
> Who in the *Secret*, deals in Stocks secure,
> And cheats th'unknowing Widow and the Poor?
> Who makes a *Trust*, or *Charity*, a Job,
> And gets an Act of Parliament to rob?   (138–43)

The abuse of financial power, including ministerial insider-trading, is
again up for exposure by way of preparing for the criminal expropriation of funds designed to help the poor. In 1732, directors of London's

Charitable Corporation were found guilty of embezzlement, and we watch Pope orchestrate his satirical campaign against Walpole's administration by weaving in and out of events currently reported in the public prints and debated in London's coffee-shops. Monetary subornation in *Donne IV* also works retrospectively to expose the glittering attractions of a world more enticingly presented in *The Rape of the Lock*. Charm there gives way now to changing perceptions, and what was earlier cause for celebration, however ambivalently modulated, is now infected by a sense of disabused knowingness. 'And why not Players strut in Courtiers Cloaths? / For these are Actors too, as well as those', is a proposition that could have applied to the *beau-monde* of Belinda's existence except that 'pay', 'pawn', 'cheat', 'sell', 'get', 'have', 'robs'; all of these transform the earlier context. Now venereal infection becomes an item of commercial transaction, while the scintillating commodification of the earlier poem has become a condition of explicit servitude:

> '*Dear Countess*! you have Charms all Hearts to hit!'
> And '*sweet Sir Fopling*! you have so much wit!'
> Such Wits and beauties are not prais'd for nought,
> For both the Beauty and the Wit are *bought*.   (232–5)

And in keeping with a developing strategy of intertextual implication, behind the *Captain* who enters to establish his authority at the close of the poem, 'whose very Look's an Oath' and who 'Confounds the Civil, keeps the Rude in awe', hovers the determining figure of the First Minister, Walpole again.

In 1734, 'The Second Satire of the Second Book of Horace Paraphrased' went in search of the 'wholesome Solitude' so manifestly denied in *Donne IV*, and the poem's closing couplet: 'Let Lands and Houses have what Lords they will, / Let Us be fix'd, and our own Masters still' (179–80), reminds us of Pope's paradoxical insertion into a preferred network of landed values which we see in *Burlington's* image of the positive responsibilities of independent property-ownership: a paradigm of propertied virtue designed to linger in the mind as refuge from the marauding corruption all around:

> His Father's Acres who enjoys in peace,
> Or makes his Neighbours glad, if he encrease;
> Whose chearful tenants bless their yearly toil,
> Yet to their Lord owe more than to the soil;
> Whose ample Lawns are not asham'd to feed
> The milky heifer and deserving steed;
> Whose rising Forests, not for pride or show,

But future Buildings, future Navies grow:
Let his plantations stretch from down to down,
First shade a Country, and then raise a Town.   (181–90)

As Pope turns pastoral imagery to the service of agrarian improvement, we watch an idealised version of English landed virtue in the making. The timelessness which is a calculated effect of this pastoral usage, lending durability and above all attractiveness – 'enjoys', 'glad', 'chearful', 'ample' – to propertied stability, is effectively incorporated into an image of ideal economy, with Aristotle's notions of a proper foundation for civic virtue strengthening the definition of attitude in much of this poetry:

In the state with the finest constitution, which possesses just men who are just absolutely and not relatively to the assumed situation, the citizens must not live a mechanical or commercial life. Such a life is not noble and it militates against virtue. Nor must those who are to be citizens be agricultural workers, for they must have leisure to develop their virtue, and for the activities of a citizen.[32]

The idealisation in Pope's portraits of landed justice and benevolence is evidently an ideological calculation, and forms an integral part of his scripted design for a balanced commonwealth of landed magnates and the less substantial but more numerous free-holders of property who comprised England's squirearchy. But the *Burlington* construction of a happy neighbourhood of mutually sustaining tenants and landowners comes into specific conflict with literary senses of continuity linking it with country house centres of community as Marvell or Herrick envisaged them. The last attempt to legislate against depopulating enclosures had been defeated in Parliament as long ago as 1656,[33] and as an idealised structure of specific power, Pope's presentations of propertied responsibility would flatter a substantial constituency. But from before the Civil War the aim of improving landlords had been to substitute determinable contracts for the indeterminate, traditional and customary rights of a medieval peasantry. 'Racking of rents, raising fines, enclosure, all the familiar techniques of estate management, increased landlords' revenues, either by curtailing the consumption of the old-established tillers of the soil, or by evicting them and replacing them by capitalist farmers who could afford the new agricultural methods.'[34] Not only did these men of landed property continue to dominate the villages and most of the towns of England; for most people the landed

---

[32] Aristotle, *The Politics* (Harmondsworth, 1962), Bk VII, ch. ix , p. 415.
[33] Christopher Hill, *Puritanism and Revolution* (London, 1958; rpt. 1968), p. 274.
[34] Ibid., pp. 156–7.

estate was still the sole centre of political authority they encountered, and over most of the countryside the manorial courts still exercised jurisdiction.[35] England's aristocracy wielded real power, and Pope presented in durable ways a version of their campaign for continued national rule.

Since post-Revolutionary movements in property-ownership became a politically motivated image with which Pope troubled and disturbed his readers, it is worth reminding ourselves that the Revolution of 1688 involved a significant restoration of power to England's traditional rulers, including the shire gentry and town merchants, which confirmed a monopoly of control over the spoils of government by a narrow social élite.[36] But it was becoming apparent that nothing could prevent the installation and development of financial agencies and instruments that would henceforth significantly direct and mediate political power. In Westminster Hall, as elsewhere, money increasingly did the talking. Already in 1674 a former landowner was acknowledging: 'I choose rather to keep my estate in money than in land, for I can make twice as much of it that way, considering what taxes are upon land and what advantages there are of making money upon the public funds.'[37] People who disliked these developments were among the constituency Swift's *Examiner* addressed, and they formed an important plank in the Opposition platform of the 1730s. By changing its name to the *Country Journal: or The Craftsman*, Bolingbroke's newspaper had identified itself more definitely with the country interest Pope sought to confirm by seeking out examples of this kind of right living. Whereas the Man of Ross focused this virtue in the *Epistle to Bathurst*, Pope took advantage of Horace to promote the frugality of his own personal circumstances as a locus of resistance to corruption everywhere else. The image is presented of an island of value and practice divorced from the fantasies of property-owning wealth inspired by expectation of stock market profits:

> In *South-sea* days not happier, when surmis'd
> the Lord of thousands, than if now *Excis'd*;
> In Forest planted by a Father's hand,
> Than in five acres now of rented land.
> Content with little, I can piddle here
> On Broccoli and mutton, round the year.
>
> (*Satire II*, i, 133–8)

[35] Dickinson, *Liberty and Property*, p. 21.
[36] Christopher Hill, *The Century of Revolution*, p. 235.
[37] Quoted in *The Century of Revolution*, p. 233.

The homeliness of detail here and elsewhere in the epistle has been read as central to its design of balancing simple human need against the extravagance of South Sea speculation, with the weary melancholy of the poem's concluding lines aptly expressing the chances and changes of the world of affairs:[38]

> What's *Property*? dear Swift! you see it alter
> From you to me, from me to Peter Walter,
> Or, in a mortgage, prove a Lawyer's share,
> Or, in a jointure, vanish from the Heir.   (167–70)

Pope's disbarment from property-ownership on the grounds of his religion also gives the fey resignation of these lines an autobiographical corollary: 'I am but a *Lodger* here', he wrote to Bethel in 1726: 'this is not an abiding City. I am only to stay out my lease, for what has Perpetuity and mortal man to do with each other? But I could be glad you would take with an Inn at Twitenham, as long as I am Host of it' (*P. Corr.* II, p. 387). Excluded from house-ownership because of his Roman Catholicism, Pope nonetheless became a leading voice on behalf of the political virtue of landed property, and his position sometimes troubled him. Towards the end of 1736 he writes to William Fortescue: 'You can cast a Glympse at Posterity, in your Daughter, & please yourself in the thought of your Childrens Children enjoying it: I see nothing but Mrs Vernon [from whom he rented his Villa], or a sugar-baker, to succeed to my plantations (*P. Corr.* IV, p. 34). We catch occasional echoes of this in the poetry, sometimes with a sense of its injustice:

> I've often wished that I had clear
> For life, six hundred Pounds a year,
> A handsome House to Lodge a Friend,
> A river at my garden's end,
> A terras-walk, and half a Rood
> Of land, set out to plant a Wood.
> Well, now I have all this and more,
> I ask not to increase my store;
> But here a grievance seems to lie,
> All this is mine but till I die;
> I can't but think 'twould sound more clever,
> To me and to my Heirs for ever.   (*Satire II*, vi, 1–12)

Although 'clever' maintains a bantering tone, there is a feeling that Pope's care and effort to develop his rented property at Twickenham will be transient sooner than others. It remains a contradiction that

[38] Erskine-Hill, *The Social Milieu*, pp. 315–6.

while his ability to exploit a developing literary market allowed him to claim for himself the kind of independence appropriate for a Country Ideology spokesman, his position in society meant that money and not land was to be the means by which this independence could be achieved and sustained. His poetry, in consequence, also records aspects of the ensuing conflict between private action and public profession, between the personal and the social.

The search for examples of preferred forms of virtue continued, however, and in *Satire II*, ii, it proceeds by way of a consideration of the use and ownership of property at a time when profits from London's money markets enabled land to change hands in disturbing ways for traditionalists – 'Slid[ing] to a Scriv'ner or a City Knight'. The poem ruefully acknowledges that in contemporary England: 'Shades that to Bacon could retreat afford, / Become the portion of a booby Lord', while references to Peter Walter here and elsewhere play a steady focus on false stewardship as a subversion of the virtuous independence guaranteed by freehold property-rights. By sheer dint of repetition Walter achieves symbolic significance as an embodiment of callous money-making, and the fuller sense we now have of his abilities allows us to see nonetheless a prejudiced and parsimonious character singularly unattractive in several ways and not least when he was acting as managing factor and steward for other people's estates.[39] Walter's actual and symbolic function as a representative of monetarist values threatening traditional dispositions and relationships becomes clearer, allowing us to understand in additional ways the almost neurotic attention paid to this figure in poem after poem. 'What always *Peter*?' cries the satiric adversary in *Epilogue to the Satires* (*Dialogue II*): '*Peter* thinks you mad, / You make men desp'rate if they once are bad' (58–9).[40] But these repetitions also suggest a kind of omnipresence beyond any couplet confinement. If Blunt and Walpole together shimmer and merge as presiding evil geniuses within the structured world of *Bathurst*, over all the satires of the 1730s Walpole and Walter are suggestively interwoven, with Walter's commercialisation of an agrarian economy through the rigorous application of profit-maximising procedures playing a dual and responsive role to Walpole's policy of non-resistance to the moneyed interest.

In the lascivious world of 'Sober Advice From Horace',[41] landed

---

[39] Ibid., esp. pp. 8–11, 103–31, 243–57.

[40] Erskine-Hill lists the ten occasions Pope attacks Walters (*The Social Milieu*, p. 103, n. 2).

[41] 'Sober Advice from Horace, to the Young Gentlemen about Town', in *Poems of Alexander Pope*, edited by John Butt, vol. IV (London, 1939), pp. 71–89. Subsequent citations are given by line parenthetically in the text.

virtue is differently betrayed when saturnalian imagery of carnal satisfaction produces almost surreal effects: 'And Lands and Tenements go
down her Throat' (14): a delirium of consumption showing that Pope
knew something about fantasy. As arresting is his portrait of debased
woman so possessed by monetary values that they have now become the
estranged essence of her existence to the point of reconstructing sibling
relationships in stock market terms:

> *Fuvidia* thrives in Money, Land and Stocks:
> For Int'rest, ten *per cent.* her constant rate is;
> Her Body? hopeful Heirs may have it *gratis.*
> She turns her very sister to a Job,
> And, in the Happy minute, picks your Fob.   (18–22)

There is Rabelaisian burlesque here which the macaronic rhyme serves
to accentuate for the edge of acquisitive craving it depicts to be carried
over into corrupt desire: what was once orgasmic is now merely an
opportunity for illicit enrichment. Personality and property are interacting in disturbing ways, and where appetite and desire so differently
consort, it will hardly be accidental that when one individual has the
means to purchase gratification from another, even if 'diff'rent Taste in
diff'rent Men prevails, / And one is fired by heads and one by Tails'
(35–6), the lines rewrite as libidinal excess a classical constraint for
which Pope's *Essay on Criticism* had striven more than twenty years
earlier, where 'diff'rent *styles* with diff'rent subjects sort, / As several
garbs with Country, Town, and Court' (322–3). Certainly writing is
not exempt from contamination, as the early *Dunciad* had emphasised,
and *The Second Satire of Dr. John Donne* (*TE* IV, pp. 129–45) further
elaborates by initially identifying verse itself as the 'Giant-Vice'
enthralling the town, before sharpening the satire in ironic promotion
of the stock market's seductive lure:

> What further could I wish the Fop to do,
> But turn a Wit, and scribble verses too?
> Pierce the soft Lab'rinth of a Lady's ear
> With rhymes of this *per Cent.* and that *per year*?   (53–6)

Pope has ideas about the stimulation of fantasy both sexual and acquisitive. But what is being postponed is the most sustained attack on Peter
Walter that he launched, the focus this time being specifically the role
of attorneys in legally sanctioned shifts in traditional patterns of
property-ownership, and the contribution of gambling to the structure
of indebtedness that makes such transferrals both necessary and pos-

sible. After a glance at voluptuous pleasure expensively purchased, thereby turning fantasy into experience, the movement of the verse expands tidally from small beginnings:

> In shillings and in pence at first they deal,
> and steal so little, few perceive they steal;
> Till like the Sea, they compass all the land,
> From Scots to Wight, from Mount to Dover Strand.
> And when rank Widows purchase luscious nights,
> Or when a Duke to Jansen punts at White's,
> Or City heir in mortgage melts away,
> Satan himself feels far less joy than they.
> Piecemeal they win this Acre first, then that,
> Glean on, and gather up the whole Estate:
> Then strongly fencing ill-got wealth by law
> Indentures, Cov'nants, Articles they draw;
> Large as the Fields themselves, and larger far
> Than Civil Codes, with all their glosses, are:
> So vast, our new Divines, we must confess,
> Are Fathers of the Church for writing less.   (83–98)

In this rising flood of altered possession, itself a recurrent metaphor, landed property comes under threat when the customary terms and usages of management and natural harvesting are converted into changed ownership. We watch the implicit metamorphosis of farming activity – gleaning, gathering and the fencing of fields – into the sense of farm as a monetary arrangement: 'to take or hold for a term at a fixed payment' (*OED*). In a slippage from divine to civil, codes of biblical stewardship are corrupted by a newly dominant secular clerisy which controls and adapts language for its own purposes, and again we are confronted with writing complicit in a process that incorporates the worlds of print and the law as agents in the engrossing of land. What passes out of use once 'Lands are bought', are the cherished and politically salvational benevolence and responsibility of a proprietorial lord to his dependants:

> No Kitchens emulate the Vestal fire.
> Where are those Troops of poor, that throng'd of yore
> The good old Landlord's hospitable door?   (112–14)

For the image to hold, property would have to continue to pass in secure possession and inheritance, and that was increasingly a problem. How far Pope's perceptions of its surviving integrity had matured is suggested by comparing the youthfully confident and self-sustaining dispositions of his *Ode on Solitude*:

> Happy the man, whose wish and care
> A few paternal acres bound,
> Content to breathe his native air,
> In his own ground.
>
> Whose herds with milk, whose fields with bread,
> Whose flocks supply him with attire;
> Whose trees in summer yield him shade,
> In winter fire   (1–8)

with *Epistle II*, ii, first published in 1737.[42] There, a monetarised world of values now rendering all titles and terms of ownership insecure, the paper-credit that in Pope's scheme of things lends corruption lighter wings to fly is actively assisting the transfer of property ownership:

> Estates have wings, and hang in Fortune's pow'r
> Loose on the point of ev'ry wav'ring Hour.   (248–9)

What Pope conveys, ultimately, is a troubling uncertainty about the future survival of those landed estates as are managed by such figures of proprietorial virtue in Pope's pantheon of praise as the Man of Ross, Burlington and Bathurst.

Albert Hirschman's reading of the conflict between the Passions and the Interests as an Enlightenment advocacy of bourgeois self-interest against aristocratic pride[43] suggests both the serious level at which the debate about virtue was conducted and the equally serious problems Pope has in engaging with it. Like *Gulliver's Travels*, the *Essay on Man*'s concern with the fraught and difficult relations between Reason and the Passions articulates a social and political conflict between landed Reason and the passionate acquisition of the new men of money, and in this respect the *Essay*'s opening address to Bolingbroke in an easy and affable tone of conversational intimacy during a stroll through extensive property emphasises its ideological orientation. A gentlemanly political sensibility is explored in terms of proprietorial metaphor:

> Together let us beat this ample field,
> Try what the open, what the covert yield;
> The latent tracts, the giddy heights explore
> Of all who blindly creep, or sightless soar;
> Eye Nature's walks, shoot Folly as it flies,
> And catch the Manners living as they rise.   (I, 9–14)

---

[42] 'The Second Satire of the Second Book of Horace Paraphrased', in *Poems*, ed. Butt, pp. 51–69. Subsequent citations are given by line parenthetically in the text.

[43] Albert O. Hirschman, *The Passions and the Interests: Political Arguments for Capitalism Before its Triumph* (Princeton, NJ, 1977).

Within a gracious seat of landed self-sufficiency, Pope enthrones Reason and the reasonable man for an ordered survey of hierarchy in Creation to proceed. The first epistle derives divine authority for an authoritarian social structure by translating the hierarchy envisaged in heaven and in nature as the appropriate form of political organisation. The second epistle includes a defence of natural order and human sociality in terms of agricultural improvement (II, 181–6), and the third images power as land-management, drawing strength from a perception of manorial responsibility flattering its possessor:

> Man cares for all: to birds he gives his woods,
> To beasts his pastures, and to fish his floods;
> For some his Int'rest prompts him to provide,
> For more his pleasure, yet for more his pride.   (III, 57–60)

As this third epistle launches post-lapsarian man out into animal- and field-husbandry and on to mercantile endeavour, it adapts Mandeville's metaphor into an image of monarchy as guarantor of landed self-sufficiency:

> The Ant's republic, and the realm of bees;
> How those in common all their wealth bestow,
> And Anarchy without confusion know;
> And these for ever, tho' a monarch reign,
> Their sep'rate cells and properties maintain.   (III, 184–7)

Self-evidently the *Essay* promotes forms of order and equilibrium tied to images of propertied integrity. Its reconstruction of a Renaissance 'great chain of being' and its idealisation of benign patriarchy are central to the poem's design and it will touch wrathful melodrama at any attempted infringement:

> All this dread ORDER break – for whom? for thee?
> Vile worm! – oh Madness, Pride, Impiety!   (I, 257–8)

But the 'Design' prefixed after 1743 states a concern with the commercial and the personal – '*Men's Business and Bosoms*' (*TE* III, i, p. 7). And while it dissociates itself from particular political organisation: 'For forms of Government let fools contend' (III, 303), the poem keeps an appropriate civic ethics in mind; an ethics that has to negotiate the unsettling of orderly constraints upon Reason and Passion so that we watch 'each by turns the other's bound invade'. It may be that there is anyway a more directly political element to these invasive pressures in the writing, since out in the world of affairs there was no clear division between Court and Country ideologies as far as the practicalities of power and wealth were concerned. Neither was homogeneous: the joint-stock trading companies had their quota of Tory directors as well as of Tory shareholders,[44] and such a sharply prescribed inter-dependence between Court and Country would mean that neither ideological position could be propounded without making some concession to the other. While the rhyming couplet aspires to containment, Pope's narrative strives to be as accommodating as possible.

Given this drive to inclusivity, we do the poem a disservice by reinforcing its evident authoritarian tendencies through modes of reading dedicated to the reproduction of unchanging order, of enveloping unity or of rigid scales of value, and it is instructive to watch its Twickenham editor guarding against the tendency. Pope 'liked too well ... to house with both Whig and Tory, Locke and Montaigne, Aristippus and St Paul'; and he 'may have wished to have it both ways ... [wanting to] tell the truth as he conceived it, without wanting to be un-Christian or start a fight': his philosophical theory 'is not in any case an adequate one'. Because it 'ignores too many subjects ... the *Essay* is also short in the logical virtues of delimitation and consistency ... [and] is incomplete or incoherent at some points' (*TE* III, i, pp. xxiv, xxv, xliii). Mack was writing when the priorities of American 'New Criticism' were being developed and it seems, now, appropriate to record more openly that the *Essay* in effect, and in apparent conflict with its professed intention, mounts an internal critique of the laws of creation and order where its express purpose is to codify and legitimise. Within the garden metaphor that stabilises the poem's landed ambience, Man is as much a violator as a preserver of order and the end of the second epistle acknowledges that history belongs to the victors; that optimistic expectation will continue to stimulate hope even if human happiness is itself a project for which 'bubble' (II, 288) would echo plangently enough. But the terms of innovation are accepted: it may all be folly, and Pope may have to insist that 'Tho' Man's a fool, yet GOD IS WISE' (II, 294), yet altered perceptions of progress are making themselves felt. Preaching that self-love will eventually constrain itself, the third epistle proposes an image of acquisitive egos engaging in social transactions that co-ordinates with the principles and practices of insurance companies to become a kind of enforced virtue:

> How shall he keep, what, sleeping or awake,
> A weaker may surprise, a stronger take?
> His safety must his liberty restrain:

[44] Geoffrey Holmes, *British Politics*, p. 167.

All join to guard what each desires to gain.
Forc'd into virtue thus by Self-defence,
Ev'n Kings learn'd justice and benevolence:
Self-love forsook the path it first pursu'd,
And found the private in the public good.   (III, 275–82)

Not for the only time, Pope bends Mandeville to Country ideology, and readers of the *Essay* agree that it frequently achieves its liveliest effects from apparent conflicts with its express design of hierarchy, order and subordination. Although Pope's theory of the ruling passion is designed to account for order in Divine creation, his collocations of reason and passion and of virtue and self-love have been read as constituting the very inconsistencies it is the *Essay*'s presumed business to smooth away.[45] An attempt to codify and bring under formal control newly acclimatised motives and appetites in a massively expanding market is coming into conflict with the energies thereby socially released. For the survival of a landed interest in this society Pope promotes an ethic of improvement through productive invest-ment in the *Epistle to Burlington* and goes on to elaborate in the *Essay on Man* what we might now recognise as a morality of enlightened self-interest appropriate to such activity. The largely inherited rhetoric of abstractions used to conduct his search for a harmonious balance, a 'golden mean' in appetite and behaviour, produces that golden mean by combining the public and personal codes of propriety Pope intends to justify and endorse. Virtue and self-love come together as a kind of virtuous self-help; a profitable virtue in the service of an acquisitive morality thereby suitably restrained. In these ways, the *Essay on Man* attempts to incorporate expanding social activities and aspirations within a prior system of moral regulation, and it then becomes appropriate to describe the poem as philosophically suspended between a capitalist ethic and traditional Christian morality, docu-menting in its own contradictions the appropriation of the passions by a new ideological system and the individualist possibilities it pro-moted.[46] Since it has also been suggested that interpretations of the poem are a good deal more coherent, more consistent and more fully integrated than the poem itself,[47] perhaps as a precautionary measure the famous lines apotheosising Man in his newly structured ambi-valence which open the *Essay*'s second epistle should be allowed greater emphasis:

---

[45] Laura Brown, *Alexander Pope*, pp. 68–93.   [46] Ibid., p. 91.
[47] Miriam Leranbaum, *Alexander Pope's 'Opus Magnum', 1729–1744* (Oxford, 1977), p. 38.

> Alike in ignorance, his reason such,
> Whether he thinks too little or too much:
> Chaos of Thought and Passion, all confus'd;
> Still by himself abus'd, or disabus'd;
> Created half to rise, and half to fall;
> Great lord of all things, yet a prey to all;
> Sole judge of truth, in endless Error hurl'd:
> The glory, jest, and riddle of the world!   (11–18)

Within a maze of paradox, the political nature of Pope's concept of virtue is elaborated, and since as precept and practice, civic virtue was mutating as he wrote, the *Essay* stretches the term towards a variety of applications. It appears more than thirty times in different contexts including specifications of its theological and moral significance, with Pope making every effort to accommodate as much as he can of the liberalising tendencies all around him. But when the third epistle turns to what Pope's note identifies as the 'Origine of POLITICAL SOCIETIES' and follows it with lines on the 'Origine of MONARCHY' and then 'of PATRIARCHAL GOVERNMENT', we see a naturally assumed linkage of hierarchical authority in social organisation:

> 'Twas VIRTUE ONLY (or in arts or arms,
> Diffusing blessings, or averting harms)
> The same which in a Sire the Son's obey'd,
> A Prince the Father of a People made.   (III, 211–14)

If *Paradise Lost* told an English story of successful if fateful rebellion, the *Essay on Man* presents a bourgeois royalist's plea for the restoration of an appropriate king to rule over a changing England: a king to gladden Patriot hearts. With the fourth epistle's extended hymn to Virtue as benevolence and charity, as well as its adaptation as a mode of optimism, it becomes apparent that in important ways the *Essay on Man* should be read as a contribution to that cross-weave in contemporary politics known as the 'Country Opposition' to Walpole:

Country ideology was founded on an ethic of civic virtue that maintained that civilised society and civil government could be preserved only by the patriotic actions and the public spirit of men of landed property. Those who possessed a real and substantial stake in the country were the only true citizens and were the natural leaders of those who were merely inhabitants. Their property gave them independence and a sense of responsibility; hence they alone were in a position to act in the best interests of the nation as a whole. It was essential for such men to play the dominant role in society if harmony and stability were to be achieved and social discord was to be avoided. The landed proprietors must concern themselves with the welfare and morality of those below them in the social hierarchy and they must promote moderation, taste and decorum rather than pursue material advancement or personal ambition. Only by such means could men sustain the traditional moral economy, in which landlords and their rural neighbours were united together in a reciprocal bond of rights and duties.[48]

In this light, we discover that Pope is best described as one of the most memorable voices raised in support of Country or Patriot principles. It was country ideology, with its appeal both to Tories and to Opposition Whigs to unite in a cross-party campaign to restore public virtue, that won Pope's political and imaginative loyalties in the 1730s, and he was active in its service. So Pope's warning that he is 'arm'd for *Virtue*' when he points the pen (*Satire II*, i), is still a girding on behalf of specific political emphases, just as there are identifiable personalities behind his subsequent assertion that he is 'To VIRTUE ONLY and HER FRIENDS, A FRIEND' (121). In the *Politics*, Aristotle's determination that in active life the highest role was that of the citizen who ruled as head of his household and so took part in the framing of legislation by a community of equal heads making decisions that were binding on all, repeatedly provides Pope with suitable classical credentials for his imaginative interventions. The *Epistle to Burlington* is then usefully read as a proclamation of an appropriate politics to contend with the corruption of power in Walpole's England.

As well as the inauguration of the money markets and their modern banking systems, Pope also saw a profit-led modernisation of agriculture by an agrarian bourgeoisie actively developing its estates. In these processes there would be gains and losses of a moral and ethical, as well as of material kinds, from changed attitudes towards productive investment. Much of the *Epistle to Burlington*, Raymond Williams suggested, is representative of a significant tradition of eighteenth-century writing about house-building and landscape-gardening in which, 'as the outward sign of the new morality of improvement, the country was reshaped and redesigned'.[49] An increasingly utilitarian agrarian economy requires particular kinds of stewardship from the landed magnates to whom Pope looks as possible sources for the political regeneration of a culture in transformation:

> Who then shall grace, or who improve the soil?
> Who plants like BATHURST, or who builds like BOYLE.

[48] Dickinson, 'The Politics of Pope', pp. 12–13.
[49] Raymond Williams, *The Country and the City* (London, 1973), p. 77.

'Tis Use alone that sanctifies Expence,
And Splendor borrows all her rays from Sense.
(Epistle to Burlington, 177–82)

In John Kyrle, the Man of Ross, Pope had proposed a figure in whom the values and obligations of the ancient feudum were ideally incorporated. On the other hand, as his satire repeatedly emphasises, corruptions of responsible stewardship both of the land and the communities it sustained, jeopardised this patriarchal ideal and frequently led to transfers of ownership or a developing obligation to people whose concerns and priorities involved a wholesale traduction of traditional duties and relationships.

Pope's angry suggestion in the *Epistle to Cobham*, that monetary calculation is the only acceptable calibration of worth at Court: 'Court-virtues bear, like Gems, the highest rate, / Born where Heav'n's influence scarce can penetrate' (93–4), forms part of the same Country Party propaganda campaign. Conversely, by attaching his own frugal habits – 'the Virtue and the Art / To live on little with a chearful heart' – to a domestic economy of hospitality and moderate living, Pope makes clear his own preferred identifications. To flesh out this political design, by picturing himself contentedly living 'in five acres of rented land' he makes a direct bid for identification with those lesser levels of gentry society to whom Bolingbroke was also appealing. And when, in 1738, Pope addressed *Epistle I*, i to St John, he made explicit the contrast between Country virtue and the new methods of national accountancy and management which displace traditional Christian morality regardless of theological bias:

> Here, Wisdom calls: 'Seek Virtue first! be bold!
> As Gold to Silver, Virtue is to Gold.'
> There, London's voice: 'Get Mony, Mony still!
> And then let Virtue follow, if she will.'
> This, this the saving doctrine, preach'd to all,
> From low St James's up to high St Paul;
> From him whose quills stand quiver'd at his ear,
> To him who notches Sticks at Westminster.   (77–84)

The sense of an irresistible chorus tempting the unwary across society from pulpit to national Exchequer is effectively caught, leaving Country virtue in possession of ancient values while the Court usurps traditional norms:

> And say, to which shall our applause belong,
> This new Court jargon, or the good old song?
> The modern language of corrupted Peers,

> Or what was spoke at CRESSY AND POITIERS?
> Who counsels best? who whispers, 'Be but Great,
> With Praise or Infamy, leave that to fate;
> Get Place and Wealth, if possible, with Grace;
> If not by any means get Wealth and Place.'   (97–104)

A resilient irony is directed at a pervasive pursuit of personal advancement regardless of the cost either to individual morality or to civic virtue as Pope's friends understood those terms, and Walpole is never far away in this writing: '*He* makes *Secretaries*: *He* makes *Governors*: *He* makes *Chaplains* to their *Factories*: He makes their *Officers* and *Soldiers*: and, to sum up all, He has made to himself an *immense Fortune*.'[50]

By 1738, though, it was already evident that the changes presided over by Walpole were as irreversible as his tenure in office appeared interminable, and the first of the *Epilogues to the Satires* to be published in that year issues an invitation to go and see 'Sir Robert' early in its unfolding design, and ends with a quasi-allegorical image of Vice triumphant. But whereas '*Virtue* may chuse the high or low Degree' and remain 'still the same, belov'd, contented thing', the ethical levelling which an all-pervasive corruption entails is one of its most dangerous attributes. In a bravura performance, Pope images the conquering progess of Vice through Church and State as a kingdom's whore leading a carnival of degradation, where those drawn to the idol of self-interest can offer up in sacrifice their country, their families and themselves. Her control over civil and political society, Patriot Opposition as well as government minions, is unchallenged and seemingly unchallengeable. In this figure a new hegemony is manifest:

> In golden Chains the willing World she draws,
> And hers the Gospel is, and hers the Laws:
> Mounts the Tribunal, lifts her scarlet head,
> And sees pale Virtue carted in her stead!
> Lo! at the Wheels of her Triumphal Car,
> Old *England*'s Genius, rough with many a Scar
> Dragg'd in the Dust! his Arms hang idly round,
> His Flag inverted trails along the ground!
> Our Youth, all liv'ry'd o'er with foreign Gold,
> Before her dance; behind her crawl the Old!
> See thronging Millions to the Pagod run,
> And offer Country, Parent, Wife, or Son!
> Hear her black Trumpet thro' the Land proclaim,
> That 'Not to be corrupted is the shame.'

---

[50] *The Craftsman*, ed. D'Anvers, no. 13 (16 January 1727).

In Soldier, Churchman, Patriot, Man in Pow'r,
'Tis Av'rice all, Ambition is no more!
See, all our Nobles begging to be Slaves!
See, all our Fools aspiring to be Knaves!
The Wit of Cheats, the Courage of a Whore,
Are what ten thousand envy and adore.
All, all look up, with reverential Awe,
On Crimes that scape, or triumph o'er the Law:
While Truth, Worth, Wisdom, daily they decry –
'Nothing is Sacred now but Villainy.'   (147–70)

If the sacking of Rome is implicitly conjured, there is also something of an Old Testamentary excess in all of this, which Pope is drawing upon to clinch his presentation of nefarious attainment and fruition.[51] A supple dramatisation presents its pomp as a consummation of pagany, whose conquering heroine takes possession of the country, and prefigures the culturally triumphant goddess of *The Dunciad*'s fourth book. Beginning with rhetoric of a Christian provenance, the verse paragraph which the quoted lines conclude proceeds through a relentless desecration: from 'preaching well' through 'Monk', 'Bishops', 'Gospel', to 'adore' and 'reverential Awe', it maintains a steady orientation towards the perversion of the sacred it charts until the last line inserts villainy as this created world's proper object for worship. And since 'carting', or displaying in a cart, was a punishment for prostitutes, then to 'see pale Virtue carted in her stead' is to witness the prostitution of values dear to Pope and his friends. In the pageant of perversion thus presented, the figure which Vice makes, and which Dulness is shortly to assume, both penetrates a world *and* oppresses it. The institutions of civil society are suborned and possessed while the structures of political society – 'Soldier, Churchman, Patriot, Man in Pow'r' – are equally brought under an irresistible domination. The city of dreadful night that will shortly bring *The Dunciad* to its climax is here invaded and subordinated, as the virtuous independence promoted elsewhere in the poetry is abolished. The values according to which the sovereign power of a landed aristocracy had legitimised its own rule and validated its divine right to succession, are now dissolved and replaced by corrupting forms of control actively alienating relationships which had hitherto defined and bound communities together.

Although this allegorised figure holds sway over all areas of life, hers

---

[51] For a consideration of the more immediately political resonances in this passage see J. M. Osborn, 'Pope, the Byzantine Empress, and Walpole's Whore', *Review of English Studies*, new series, 6 (1955), pp. 372–82.

is a mode of power still effectively mediated by willing servants busily spinning the conditions of that coming darkness, as *Dialogue II* of the *Epilogue to the Satires* makes clear:

> Ye tinsel Insects! whom a Court maintains,
> That counts your Beauties only by your Stains,
> Spin all your Cobweb's o'er the Eye of Day!
> The Muse's wing shall brush you all away:
> All his Grace preaches, all his Lordship sings,
> All that makes Saints of Queens, and Gods of Kings,
> All, all but Truth, drops dead-born from the Press,
> Like the last Gazette, or the last Address.   (220–7)

Because probity has been sacrificed by the maladministration of Justice (in the reference to [Westminister] Hall), Pope's ironic apostrophe intimates that satire becomes an almost religious duty: 'To rowze the Watchmen of the Publick Weal, / To Virtue's Work provoke the tardy Hall'. With this goes a developing recognition that politics itself (in the reference to the 'last Address', the King's speech at the opening of Parliament), has now become an alien activity, no longer an expression of virtuous integrity. As far as the structures of power were concerned, the struggle for possession was lost: but Pope was girding for his final assault.

6

'Illusion on the town': figuring out credit in *The Dunciad*

Drury Lane's vigorous effort in support of the Hanoverians reached a climax with [Cibber's] *The Non-Juror*. Produced in December 1717, when the excitement over the rebellion of two years earlier was subsiding, the play excoriated the Jacobites with a jingoistic fury. All the subtlety of Molière's *Tartuffe*, from which it is adapted, is lost in this blatant exercise in demagoguery, produced after the cause it purported to defend was already won. Yet the play was an immense success. It ran sixteen nights in December and was afterwards revived. Cibber received permission to dedicate it to the King, an honour that was accompanied by a gift of £200. Thereafter until his death Cibber's voice was among the loudest in the chorus of praise of the Hanoverians, whose Poet Laureate he became in 1730.[1]

In 1736, Pope outlined to Swift a plan he never realised for four epistles which naturally followed the *Essay on Man*: 'It will conclude with a satire ... exemplified by pictures, characters, and examples' (*P. Corr.* IV, p. 5). Throughout the 1730s Pope had been shaping a poetic persona that gave effective voice to values of a social and moral order increasingly of the past. By positioning his persona to address its representations directly to the landlords and squires of England, as well as to anyone else who might be expected or persuaded to share their values and attitudes, he elected to speak to and for a significant sector of economically powerful individuals. No matter what was happening in the City, agriculture was, and for more than a century remained, the main system of domestic production, enabling England's landowners to feel that they had everything to play for. They enjoyed, moreover, the great advantage of being the natural inheritors of a language of ethics developed over the preceding century to justify their ruling position. By revivifying this traditional lexicon Pope sought to stage a developing

[1] Loftis, *Politics of Drama*, p. 72.

177

world-historical scene in a preferred guise and language. Insofar as Pope was constructing a myth for the times, we are usefully reminded that the unity of such a myth is itself a phenomenon of the imagination, 'resulting from the attempt at interpretation; and its function is to endow the myth with synthetic form and to prevent its disintegration into a confusion of opposites'.[2] By tailoring his own personality and circumstances as an investiture of preferred attitudes Pope sought representative status in his writing for which his secure possession of form and technique to promote traditional emblems of honour and virtue would offer a guarantee of probity and integrity.

But Cibber's inheritance in *The Dunciad*'s final version of Theobald's library from the 1727 poem already shows a compromised and uncomfortable cultural inheritance disrupting a prior formal integrity. Moreover, the concept of virtue Pope had elsewhere enlisted and promoted included honesty, loyalty, benevolence, selflessness, reliability and helpfulness as forms of regard for the interests of others. Such a conspectus could appear hopeless in a society whose participants, as *The Dunciad* now puts it, seemed perfectly able and willing to bury such notions, to 'Find Virtue local, all Relation scorn, / See all in *Self*, and but for self be born' (IV, 479–80). The political campaign of the 1730s had failed and *The Dunciad* was assuming its final form: 1743 was not 1728 and changing circumstances required other changes including the installation of a different anti-hero. Walpole retired in early February, 1742, and the separate Book IV of the *New Dunciad* was published in March. A year and a half later, on 29 October 1743, the day before George II's birthday, the publication of the revised *Dunciad* in four books, with Cibber as hero, was, as Sherburn comments, almost a birthday present for the King (*TE* V, p. xxxii, n. 3). Sherburn elsewhere points out the resemblance between Dulness's distribution of awards and the honours list of a royal birthday.[3] Pope was aiming high, but he badly needed an appropriate court-jester to serve as King of the Dunces, and when Colley Cibber published in 1740 what his most recent editor describes as pathetic efforts to show the world that his public figure was a caricature of a wise man who could recognise his own vanity,[4] he made the biggest mistake of his life. With the best will

---

[2] Claude Lévi-Strauss, *The Raw and the Cooked: Introduction to a Science of Mythology*: 1, translated by J. & D. Weightman (London, 1970), p. 5.

[3] George Sherburn, '*The Dunciad*, Book IV', *Texas Studies in Language and Literature*, 24 (1944), pp. 197–210.

[4] *A Critical Edition of: 'An Apology for the Life of Colley Cibber, Comedian'* (New York, 1987), edited by John Maurice Evans, p. xxxii. Subsequent citations are given parenthetically in the text.

in the world it is difficult not to read Cibber's autobiography as a caricature of a man frequently unable to draw the line between openness to his own faults and shameless self-exposure. There was already, and most usefully, a fashion in print of associating Cibber with his political master so that damning one damned the other by implication,[5] and as an additional spur Cibber had recently published an account of a visit to a brothel with the young Pope and the Earl of Warwick which had become the talk of the town when *The Universal Spectator* printed a cartoon of the poet on the lap of a whore.[6] Pope would have enjoyed his own image of Cibber reclining in the lap of Dulness but anyway, and for several reasons, *An Apology for the Life of Mr Colley Cibber, Comedian* was a gift outright to the revised *Dunciad*, and Pope accepted. As the officially presiding literary figure during the decade of Pope's developing opposition to Walpole's administration and what it represented, Cibber's prosaic exposure of his own personality and history made him an irresistible candidate for literary rule in the empire of Dulness. 'I cannot say I have much improved by Study', England's laureate allows, 'a giddy Negligence always posses'd me ... It is not on what I write, but on my Reader's Curiosity I rely to be read through' (pp. 5, 7), and in that last respect he is telling the truth. A sometimes efficient dramatist and an execrable poet, Cibber's acting abilities had shone to best effect in the role of the coxcomb, a fact that he also blithely acknowledges: 'Nothing gives a Coxcomb more Delight, than when you suffer him to talk of himself; which sweet Liberty I here enjoy for a whole volume together' (p. 18).

The bland disclosure of motive and intent which *An Apology* produces goes hand in hand with a recurrent tendency to equate the state of theatres with the theatre of state, and with Cibber himself as often as not at stage-centre. 'You cannot but observe', he says with reference to the tumultuous events of 1688 when he was seventeen and had not yet gained a toehold in the acting profession, 'that the Fate of King *James*, and of the prince of *Orange*, and that of so minute a being as my self were all at once upon the Anvil' (p. 37). It was, at least, a way of contextualising an upwardly mobile career towards the highest rungs of fashionable society, and as his story of a life on the London stage develops into one of theatre management, Cibber frequently constructs his activities as a paradigm of the social and political culture he entertained and served. He will (justifiably) present a dispute with the Lord Chamber-

---

5 *The Garden and the City*, pp. 155–62.
6 Mack, *Alexander Pope: A Life* (Yale, 1985), pp. 292–3.

lain as a struggle in defence of the liberty of the individual against the exercise of arbitrary power (p. 204); will consider 'that the Talents requisite to form good Actors, great Writers, and true Judges, were like those of wise and memorable Ministers' (p. 210); and will reflect similarly upon an episode involving players and management in litigation to determine a fair method of payment: 'How often does History show us, in the same State of Courts, the same Politicks have been practis'd' (p. 236). Cibber speaks a post-revolutionary political culture and his narrative is a revealing document. He will recall, when comparing 'the Government of a well-establish'd Theatre ... to that of a Nation', that 'one of our Princes, in the last Century, lost his Crown, by too arbitrary a Use of his Power', and will ask 'why should we wonder, that the same Passions taking Possession of men, in lower Life, by an equally impolitick Usage of their Theatrical Subjects, should have involved the patentees, in proportionable Calamities' (pp. 238–9). He will remember a time when newspapers attacked theatre management 'with the same Freedom and Severity, as if we had been so many Ministers of State' (p. 292), and towards the end of his 'Theatrical History', will acknowledge his ingrained habit of political comparison: 'I have so often had occasion to compare the State of the Stage to the State of the Nation, that I yet feel the Reluctancy to drop the Comparison, or to speak of the one, without some Application to the other' (p. 323). And so he continues:

How many *Whigs*, and *Tories* have chang'd their Parties, when their good and bad Pretensions have met with a Check to their higher Preferment?
    Thus, we see, let the Degrees, the Rank of Men, be ever so unequal, Nature throws out their Passions, from the same Motives; ... The Courtier, and the Comedian, when their Ambition is out of Humour, take just the same measures to right themselves.   (p. 326)

Cibber had an eventful and evidently a satisfying life, but for Pope it was all far too mobile, and given Cibber's profession it could all-too-easily seem that the make-believe, play-acting world of *The Rape of the Lock* had come absurdly home to roost in the corridors of power. So Cibber comes a sacrificial lamb to Pope's Queen of Dulness for reasons beyond either his self-serving vanity or his tepid prose. As one of London's first business-managers of the stage, money is Cibber's constant theme. His *Apology* details funding and finances, and foregrounds money-payments as the prime structure of agency in the administration and organisation of the London stage from the Restoration onwards; with Cibber's own salary, and that of other actors and managers, as well as the distribution of profits among shareholders and players, occupying pages of his attention. After competition opened up in 1695, with money for a new theatre at Lincoln's Inn Fields being raised by voluntary subscription 'of twenty, and some of forty guineas apiece', Cibber records how the writing of a prologue marked the occasion when his Muse 'brought forth the first Fruit that was ever made publick' (p. 113). The company accepted his prologue but refused to allow him to speak it:

You may imagine how hard I thought it, that they durst not trust my poor poetical Brat, to my own care. But since I found it was to be given into other Hands, I insisted that two Guineas should be the price of my parting with it; which with a Sigh I receiv'd, and *Powel* spoke the Prologue: But every Line, that was applauded, went sorely to my Heart, when I reflected, that the same Praise might have been given to my own speaking it.   (p. 114)

While Pope was an effective entrepreneur in the literary market-place, Cibber speaks far more openly of the opportunities and disappointments occasioned by the economic individualism of his times. In marked contrast, Pope's carefully stage-managed public image of virtue and propriety had the effect of concealing such things as his denial of collaboration on *The Odyssey*; an episode that Mack describes as 'a shabby business all round . . . a dishonest cover-up for the sake of gain'.[7] By creating a schematic typology for the contemporary world, organised around the treatment of financial matters, Pope constructed a space for himself where a golden mean in all things would be the effective example,[8] whereas Cibber's self-revelations are less engineered, to the extent that he sometimes seems unaware of the ironies his text generates. His express dislike of the first alienation of his literary property is formulated in a text that elsewhere draws upon monetary metaphor to represent cultural values (while quipping in habitually Whiggish ways):

Praise, tho' it might be our due, is not like a *Bank-Bill*, to be paid upon Demand; to be valuable, it must be voluntary. When we are dun'd for it, we have a Right and Privilege to refuse it. If Compulsion insists upon it, it can only be paid as Persecution in Points of faith . . . in a counterfeit coin: And who, ever, believ'd Occasional Conformity to be sincere?   (p. 22)

When, therefore, a determin'd Critick comes arm'd with Wit and Outrage, to take from me that small Pittance I have, I would no more dispute with him, than I would resist a gentleman of the Road, to save a little Pocket-Money.
                                    (p. 26)

[7] Ibid., p. 414.
[8] Ian A. Bell, ' "Not Lucre's Madman": Pope, Money and Independence', in *Pope: Essays for the Tercentenary*, pp. 53–67.

In informative ways *An Apology* records the processes by which post-Restoration London theatres evolved into business ventures run for profit as share-holding companies:

> The profits of acting were then divided into twenty Shares, ten of which went to the proprietors, and the other Moiety to the principal Actors, in such sub-divisions as their different merit might pretend to. These shares of the patentees were promiscuously sold out to Mony-making Persons, call'd Adventurers, who, tho' utterly ignorant of Theatrical Affairs, were still admitted to a proportionate Vote in the Management of them; all particular Encouragements to Actors were by them, of consequence, look'd upon as so many sums deducted from their private Dividends. While therefore the Theatrical Hive had so many Drones in it, the labouring Actors, sure, were under the highest Discouragement, if not a direct State of Oppression. (p. 58)

Mandeville's metaphor surfaces again, as Whig systems of financial management are foregrounded. And subsequently, in the course of complaining about the severity with which new theatrical productions are damned by some critics while others are warmly appreciative, Cibber blends politics with economics:

> In this sort of Civil War, the unhappy Author, Like a good Prince, while his subjects are at mortal Variance, is sure to be a Loser by a Victory on either Side; for still the Commonwealth, his Play, is, during the conflict, torn to Pieces. While this is the Case, while the Theatre is so turbulent a Sea, and so infested with Pirates, what Poetical Merchant, of any Substance, will venture to trade in it? (p. 104)

In the course of explaining how a scarce labour-market had led to a pay-rise, he tells us how he felt at being bought and sold:

> As for my self, I was then too insignificant to be taken into their Councils, and consequently stood among those of little Importance, like Cattle in a Market, to be sold to the first Bidder. But the Patentees seeming in the greater Distress for Actors, condescended to purchase me. Thus, without any farther Merit, than that of being a scarce Commodity, I was advanc'd to thirty Shillings a Week. (p. 112)

When economic man and Whig man of letters thus joined in one figure, *The Dunciad* had found a hero for its times. For his mock celebration of the final destruction of English civilisation as he knew it and preferred it to remain, Pope had been presented with a figure who seemed to embody all the substantial and accidental causes that were leading to its eclipse.[9]

---

[9] *An Apology*, p. xxxvii.

In *The Dunciad* the terms of Cibber's address to Dulness gain point from his own representative status as a writer in the managerial service of the new order of things:

> Then he: 'Great Tamer of all human art!
> First in my care, and ever at my heart;
> With whom my Muse began, with whom shall end;
> E'er since Sir Fopling's Periwig was Praise,
> To the last honours of the Butt and Bays:
> O thou! of Bus'ness the directing soul!
> To this our head like byass to the bowl,
> Which, as more pond'rous, made its aim more true,
> Obliquely wadling to the mark in view ...'   (I, 163–72)

Cibber had directed his own business in Drury Lane with some success and in variation upon the earlier *Dunciad*, what are now Cibber's lines are tailored to his political alignments, bringing into focus the cultural politics of Walpole's era: 'Hold – to the Minister I more incline; / To serve his cause, O Queen! is serving thine' (I, 213–14). In its revised form the poem also rings the changes upon its original opening lines to emphasise Walpole's role in the creation of a fit laureate for the House of Hanover by offering mock praise to: 'The Mighty Mother, and her Son who brings / The Smithfield Muses to the ear of Kings'. Cibber was Walpole's laureate, although Pope could relish the additional irony that the Great Man had also presented the original *Dunciad* at Court. Then, to match Cibber's self-identification with the House of Hanover, Pope's hostile recognition that 'Still Dunce the Second reigns like Dunce the First' includes the Hanoverian succession as an inevitable consequence of the culture brought into being with the Revolution Settlement and nurtured to maturity by the Queen of Credit. It is this mother and not her several sons who is the true agent of the narrative, actively promoting and facilitating what for Pope would be a cultural debasement of classical verities. So Pope makes sport of the fact that 'the ancient Golden Age is by Poets stiled *Saturnian*; but in the Chymical language, *Saturn* is Lead' (*TE* V, p. 63, n. 26), when he invites Swift to consider the cultural ascendancy of his fertile Goddess:

> Here pleas'd behold her mighty wings out-spread,
> To hatch a new Saturnian age of Lead.   (I, 27–8)

His first version had discovered its queen in a cheapening image of commerce as the rag-trade, 'Where wave the tatter'd ensigns of Rag-Fair' (I[A], 27), but for his 1743 poem Pope situates his protagonist differently. Swift had depicted the ravings of a 'deluded bankrupt' placing 'all upon a desp'rate Bett' in a world where 'Fools will see as Wise men please',[10] while John Gay placed the banker and poet who delude themselves and each other in adjoining cells in the asylum at Bedlam. These figures merge in the goddess of Dulness to produce an equally fantastic image of a delusive power at once soporific and all-embracing, with Pope taking incidental advantage of the fact that Cibber's father had carved the two statues of lunatics at Bedlam's gates, to return there for the beginning of his tale:

> Close to those walls where Folly holds her throne,
> And laughs to think Monroe would take her down,
> Where o'er the gates, by his fam'd father's hand
> Great Cibber's brazen, brainless brothers stand;
> One Cell there is, conceal'd from vulgar eye,
> The Cave of Poverty and Poetry.   (I, 29–34)

It is an unsettling irony that these statues, 'Raving Madness' and 'Melancholy Madness' have been preserved and now stand sentinel at London's Royal Exchange, but if Gay had seen Bedlam as the proper setting for banker and poet to relate to each other and to the comic damnation of both, Pope sees emanating from the same place of perverse imaginings a deranged cultural order, from pantomime to the publishing of newspapers and broadsheets and to the inspiring of poetry:

> Hence Bards, like Proteus long in vain ty'd down,
> Escape in Monsters, and amaze the town.
> Hence Miscellanies spring, the weekly boast
> of Curl's chaste press, and Lintot's rubric post:
> Hence hymning Tyburn's elegiac lines,
> Hence Journals, Medleys, Merc'ries, Magazines:
> Sepulchral Lyes, our holy walls to grace,
> And New-year Odes and all the Grub-street race.
> In clouded Majesty here Dulness shone.   (I, 37–45)

At the opening of Book Three, this lunatic queen returns to her temple to track the source of Cibber's inspiration and to link it with fictions stimulated in a new financial era:

> Hence, from the straw where Bedlam's Prophet nods,
> He hears loud Oracles, and talks with Gods:
> Hence the Fool's Paradise, the Statesman's Scheme,
> the air-built Castle, and the golden Dream.   (III, 7–10)

[10] *Swift's Poems*, I, p. 251, 257.

While *The Dunciad* castigates a debauched literary culture, its satire centres upon a perceived slippage towards ever more fantastic foundations.

For the previous decade Pope's assault on a notoriously corrupt administration had been ingenious and sustained, rising and falling as political opportunities to challenge Walpole's tenure of office came and went, and in what remains the most tactful and sensitive account, Maynard Mack has traced the later evolution of Pope's engagement with his society. For some time during the late 1730s, Pope had been threatening opponents with inclusion in a revised *Dunciad*, but Walpole's intimidating power prevented the wasp of Twickenham from being as merciless with the First Minister as he might. Now, that threat was removed and Mack notes the difference of the fourth book: 'Once the *New Dunciad* had actually appeared, it was evident to all of Pope's informed readers that the fall of Walpole had brought forth a satire of 600–odd lines of unparalleled specificity and boldness, attributing to the Hanoverian court and its former first minister primary responsibility for a general moral and cultural decay which since the middle 30s even Whig observers had been deploring.' Without doubt, in the new poem of 1742 'the goddess Dulness of the 1729 Variorum unmistakably "mounts" a political throne',[11] as Pope's Cibber proclaims, and Mack's informed readings show us patterns of figurative subterfuge and historical innuendo in which poetry and politics unfold together. Specific reference and boldness of address we certainly get in the final poem, but combined with a scornful and angry sense of irretrievable loss. The lights were going out for Pope's espoused ideology, as the political values he supported and promoted were overwhelmed by alternative ways of conducting the nation's business culture. Over forty years earlier Davenant had warned that mixed government, once corrupted, was 'the greatest tyranny in the world, it is tyranny established by a law, it is authorised by consent, and such a people are bound by fetters of their own making'. *The Dunciad* satirises a world that Davenant predicted:

A tyranny that governs by the sword, has few friends but men of the sword; but a legal tyranny (where people are only called upon to confirm iniquity with their own voices) has of its side the rich, the fearful, the lazy, those that know the law and get by it, ambitious churchmen, and all those whose livelihood depends upon the quiet posture of affairs.[12]

---

11 *The Garden and the City*, p. 152–3.
12 Charles Davenant, 'An Essay upon the Possible Methods of Making a People Gainers in the Balance of Trade', *Works*, II, pp. 209, 231.

Davenant was nonetheless able to retain a certain optimism whereas Pope's mockery testifies to both lazy acquiescence in and vociferous confirmation of what for him were corrupting iniquities. In the face of repeated scandals a quiet posture of affairs had been sedulously courted through a sustained political willingness to let sleeping dogs lie. Non-resistance to the financial interest had become a hall-mark of Walpole's regime and what had not long before been a fledgling system of economic management had developed remarkable powers of survival. As far as its installation as the economic Areopagus of the nation[13] was concerned, the reign of Credit was secure and fantasies of wealth proliferated. Cibber's air-built castle and golden dream connect with Maria dreaming of 'Hereditary realms and worlds of gold' in the *Epistle to Bathurst* (131–2) and with a Bank of England Director waking up in *The Dunciad* 'From dreams of millions, and three groats to pay' (IV, 283). Pope's enabling goddess moves towards her ascendancy during the poems of the 1730s through an equally various display of conjurings, invocations to wizards, dreams of devils and the dark fantastic: all of which compose shouts and whisperings of a despised but seductive and unsettling power in society, and all of which helps to create the environment for the goddess's ultimately triumphant apocalypse of the banal in the poem of 1743. Pope's verse unfolds a process whereby 'the Avarice of Pow'r' came to threaten and displace what for him were reasonable attitudes:

> Can Reason hold her throne,
> Despise the known, nor tremble at th'unknown?
> Survey both worlds, intrepid and entire,
> In spite of Witches, Devils, Dreams, and Fire?
>
> (*Ep. II*, ii, 310–13)

Not easily, it appears, when individual dreams of fantastic acquisition unleashed by Public Credit after the Revolution Settlement become *The Dunciad*'s collective cultural nightmare.

In an effort to communicate an equally politically motivated notion of public Credit stressing its transcendent glory, Defoe had made God chairman of the greatest trading company of them all, with Credit as a kind of handmaiden: 'Credit is not the effect of this or that wheel in the Government ... but of the whole movement, acting ... according to the exquisite design of the Director of the whole frame.' In the same essay Defoe had already represented the insubstantiality of Credit as: 'like the

[13] Marx, *Early Writings*, p. 264.

soul in the body [which] acts all substance yet is itself immaterial; it gives motion, yet itself cannot be said to exist, it is neither quantity nor quality ... it is the essential shadow of something that is not'.[14] This moving spirit of a developing political economy has already appropriated to itself terms and capacities that John Locke had reserved to the legislative function of parliamentary rule:

'Tis in their *Legislative*, that the Members of a Commonwealth are united, and combined together into one coherent living Body. This *is the Soul that gives Form, Life, and Unity* to the Commonwealth: From hence the several Members have their mutual Influence, Sympathy and Connexion: ... For the *Essence and Union of the Society* consisting in having one Will, the Legislative, when once established by the Majority, has the declaring, and as it were the keeping of that Will.[15]

The shaping of that will becomes a shared perception of subsequent decades, and Defoe repeatedly testifies to the defining agency of public credit in the process:

Without *Credit*, we can neither make War, nor make Peace; we can neither Trade, nor live without Trade; neither go Abroad, nor stay at Home; we are muzzl'd in our Commerce, ty'd Hand and Foot in our Politicks, and in short, are given up to Enemies ... Credit must be maintain'd, or all is lost, and the very Welfare of the Nation, depends upon the Credit of the Nation.[16]

Defoe was concerned to persuade his audience that it was possible to discern the difference between 'Real and Imaginary ... Substance and Vogue', while conceding that 'All Credit built upon the Foundation of Project, is a *Deceptio visus* upon the Imagination'.[17] Pope recognised the validity of Defoe's description in different ways: for him the welfare of the nation is now beyond redemption; the real and the unreal increasingly indiscernible and he is intent upon personalising the cultural effects of what he constructs as an irresistibly corrupting power. When we substitute Cibber for Tibbald, the adaptable ironies of the 'Prolegomena of Martinus Scriblerus', attached to the 1729 *Dunciad Variorum* extend easily enough in his direction:

A *Person* must be fix'd upon to support this action ... This *Phantom* in the poet's mind must have a *name* ... He finds his name to be [*Cibber*], and he becomes of course the hero of the poem.   (*TE* V, p. 51)

---

[14] Defoe, *Essay Upon the Public Credit*, p. 13, 6.
[15] Locke, *Two Treatises of Government*, p. 407.
[16] Defoe, *Review*, 7, no. 117, p. 467 (facsimile book 18).
[17] *Review* 3, no. 126, p. 503 (facsimile book 8).

Phantoms within phantoms in effect, since like everyone else in the poem, Cibber serves the dusky Queen. In *The Dunciad* we move in Credit's ghostly realm, while in Exchange Alley nervous worries are being expressed because: 'to the disadvantage of the whole community, private persons are made immoderately rich, and every day growing richer by artificial rumours, whereby self-interested men affect the public funds, for their own gain, tho' to the apparent hazard of their country'.[18] The Houyhnhnms, we recall, had difficulty with beings who said the thing which was not: yet with or without the consent of Parliament the shadow of something that is not was visibly reconstructing English society. Bringing literary production and social developments together, the 'Argument' of *The Dunciad*'s third book makes ironic reference to these contexts:

The Goddess transports [Cibber] to her Temple, and there lays him to slumber with his head on her lap; a position of marvellous virtue, which causes all the visions of wild enthusiasts, projectors, inamoratos, castle-builders, chemists and poets.   (*TE* V, p. 319)

The perspective darkens as the poem acknowledges the irreversibility of things. It had become depressingly clear to Pope that in terms of parliamentary power, the Opposition failure to unseat Walpole in 1734 had been a watershed for Country Party aspirations; a failure from which there seemed no hope of recovery. 'Let confusion reign', John Blunt had roared in the year of the Bubble, and since then a market-led assault upon traditional categories and valorisations of virtuous activity had been relentless: it now appeared culturally triumphant. The figure of female inconstancy which entertained writers on both sides of the political divide in earlier years had matured into the deadliest of Pope's emblems for which uncertainty is its most enabling attribute: the 'cloud-compelling Queen' (I, 79) is aptly named.

The myriad personal references that have been read as disfigurements of the poem may well, many of them, be additionally motivated by professional or personal malice on Pope's part. But practically all of those so scathingly included had associated with the ministry which stabilised and protected the institutions that enriched them all. Insofar as they actively supported Walpole's administration with their pens, and a vast majority of them did, they function in Pope's satirical reaction as a clerisy of the damned, their Lilliputian scribblings forming part of the infrastructure of a power system that created, dwarfed and

[18] Richard Steele, 'A Nation a Family: Being a Sequel to the Crisis of Property', in *Tracts and Pamphlets by Richard Steele* (Oxford, 1944), edited by Rae Blanchard, p. 581.

transcended them. In his view these sorry successors to the aediles of ancient Rome were, or they assisted, the functionaries who first either serviced or piloted the huge impersonal machinery of a bureaucratic state significantly developed by Walpole. What then becomes a singular emphasis in the poem is the great number of these figures who are *not* named, but who go to make up the poem's overwhelming sense of an embracing cultural movement:

> Sons of a Day! just buoyant on the flood,
> Then number'd with the puppies in the mud.
> Ask ye their names? I could as soon disclose
> The names of these blind puppies as of those.   (II, 307–10)

The anonymity of Walpole's supporters composes something of a refrain: Cibber sees 'Millions and millions' of them (III, 31), and the goddess subsequently invites him to consider 'An hundred sons, and ev'ry son a God: / ... Behold an hundred sons, and each a Dunce' (III, 134, 138). This then becomes: 'ev'ry nameless name, / All crowd, who foremost shall be damn'd to Fame' (III, 157–8), before the final book revisits the closing image of the first *Epilogue to the Satires*, to show an England seduced by the goddess's power:

> The gath'ring number, as it moves along,
> Involves a vast involuntary throng,
> Who gently drawn, and struggling less and less,
> Roll in her Vortex and her pow'r confess.
> Not those alone who passive own her laws,
> But who, weak rebels, more advance her cause.   (IV, 81–6)

Those who are called by name are often being identified in order to be further diminished as part of a plague of 'Locusts black'ning all the ground' (IV, 397), although for writers active in the service of the government Pope does reserve particular scorn. 'These are', the verse falters over such ephemeral officers of the commercial state in a comic deconstruction of its epitaph for them, ' – ah no! these were, the Gazetteers' (II, 314). Like so many of the jokes in *The Dunciad*, this one also detonates in the machinery of annotation into which the rhyming couplets spill. Quoting from a report of the Parliamentary Committee of Secrecy (1742) to the effect that upwards of fifty thousand pounds had been paid out to authors and contributors to government newspapers in the decade from 1731 to 1741, the note concludes: 'Which shows the benevolence of One Minister to have expended, for the current dulness of ten years in Britain, double the sum which gained

Louis XIV so much honour in annual Pensions to learned men all over Europe' (II, 314, n.). Naturally enough, Walpole himself eventually falls victim to the powers for which he had acted as such an astute midwife and manager. When the goddess asserts that 'Princes are but things / Born for First ministers' (IV, 601–2), it must inevitably follow that at her yawn, as part of 'the Nation's sense' being lost, 'Ev'n Palinurus [Walpole] nodded at the helm' (IV, 611, 614).

But this bold specificity in the final *Dunciad* combines with a rival tendency towards generalising and also towards abstraction:

> Say great Patricians! (Since your selves inspire
> These wondrous works; so Jove and Fate require)   (I [A], 4–5)

in the first version, becomes in the later one:

> Say you, her instruments the Great!
> Call'd to this work by Dulness, Jove and Fate.   (I, 3–4)

The great patricians of the Whig aristocracy, also known as the Junto, who had secured their share of power through the Revolution Settlement and who were active in bringing the Hanoverians to England after the death of Queen Anne in 1714, become subordinated now as mere 'instruments' to a culture that brooks no resistance. As Dulness displaces Jove, a governing patriciate becomes a governed instrumentality: from being instigators of action their status shifts to one of submission to a decidedly non-classical deity. Classical antecedents of fructifying and invigorating gods and goddesses that had once provided a persuasive contrast and corrective for contemporary departures are now demoted themselves by Dulness's triumphant penetration and possession of the British state in the world of the poem. With the poetry of the 1730s behind it, one of the ways in which *The Dunciad* mocks this gathering historical transformation as a wholesale degradation of epic virtue and classical decorum is by insinuating that within and behind the decomposing shadow of its ubiquitous queen hovers the plundered Republic of Rome. At times Pope stretches epic contrast into melodramatic excess to imagine the scope of a new power organising his society: certainly his queen's symbolic significance transcends the lesser figures who cluster at her throne. Her 'ample presence' (I, 261) displaces even the colossal domination that was Walpole's particular achievement in political affairs: the First Minister of the House of Hanover is no more than her 'bonded son', while a display of nominalising inventiveness disseminates Dulness throughout the text, her various identities creating a sense of inexorable omnipresence. The 'mighty mother' (I, 1) is also the 'Daughter of Chaos and eternal Night' (I, 12). In her 'clouded

Majesty' (I, 45) she is the 'Great Tamer of all Human Art' (I, 163), and from being 'the Great Mother dearer held than all' (I, 269), the 'great Empress' (IV, 282) mutates into the 'Great Anarch' who drops the final curtain on the poem's presentation of her native city's performance. Cibber's career in the theatre lends a personal edge to this choice of puppet-show closure: Pope was showing him how a Patriot laureate writes.

Through their control of parliament, meanwhile, the institutions of the City of London had effectively displaced their terrestrial monarch as the ruling power in the land and by starting the action of his poem from Bedlam on a Lord Mayor's Day, and linking its degraded rituals to a Lord Mayor's procession Pope specifies a target that is already an historical culture. An 'Appendix' informs us that: 'The time and date of the Action is evidently in the last reign, when the office of City Poet expir'd upon the death of *Elkanah Settle*' (*TE* V, p. 205). Settle, who died in 1724, had been appointed poet to the City of London in 1691, establishing a link closer in time to the Revolution Settlement and its financial culture whose present dominance Pope satirises. Because at Settle's death no one was appointed fill his place: 'This important point of time our Poet has chosen', a note informs us, 'as the Crisis of the Kingdom of *Dulness*, who thereupon decrees to remove her imperial seat from the City, and overspread all other parts of the town: to which great Enterprize all things being now ripe, she calls the Hero of this Poem' (*TE* V, p. 70, n. 88). In synchrony with a revolutionary transformation of England's economic dispositions the goddess Dulness spreads her wings and takes flight, from the lunatic transfigurings of Bedlam into the City of London and then on to incorporate the cultural life of the nation.

Bernard Mandeville had represented good springing up 'and pullulat-[ing] from evil as naturally as chickens do from eggs'[19] and from his different perspective Pope is frequently fascinated by a related imagery of incubation, but from lower down the scale and involving a more threatening germination of wealth:

> Riches, like insects, when conceal'd they lie,
> Wait but for wings, and in their season, fly.
>
> (*To Bathurst*, 171–2)

When Pope contemplates people living off unearned income, the 'silent growth of ten per cent' which sustains them takes place where 'In dirt

---

19 *Fable of the Bees*, I, p. 91.

and darkness hundreds stink content' (*Epistle I*, i, 132–3). He images
notes of credit flitting from place to place 'pregnant with thousands'
(*To Bathurst*, 77), and calls upon Swift to watch his goddess 'hatch a
new Saturnian age of Lead'. This insect life infects writing: 'Now Times
are chang'd, and one Poetick Itch / Has seiz'd the Court and City, Poor
and Rich' (*Epistle II*, i, 169–70), and finally infiltrates society so
successfully as to render it beyond political redemption, as Pope infers
by including in his unfinished satire *One Thousand Seven Hundred and
Forty*, the couplet:

> The Plague is on thee, Britain, and who tries
> To save thee in th'infectious office *dies*.   (*TE* V, p. 336)

Something different was breeding in society, wrecking established hierarchies and proprieties, and an early fascination with its apparently
autonomous reproduction is registered in a letter to Broome:

Every valuable, every pleasant thing is sunk in an ocean of avarice and
corruption. The son of a first minister is a proper match for a daughter of a late
South Sea Director, – so money upon money increases, copulates, and multiplies, and guineas beget guineas in saecular saeculorum.   (*P. Corr.* II, p. 182)

Given the fictional, imaginary element which many alluded to
whenever credit was being discussed, *The Dunciad*'s focus in Book One
upon the race to gain a 'poet's form' which then dissolves into nothing
seems particularly apt. The goddess had 'form'd this image of well-
body'd air' (II, 42), calling to mind Defoe's description of a 'Multitude
of projectors ... who besides the Innumerable conceptions which die in
the bringing forth, and (like Abortions of the Brain) only come into the
Air, and dissolve, do really every day produce new Contrivances,
Engines, and Projects to get money, never before thought of.'[20] When
Dulness contemplates 'where nameless Somethings in their causes
sleep', poetic incubation forms unnerving continuities with Pope's 'dirt
and darkness' of speculative gain:

> Till genial Jacob, or a warm Third day,
> Call forth each mass, a poem, or a Play:
> How hints, like spawn, scarce quick in embryo lie,
> how new-born nonsense first is taught to cry,
> Maggots half-form'd in Rhyme exactly meet,
> And learn to crawl upon poetic feet.   (I, 57–63)

Pope is constructing a satirical pageant appropriate to an entirely
bought culture for which he cultivates appropriate imagery. When

---

[20] Defoe, *Essay Upon Projects*, p. 4.

Dulness surveys past City laureates: 'She saw with joy the line immortal run, / each sire imprest and glaring in his son' (I, 97–8), and while there may well be a topical reference here to the new gold, silver and copper coinage struck for the accession of George II, the image is interesting for its application of terms from coin-milling to the creation of poets and the invention of poetry. Coinage and Cibber engender metaphor together on other occasions; to speak the currency of his own reified servitude: 'This brazen Brightness, to the 'Squire so dear; / This polish'd Hard-ness, that reflects the Peer' (I, 219–20), and also to articulate the monetarised culture it was his business to stimulate: 'His Peers Shine round him with reflected grace, / New edge their dulness, and new bronze their face' (II, 9–10). Whereas Defoe had figured credit as money's younger sister, though able to produce considerable effects, *The Dunciad*'s coined countenances gather around the throne of dulness abject before her power. So when the goddess rejoices at a system of production that integrates capital with cultural credit, her pleasure springs from a recognition of the dominance of City values. Inheritance is moving in different channels to produce an appropriate genealogy for *The Dunciad*'s contempt: 'She saw old Pryn in restless Daniel shine, / And Eusden eke out Blackmore's endless line; . . . In each she marks her Image full exprest' (I, 103–7).

The Dunciad is marking out its own imaginative lineage: Blackmore's endless line leads all the way back to 1700 and his *Satyr Against Wit* which speaks economic metaphor for middle-class men of sense against aristocratic wit. Because of the 'vast Destruction' wit has made of letters, the *Satyr* claims, unless 'a Fund were settled once that cou'd/ Make our deficient Sense and Learning good':

> Nothing can be expected, for the Debt
> By this loose Age contracted, is so great,
> To set the Muses mortgag'd Acres free,
> Our Bankrupt Sons must sell out-right the Fee.

However, 'If once the Muses Chequer would deny / To take false Wit, 'twould lose its Currency', and to this end *A Satyr Against Wit* calls upon figures from the Whig Junto now displaced by Dulness in Pope's scheme 'to oversee the Coining of our Wit'. In a provocative appropriation of the terms and ordinances of Whig financial culture Blackmore proposes the reconstitution of Parnassus as a process of economic renewal requir-ing re-smelting and new minting; a process in which the wit of a poet like Dryden, 'When once his boasted heaps are melted down, / A Chest full scarce will yield one Sterling Crown'. But *A Satyr* is concerned with future investment in learning, with maintaining what it calls the 'Muses learned Commerce'. 'Let us', it proposes, 'erect a Bank for Wit and Sense, / A Bank whose current Bills may Payment make, / Till new Mill'd Wit shall from the Mint come back.' The terms of a monetarised culture find versified integration while Blackmore seeks credit-worthiness for 'Funds of Standard-Sense [which] need no Allay'.[21] *The Dunciad* takes issue with these grounding assumptions and the culture thus called into being: the 'proud Parnassian sneer' (II, 5) that Cibber wears marks him out as successful subscriber in Blackmore's project. In 1735, with the addition of an 'author's DECLARATION' (*TE* V, 237), a running metaphor of the monetary corruption of preferred literary values comically subverts the metaphoric strategies of *A Satyr* by includ-ing: 'Critics and Restorers who have taken upon themselves to adul-terate the common and current sense of our Glorious Ancestors, Poets of this Realm, by clipping, coining, defacing the images, mixing their own base allay, or otherwise falsifying the same; which they publish, utter, and vend as genuine.' A careful imbrication of literary and monetary terminology satirises their integration in a process of counterfeit expres-sion at once 'invented', recorded and condemned. As process it achieves a kind of apotheosis when, in Book Two, after the prize of a poet's form has evaporated into nothing, the goddess invites the bookseller Curl to 'turn this whole illusion on the town' and presents him with a grotesque promissory note on the future. In an equation that Gay would have recognised, fraudulent equivalencies are to be the order of the day:

> Be thine my stationer! this magic gift;
> Cook shall be Prior, and Concanen, Swift:
> So shall each hostile name become our own,
> And we too boast our Garth and Addison.   (II, 137–40)

Where, in his correspondence, Pope could urge a friend to 'Turn your Eyes and Attention from this miserable mercenary Period: and turn yourself, in a just Contempt of these Sons of Mammon, to the Contem-plation of Books' (*P. Corr.* II, p. 50), in the world of the poetry no such separation seems possible and no such avenue of escape.

Appropriately enough, the fourth book of *The Dunciad* also dramatises most effectively both the reification of human aspirations and the deification of money-objects. The numismatist Mummius describes how the forger and counterfeiter Annius swallowed stolen Greek coins to conceal them from pirates:

> 'Down his own throat he risq'd the Grecian gold;
> Receiv'd each Demi-God, with pious care,

---

21 Richard Blackmore, *A Satyr Against Wit* (London, 1700), pp. 8–11.

Deep in his Entrails – I revered them there.
I bought them, shrouded in that living shrine,
And, at their second birth, they issue mine.'
'Witness great Ammon! by whose horns I swore,
(Reply'd soft Annius) this our paunch before
Still bears them faithful; and that thus I eat,
Is to refund the Medals with the meat.'   (IV, 382–90)

For this marvellously compact moment, a sentence from the young
Marx seems as marvellously apposite: 'Money has not been transcended
in man within the credit system, but man is himself transformed into
money, or, in other words, money is *incarnate* in him.'[22] A century after
Pope's death, Marx is struggling to comprehend a dislocation of value
and orientation he identified as a central characteristic of modern
political economy. Structural continuities can be traced between the
systems both writers confronted, and Marx also saw monetarised ethics
and priorities usurping older valorisations. Although it would be difficult to imagine two more different temperaments and personalities, in a
curious convergence across time and from opposite ends of the political
spectrum they share at times a tropic animus against financial instruments they saw as alienating. Both writers figure a reconstitution of
subjectivity in terms of transubstantiation:

Human individuality, human *morality*, have become both articles of commerce
and the *material* which money inhabits. The substance, the body clothing the
spirit of money is not money, paper, but instead it is my personal existence, my
flesh and blood, my social worth and status. Credit no longer actualises
money-values in actual money but in human flesh and human hearts ...
Within the credit system credit, estranged from men, functions with all the
appearance of the greatest possible recognition of man's worth by economics.[23]

Pope presents his incarnation of money as a perverse eucharistic
communion; a festival of consumption in which idolatry, blasphemy
and cuckoldry contextualise the excremental rebirth of a filched
classical symbolism. As the human form becomes a container for this
figural process of possession and displacement, so the verse contains
within itself echoes of a once divinely inspired order of epic virtue in the
world. Alexander the Great visited the oracle of the Egyptian god
Ammon, whom the Greeks identified with Zeus, and the Romans with
Jupiter, special protector of Rome. After his visit, Alexander had coins
struck showing his own head adorned with the curling ram's horns of
the Egyptian god, so an invocation of antique grandeur suffers comic
degradation as the denizens of *The Dunciad* whore after their own false

[22] Marx, *Early Writings*, p. 265.   [23] Ibid., p. 264.

gods, each of them, as it were, 'wrapt up in Self, a God without a thought' (IV, 485). We have come a long way from the *Essay on Man*'s promotion of a reasonable 'God within the mind' (II, 204) and when, after prolonged exposure to her deforming experience, 'ev'ry finished son returns' (IV, 500) to the service of the goddess, the supremacy of a usurping system of values is acknowledged, with any notion of the justly balanced 'oeconomy' celebrated in *To Bathurst* now overwhelmed by the pervading currency of Dulness's domestic empire. In the words of Silenus:

> Now to thy gentle shadow all are shrunk,
> All melted down, in Pension, or in Punk.   (IV, 509–10)

A fascination with corruptions of previously accepted definitions and assumptions about what constitutes personal and public value is constant in Pope's satire, and images of money entering or otherwise altering the human form recur. With Swift and Gay he shared a sense not only that public credit had facilitated wider access to social power but that money had thereby become the arbiter of private and social worth in more than material senses. The *Essay on Man* sought to reserve to 'the Good and Just' the reputation and trust that wealth can inspire, and while it acknowledges that 'Judges and Senates have been bought for gold' it still maintained that true 'Esteem and love were never to be sold' (IV, 187–8). But Pope had seen value going to the highest bidder often enough, and had also written: 'A Man of wealth is dubb'd a Man of worth, / Venus shall give him form, and Anstis Birth' (*Epistle I*, vi, 81–2). John Anstis was the Herald at Arms, and the lines refer to the purchase of aristocratic pedigree and to the power of money to make the unlovely attractive in public estimation. Insofar as Pope repeatedly refers to silent flights and subversive transferrals of valorising power, his articulate anger again pre-scribes some of the young Marx's moral astringency:

When, in the credit system, the granting of *moral recognition to a man*, like the placing of *confidence in the state*, takes the form of *credit*, then the mystery implicit in the lie of moral recognition, the sheer depravity of this morality, no less than the hypocrisy and egoism contained in that confidence in the state, emerges clearly and shows its true colours.[24]

Phantom images of this gradual but inexorable emergence of an alien power organising both personal and political valorisations echo and re-echo throughout Pope's poetry. In *The Dunciad*'s all-embracing

[24] Ibid., 265.

goddess we witness a darkly comic exfoliation of forces that seem to be no more than grotesque figures in the human brain and yet which effect changes in its constructed characters' behaviour. What is at first inexplicable comes to assume a natural dominance in the structure of the poem as the fantastic figures of Pope's imagination acquire social attributes and become parodied representations in an equally burlesqued history. We move uncertainly in the shadow-worlds of Pope's invention, but the goddess herself survives her alienating mission while in the society of the poem a system of education is enslaved in her service. Swift made the political implications of this clear when he dated from the Restoration: 'the corrupt Method of Education among us, and the consequences thereof, in the Necessity the Crown lay under of introducing *New Men* into the highest Employments of State, or to the office of what we now call Prime Ministers ... merely for want of a Supply among the Nobility' (*SP* XII, p. 47). Since then, *The Dunciad* informs us, the process has become sufficiently sophisticated 'to confine Youth to the study of *Words* only in schools, subject them to the authority of *Systems* in the universities, and delude them with the name of party-distinctions in the World' (IV, 501, n.).

It all sounds strangely familiar, but we are further unsettled when we recognise that ultimately *The Dunciad* both states and embodies its premise that even 'The Muse obeys the Pow'r' (IV, 268), not least because the classical order and decorum of its framework are themselves crumbling. Pope's allegiances to ancient precedent had always been self-aware – he well knew the relationships between public writing and political power and could knowledgeably compare Virgil with Walpole's gazetteers. He also told Spence that *The Aeneid* was a party piece written on the side of usurpation with not one honest line it,[25] which suggests another dimension to *The Dunciad*'s parody of its narrative events. Although Pope's unique combinations of Horatian ease with Juvenalian ferocity seem often to answer an existential need, some distancing from Horace was politically necessary. Horace was in the court party, whereas during the peak of Pope's career he was opposed to the court, and not likely to find a cultural hero associated with the minions of Walpole.[26] Howard Weinbrot has shown us how Pope's was always a 'mingled muse', compounding Horatian, Persian and Juvenalian elements to his own satirical purposes. Considering the role that

---

[25] Joseph Spence, *Observations, Anecdotes, and Characters of Books and Men Collected from Conversation*, edited by J. M. Osborne (Oxford, 1966), I, pp. 229–30.
[26] Howard D. Weinbrot, *Eighteenth-Century Satire*, p. 28.

Horace played in support of the throne of Augustus, a throne that was
coming to be seen as built on the rubble of the great republic whose
constitutional balance Augustus destroyed, Weinbrot also suggests how
mystifying it is to refer uncritically to writing in Pope's time as
Augustan. Nowhere are the tensions and ambivalences that mark
Pope's attitudes more evident than in his developing relationship with
the mock-epic. To contrast *The Rape of the Lock* as 'an exquisitely
diminished shadow cast by an entire epic poem' with *The Dunciad* as
'the ludicrous, grotesque, life-size shadow cast by a piece of an epic
poem'[27] is to half-recognise that in the early poem classical precept
could still, just, contain and present a modernising world; the couplet is
elastic enough and up to the task. In the later work modernity is too
energetically plural for such coercive enclosure and takes its revenge in
both formal and structural ways, so that we can encounter lines that
strike as self-referential to the poem's own performance:

> There motley Images [our] fancy strike,
> Figures ill pair'd, and Similes unlike.
> [We] see[] a Mob of Metaphors advance,
> Pleas'd with the madness of the mazy dance:
> How Tragedy and Comedy embrace;
> How Farce and Epic get a jumbled race;
> How time himself stands still at her command,
> Realms shift their place, and Ocean turns to land.   (I, 65–72)

The imperialising mission of new cultural dispositions carries us back to
the conjurings of solidity from liquidity in Swift's 'The Bubble', while
the all-consuming 'artifice of mind' displayed in Pope's text collapses
generic boundaries, makes equivalence out of difference and merges
rhetorical territories. In one reading, *The Dunciad* is gorged on a surfeit
of its own inventiveness, and a central deconstructive attribute might
then be read as a consequence of its own excess; that is to say, its
progressive weakening, amounting at times to a virtual dismantling of
the couplet's ability to contain the world it anathematises. In Pope's
hands, the balance, the judicious regulation and the controlled variabi-
lity of the couplet might function as a technical correlative for an ideal
society, an appropriate mode for the desired Polybian balance of a
stable, mixed constitution. Pope had been explicit about the social
responsibility he intended his form to shoulder when he co-ordinated
military conquest over France with Anglo-French aesthetic and artistic
conjunction: 'Britain to soft refinements less a foe, / Wit grew polite,

27 Geoffrey Tillotson, *On the Poetry of Pope* (London, 1938), p. 55.

and Numbers learn'd to flow.' He went on to elaborate what we might now recognise as a preferred sociology of form:

> Tho' still some traces of our rustic vein
> And splay-foot verse, remain'd, and will remain.
> Late, very late, correctness grew our care,
> When the tir'd nation breath'd from civil war.
>
> (*Ep. II*, i, 270–3)

The privileged and privileging couplet, technically 'correct' paradigm of balance and harmony, of epigrammatic containment and equilibrium, generates the appropriate rhythm for a social perspective seeking to restore traditional value and order after civil strife. As Pope manipulates it, the couplet shows a remarkable capacity for diversity and variety within its formal constraints: by imposing rhyming pentameters upon such heterogeneous material as he includes, reducing it to ordered syllables and fixed if often labile terms, he could give form to the particular kinds of accommodation that he promoted.

But in the new English state initiated so precariously after 1688, the days of this balance were to be numbered in very different senses, and one of the most telling disjunctions we recognise is that while Public Credit, a billowing stock exchange and burgeoning money markets were creating enormous and foundational opportunities for enrichment and development, by the time of his death Pope had left the capacities of his favoured form virtually exhausted. Perhaps such an explosion of socio-economic and political activity must inevitably militate against the couplet's enclosure, although it was evidently different for landed wealth, where enclosure further enriched possessors of the soil. But London's commercial culture was far too busy to brook such containment for long, and the couplet fractures, though thanks to Pope's mastery it does not disintegrate. It had evidently become too much for him to negotiate proliferating forms of fantasy and activity within the couplet's system of regulation. Something had to give and it was hardly likely to be the progress of culture and history. As it comes to us now with its Introductions, Arguments, and welter of critical machinery, *The Dunciad* is as cross-discursive and intertextual a document as *Gulliver's Travels*. Its dependence on prior codes and its infiltration by innovative ones unravels a process amounting almost to a self-deconstruction. Over the decade and a half of its incremental composition and textual complication, *The Dunciad* contrives itself as a satire on the concept of the book as a means of communication. In its pages rhyming pairs, staggering valiantly under the weight of an

endlessly fertile cross-breeding of joke and explication, of editorial
ironies and obfuscations, come to generate something of a discursive
continuity with Pope's perception of an economics where 'money upon
money increases, copulates, and multiplies . . . in saecular saeculorum.'
As we try to pursue these continuities and discontinuities we realise that
any clear sense of origins is being confounded and even the secure
construction and transmission of meaning itself at times jeopardised by
an addictive machinery of annotation that conglomerates the real with
the unreal as text and shadow-text. Which is as much a problem now as
it was then. But if a sense of origins is muddied, in its developing
multi-referentiality *The Dunciad* also shadows forth uncertain futures.
As a curtain of darkness closes its verse, inventive energies extend its
overall formal possibilities. Couplet discipline opens into textual inter-
disciplinarity while the codes of an aristocratically derived reasoning
are germinally enriched and corrupted by a magnetic irrationalism.

This crisis of form and meaning might register now as a crisis in
Pope's natural inheritance, the discourse of civic humanism which
struggled after the Restoration to continue framing the discussion of
political conduct in its preferred ethical terms; to re-impose a moral
order upon the world of its utterance. But the period was one of change
and development in some ways more radical and significant even than
that of the Civil War and Interregnum. Financial power was forging
the constitution of society towards altered priorities and in the ensuing
conflict the language of 'balanced government' and 'separation of
powers' was invested with very different meanings. By continuing to
view government as itself a mechanism for the corruption of property,
independence and virtue, traditional discourse discloses a resistance to
changing realities. It was still presenting a 'corruption' springing from
the economic dependence of members of the legislative upon resources
controlled by the executive as the principal enemy of virtue and liberty.
But 'virtue' and 'liberty' were being reconstituted by the money market
and its credit systems. Civic liberty shades into the social market
freedoms of consuming individuals to pursue their acquisitive passions;
freedoms that were often perceived by Opposition writers as dependent
upon paper-based imaginary expectations. Fictions and fantasies were
evidently re-shaping selfhood, and given a massive expansion of state
bureaucracy and its legions of associated hirelings, this inherently
unstable dependency assumed for them nation-wide dimensions. In
these contexts, their polemic against corruption became an attack upon
modernity itself. Rival constructions of a more liberalising subjectivity
were being circulated to validate and integrate a still-transforming

civic personality as the natural configuration of human possibility, but
that is not how the Scriblerians wanted to see things. Against their best
efforts, the entry into history of a new system of credit-financed trade
and a consequent insertion of altered accountancy required for a
rapidly expanding acquisitive individualism heralded the demise of
civic humanism's classical ethos, leaving the conventions of its literacy
stranded. Those conventions had not developed a sufficient vocabulary
to describe and recognise the continuing revolution with which they
had to contend.

The confrontation was still being spoken of as one between 'virtue'
and 'corruption' but already this antithesis was expressing a quarrel
between value and personality on the one hand and an on-going history
and society on the other. A gap was opening up between structures of
government and the institutions and practice of economic activity,
between governing political instrumentation and civil society's wealth-
creating procedures. Forms of governing regulation had come into
decisive conflict with the irresistible temptations of private initiative:
the individual as a self-valorising economic unit could no longer be
constrained within older integrations of community. As they exploited
this gap, political subjectivities demanded more accommodating per-
missions than inherited discourses could offer. Political economy was
moving into its early modern forms, rendering traditional codifications
of its predecessor society increasingly unviable. In what at first appears
a perverse and contradictory operation it begins to seem that the
'Ideal-Debts' in which John Gay's banker traded, the 'Ideal Values' of
the stock market to which *The Craftsman* alluded, and Richard Steele's
'Groundless Imaginary Motive' combine with the 'power of Imagination' Defoe saw operating in credit-based transactions and the 'artifice
of mind' Pope mentions to create discursive contexts for the autonomous, self-constituting and transcendental subjectivity of later provenance. But the conditions of that emergence were necessarily spelling
the end of previously established ways of seeing selfhood in society.
Mandeville was aware of this and, though its whole drift seems to
contradict the perception, in his *Essay on Man*, in many ways an elegiac
if somewhat strident hymn to the paradise lost of landed stability, Pope
had allowed his own God to glimpse:

> Atoms or systems into ruin hurl'd,
> And now a bubble burst, and now a world.   (I, 89–90)

Bibliography

Aden, John, *Pope's Once and Future Kings: Satire and Politics in the Early Career* (Knoxville, TN, 1978)

    Something Like Horace: Studies in the Art and Allusion of Pope's Horatian Satires (Vanderbilt Univ., TN, 1969)

Alpers, P. J., 'Pope's "To Bathurst" and the Mandevillian State', *English Literary History*, 25 (1958), pp. 23–42

Aristotle, *The Politics* (Harmondsworth, 1962)

Ashcraft, R., and Goldsmith, M. M., 'Locke, Revolution Principles and the Formation of Whig Ideology', *The Historical Journal*, 26, no. 4 (1983), pp. 773–800

Ashton, R., *The Crown and the Money Market, 1603–1640* (Oxford, 1960)

Ashton, T. S., *An Economic History of England: The Eighteenth Century* (London, 1955)

Audra, E. and Williams, A. (eds.), *Alexander Pope: Pastoral Poetry and An Essay on Criticism* (London, 1961)

Aylmer, G. E., *The Struggle for the Constitution: England in the Seventeenth Century* (London, 1963)

Bakhtin, Mikhail, *Problems of Dostoevsky's Poetics*, edited and translated by C. Emerson (Manchester, 1984)

    Rabelais and his World, translated by Helene Iswolsky (Bloomington, IL, 1984)

Barrell, John, *English Literature in History 1730–80: An Equal, Wide Survey* (London, 1983)

Bateson, F. W. (ed.), *Alexander Pope: Epistles to Several Persons* (London, 1951)

Battestin, M. C., *The Providence of Wit: Aspects of Form in Augustan Literature and the Arts* (Oxford, 1974)

Baxter, S. B., *The Development of the Treasury 1660–1702* (Oxford, 1960)

Beaumont, C. A., *Swift's Use of the Bible* (Atlanta, GA, 1965)

Benjamin, Walter, *Illuminations: Essays and Reflections*, edited by Hannah Arendt (New York, NY, 1968, rpt. 1985)

Bell, I. A., ' "Not Lucre's Madman": Pope, Money and Independence', in *Alexander Pope: Essays for the Tercentenary*, ed. C. Nicholson (Aberdeen, 1988), pp. 53–67

Berkeley, George, *The Works of George Berkeley, Bishop of Cloyne*, edited by A. A. Luce and T. E. Jessop, 9 vols. (London, 1948–57)

Blackmore, Richard, *A Satyr Against Wit* (London, 1700), pp. 8–11

Blunt, John, *A True State of the South Sea Scheme* (London, 1722)

Bolingbroke, Henry St. John, *Works*, 4 vols. (Philadelphia, PA, 1841)

Bond, Donald F., *The Spectator*, 5 vols. (Oxford, 1965)

Bond, Donald F. (ed.), *The Tatler*, 3 vols. (Oxford, 1987)

Boswell, James, *Boswell's Life of Johnson*, edited by R. W. Chapman (Oxford, 1904, rpt. 1961)

Brady, Frank, 'Vexations and Diversions: Three Problems in *Gulliver's Travels*, *Modern Philology*, 75 (1978), pp. 346–67

Brookes-Davis, Douglas, *Pope's 'Dunciad' and the Queen of Night: A Study in Emotional Jacobitism* (Manchester, 1985)

Brooks, Cleanth, 'The Case of Miss Arabella Fermor', in *The Well-Wrought Urn: Studies in the Structure of Poetry* (London, 1949, rpt. 1968), pp. 65–84

Brower, R. A., *Alexander Pope: The Poetry of Allusion* (Oxford, 1959)

Brown, Laura, *Alexander Pope* (Oxford, 1985)

Browning, Reed, *Political and Constitutional Ideas of the Court Whigs* (Louisiana State Univ., LA, 1982)

Burtt, Shelley, *Virtue Transformed: Political Argument in England 1688–1740* (Cambridge, 1992)

Butt, John (ed.), *Alexander Pope: Imitations of Horace* (London, 1939)

'Pope and the Opposition to Walpole's Government', in *Pope, Dickens and Others: Essays and Addresses by John Butt*, edited by Geoffrey Carnall (Edinburgh, 1969), pp. 111–26

Byrd, Max, *Visits to Bedlam: Madness and Literature in the Eighteenth Century* (South Carolina Univ., SC, 1974)

Carnochan, W. B., *Lemuel Gulliver's Mirror for Man* (Berkeley, CA, 1978)

Carretta, Vincent, 'Pope's "Epistle to Bathurst" and the South Sea Bubble', *Journal of English and Germanic Philology*, 77 (1978), pp. 212–31

The Snarling Muse: Verbal and Visual Political Satire from Pope to Churchill (Philadelphia, PA, 1983)

Carswell, John, *The South Sea Bubble* (London, 1960)

Cartwright, J. J. (ed.), *The Wentworth Papers* (London, 1883)

Case, A. E., *Four Essays on Gulliver's Travels* (Gloucester, MA, 1944)

Cohen, Ralph, 'Transformation in "The Rape of the Lock" ', *Eighteenth Century Studies*, 2, no. 3 (1969), pp. 205–24.

Cowles, Virginia, *The Great Swindle: The Story of the South Sea Bubble* (London, 1960)

Cunningham, J. S., *Pope: 'The Rape of the Lock'* (London, 1961)

D'Anvers, Caleb, *The Craftsman: Being a Critique of the Times*, 2 vols. (London, 1728)

Davenant, Charles, 'An Essay upon Ways and Means of Supplying the War', in *Works*, edited by Sir Charles Whitworth, 5 vols. (London, 1771), vol. I, pp. 73–81

'An Essay upon the Probable Ways of Making a People Gainers in the Balance of Trade' (London, 1699), in *Works*, ed. Whitworth, II, pp. 165–381

'Discourses on the Public Revenues' (London, 1698), in *Works*, ed. Whitworth, I, pp. 150–459

The True Picture of a Modern Whig: set forth in a dialogue between Mr Whiplash and Mr Double, two under-spur-leathers to the late ministry. 6th edn [anon.] (London, 1701)

Defoe, Daniel, *A Review of the State of the English Nation* (London, 1704–13), edited in 22 facsimile books by A. W. Secord (Columbia, 1938)

'An Essay Upon Projects' (London, 1697)

'An Essay Upon the Public Credit' (London, 1710)

'The Anatomy of Exchange Alley' (London, 1719)

'The Villainy of Stock-Jobbers Detected' (London, 1701)

Delaney, Sheila, 'Sex and Politics in Pope's "Rape of the Lock"', *English Studies in Canada*, 1 (1975), pp. 46–61

Dennis, Nigel, *Jonathan Swift: A Short Character* (London, 1964)

DePorte, M. V., *Nightmares and Hobbyhorses: Swift, Sterne, and Augustan Ideas of Madness* (Huntington Library, NY, 1974)

Dickinson, H. T., 'The Politics of Bernard Mandeville', in *Mandeville Studies: New Explorations in the Art and Thought of Bernard Mandeville (1670–1733)*, edited by I. Primer (The Hague, 1975), pp. 80–97

Bolingbroke (London, 1970)

Liberty and Property: Political Ideology in Eighteenth-Century Britain (London, 1979)

Politics and Literature in the Eighteenth Century (London, 1974)

Walpole and the Whig Supremacy (London, 1973)

Dickson, P. G. M., *The Financial Revolution: A Study in the Development of Public Credit, 1688–1756* (London, 1967)

Dixon, Peter, *The World of Pope's Satires* (London, 1968)

Dixon, Peter (ed.), *Writers and Their Background* (London, 1972)

Dobrée, Bonamy, *English Literature in the Early Eighteenth Century* (Oxford, 1959)

Donaldson, Ian, ' "A Double Capacity": *The Beggar's Opera*', *Modern Essays on Eighteenth-Century Literature*, edited by L. Damrosch Jr (Oxford, 1988), pp. 141–58

'Concealing and Revealing: Pope's "Epistle to Arbuthnot"', *The Yearbook of English Studies*, 18 (1988), pp. 181–99

Downie, J. A., 'Political Characterisation in *Gulliver's Travels*', *The Yearbook of English Studies*, 7 (1977), pp. 108–20

Jonathan Swift: Political Writer (London, 1984)

Robert Harley and the Press: Propaganda and Public Opinion in the Age of Swift and Defoe (Cambridge, 1979)

'1688: Pope and the Rhetoric of Jacobitism', in *Pope: New Contexts*, ed. D. Fairer (London, 1990), pp. 9–24

Dryden, John, *The Poems and Fables of John Dryden*, ed. James Kinsley (London, 1962)

The Works of John Dryden, edited by E. N. Hooker, H. T. Swedenberg Jr, S. H. Monk, E. Miner, G. Guffey and A. Roper, 20 vols. (California Univ., CA, 1956–89)

Dumont. Louis, *From Mandeville to Marx: The Genesis and Triumph of Economic Ideology* (Chicago and London, 1977)

Dunn, J., *The Political Thought of John Locke* (Cambridge, 1969)

Dussinger, J. A., ' "Christian" vs "Hollander": Swift's Satire on the Dutch East India Traders', *Notes and Queries*, 21 (1966), pp. 209–12

Eagleton, Terry, *The Function of Criticism: From 'The Spectator' to Poststructuralism* (London, 1984)

The Ideology of the Aesthetic (Oxford, 1990)

Earle, Peter, *The Making of the English Middle Class: Business, Society and Family Life in London, 1660–1730* (London, 1989)

Easthope, Antony, *British Post-Structuralism: Since 1968* (London, 1988)

Eddy, W. A., *'Gulliver's Travels': A Critical Study* (Princeton and London, 1923; rpt. Gloucester, MA, 1963)

Edwards, T. R. Jr, *This Dark Estate: A Reading of Pope* (Berkeley, CA, 1963)

Ehrenpreis, Irvin, *Literary Meaning and Augustan Values* (Columbia Univ., CA, 1974)

Swift: The Man, his Works and the Age, 3 vols. (London, 1962–83)

Empson, William, *Some Versions of Pastoral: A Study of the Pastoral Form in Literature* (London, 1935; rpt. 1950)

Erskine-Hill, Howard, 'Alexander Pope: The Political Poet in His Time', *Eighteenth Century Studies*, 15 (1981–2), pp. 123–48

'Literature and the Jacobite Cause: Was there a Rhetoric of Jacobitism?', in *Ideology and Conspiracy: Aspects of Jacobitism 1689–1959*, edited by Eveline Cruickshanks (Edinburgh, 1982), pp. 49–69

'Pope and the Financial Revolution', in *Writers and Their Background*, edited by P. Dixon (London, 1972), pp. 200–29

'The Lucky Hit in Commerce and Creation', *Notes and Queries*, new series 14 (1967), pp. 407–8

'The "New World" of Pope's *Dunciad*', *Renaissance and Modern Studies*, 6 (1962), pp. 46–67

Pope: 'The Dunciad' (London, 1972)

The Augustan Idea in English Literature (London, 1983)

The Social Milieu of Alexander Pope: Lives, Example and the Poetic Response (London, 1975)

Evans, J. M., *A Critical Edition of: 'An Apology for the Life of Colley Cibber, Comedian'* (New York, 1987)

Ewen, C. L., *Lotteries and Sweepstakes in the British Isles* (London, 1932)

Fairer, David (ed.), *Pope: New Contexts* (London, 1990)

Ferguson, Oliver, *Jonathan Swift and Ireland* (Urbana, IL, 1962)

Fielding, Henry, *An Enquiry into the Causes of the Late Increase of Robbers, and Related Writings*, edited by M. R. Zirker (Oxford. 1988)

Firth, C. H., 'The Political Significance of *Gulliver's Travels*', *Proceedings of the British Academy* (1919–20), pp. 237–59

Fish, Stanley, *Self-Consuming Artifacts: The Experience of Seventeenth Century Literature* (Berkeley, CA, 1974)

Foot, Michael, *The Pen and the Sword* (London, 1957)

Foucault, Michel, *The Archaeology of Knowledge* (New York, 1972)

Fowler, Alastair, 'The Paradoxical Machinery of *The Rape of the Lock*', in *Alexander Pope: Essays for the Tercentenary*, ed. Nicholson (Aberdeen, 1988), pp. 151–65

Frantz, R. W., 'Swift's Yahoos and the Voyagers', *Modern Philology*, 19 (1931), pp. 49–57

Fusell, Paul, *The Rhetorical World of Augustan Humanism: Ethics and Imagery from Swift to Burke* (Oxford, 1965)

Gabriner, Paul, 'Pope's "Virtue" and the Events of 1738', *Pope: Recent Essays by Various Hands*, edited by Maynard Mack and J. A. Winn (Brighton, 1980), pp. 585–611

Gay, John, *Dramatic Works*, edited by John Fuller, 2 vols. (Oxford, 1983)
   Letters of John Gay, edited by C. F. Burgess (Oxford, 1966)
   Poetry and Prose, edited by V. A. Dearing and C. E. Beckwith, 2 vols. (Oxford, 1974)

Goldgar, Bertrand A., 'Pope's Theory of the Passions: The Background of Epistle II of the *Essay on Man*', *Philological Quarterly*, 41 (1962), pp. 730–43
   Walpole and the Wits: The Relation of Politics to Literature, 1722–1742 (Nebraska Univ., NB, 1976)

Goldsmith, M. M., *Private Vices, Public Benefits: Bernard Mandeville's Social and Political Thought* (Cambridge, 1985)

Gooch, G. P., *English Democratic Ideas in the Seventeenth Century*, 2nd edn (New York, 1959)

Griffin, D. H., *Alexander Pope: The Poet in the Poems* (Princeton Univ., NJ, 1978)

Guerinot, J. V., *Pamphlet Attacks on Alexander Pope* (London, 1969)

Gunn, J. A. W., *Beyond Liberty and Property: The Process of Self-Recognition in Eighteenth-Century Political Thought* (Montreal, 1983)

Gurr, E., *Pope* (Edinburgh, 1971)

Habakkuk, H. J., 'English Landownership 1680–1740', *Economic History Review*, 10 (1939–40), pp. 2–17

Hammond, Brean, *Pope* (Brighton, 1986)
   Pope and Bolingbroke: A Study of Friendship and Influence (Columbia, MI, 1984)

Harth, P. (ed.), *New Approaches to Eighteenth-Century Literature* (Columbia Univ., CA, 1974)

Hexter, J. H., *On Historians: Reappraisals of Some of the Makers of Modern History* (London, 1979)

Higgins, Ian, 'Swift and Sparta: The Nostalgia of *Gulliver's Travels*', *Modern Language Review*, 78 (1983), pp. 513–31

Hill, Christopher, *Puritanism and Revolution* (London, 1958, rpt. 1968)
  Reformation to Industrial Revolution: A Social and Economic History of Britain 1530–1780 (London, 1967)
  Society and Puritanism in Pre-Revolutionary England (London, 1964; rpt 1969)
  The Century of Revolution: 1603–1714 (London, 1961; rpt. 1983)
Hirschman, Albert, O., *The Passions and the Interests: Political Arguments for Capitalism Before its Triumph* (Princeton Univ., NJ, 1977)
Hobbes, Thomas, *Leviathan, or the Matter, Forme and Power of a Commonwealth Ecclesiastical and Civil*, edited by Michael Oakeshott (Oxford, 1960)
Holmes, Geoffrey, *British Politics in the Age of Anne* (London, 1967)
Hopkins, R. H., 'Some Observations on Mandeville's Satire', in *Mandeville Studies: New Explorations in the Art and Thought of Bernard Mandeville (1670–1733)*, ed. I. Primer (The Hague, 1975), pp. 168–92
Hume, David, *A Treatise of Human Nature* (1739), edited by L. A. Selby-Bigge, 2nd ed., rev. by P. H. Nidditch (Oxford, 1978)
Irving, W. H., *John Gay: Favorite of the Wits* (Durham, 1940)
Jack, I., *Augustan Satire: Intention and Idiom in English Poetry 1660–1750* (Oxford, 1952)
Jeffares, A. N. (ed.), *Fair Liberty Was All His Cry: A Tercentenary Tribute to Jonathan Swift (1667–1745)* (London, 1967)
Jones, Emrys, *Pope and Dulness* (London, 1968)
Jones, R. F., *Ancients and Moderns: A Study of the Rise of the Scientific Movement in Seventeenth-Century England* (St. Louis, MI, 1961)
Kelsall, M. M., '*Iterum* Houyhnhnm: Swift's Sextumvirate and the Horses', *Essays in Criticism*, 19 (1969), pp. 35–45
Kenyon, J. P., *Revolution Principles: The Philosophy of Party 1689–1720* (Cambridge, 1977)
Kernan, A. B., *The Plot of Satire* (New Haven, CT, 1965)
Kramnick, Isaac, *Bolingbroke and his Circle: The Politics of Nostalgia in the Age of Walpole* (London, 1968)
Landa, Louis, 'Pope's Belinda, the Great Emporie of the World, and the Wondrous Worm', in *Essays in Eighteenth-Century English Literature* (Princeton Univ., NJ, 1980), pp. 178–98
Leavis, F. R., *The Common Pursuit* (London, 1953)
Leranbaum, Miriam, *Alexander Pope's 'Opus Magnum', 1729–1744* (Oxford, 1977)
Lévi-Strauss, Claude, *The Raw and the Cooked: Introduction to a Science of Mythology: I*, translated by J. and D. Weightman (London, 1970)
Lock, F. P., *The Politics of 'Gulliver's Travels'* (Oxford, 1980)
Locke, John, 'Some Considerations of the Consequences of the Lowering of Interest, and Raising the Value of Money', in *John Locke: Locke on Money*, edited by P. H. Kelly, 2 vols. (Oxford, 1991) vol. I, pp. 209–342
  An Essay Concerning Human Understanding, edited by P. H. Nidditch (Oxford, 1975, rpt. 1990)
  The Reasonableness of Christianity, edited by I. T. Ramsay (London, 1958)

Two Treatises of Government, edited by Peter Laslett (Cambridge, 1960, rpt. 1992)

Loftis, John, *The Politics of Drama in Augustan England* (Oxford, 1963)

McInnes, Angus, *Robert Harley, Puritan Politician* (London, 1970)

MacIntyre, Alasdair, *After Virtue: A Study in Moral Theory* (Notre Dame, 1981)

Mack, Maynard, *Alexander Pope: A Life* (Yale Univ., New Haven, CT, 1985)

(ed.), *Alexander Pope: An Essay on Man* (London, 1950)

The Augustans (Princeton Univ., NJ, 1961)

The Garden and the City: Retirement and Politics in the Later Poetry of Pope: 1731–1743 (Toronto, 1969)

(ed.), *Essential Articles for the Study of Alexander Pope* (London, 1964)

(ed.), *Pope: Recent Essays by Various Hands* (Brighton, 1980)

Macpherson, C. B., *The Political Theory of Possessive Individualism: Hobbes to Locke* (Oxford, 1962)

Mandeville, Bernard, *The Fable of the Bees: Or, Private Vices, Public Benefits*, edited by F. B. Kaye, 2 vols. (Oxford, 1924)

Marx, Karl, *Capital*, 3 vols. (Harmondsworth, 1976)

Grundrisse (Harmondsworth, 1973)

The Early Writings (Harmondsworth, 1975)

The Revolutions of 1848 (Harmondsworth, 1973)

Miège, Guy, *The Present State of Great Britain* (London, 1707)

Moore, J. R., 'Windsor Forest and William III', *Modern Language Notes*, 56 (1951), pp. 451–4

Namier, Lewis, *England in the Age of the American Revolution* (London, 1930)

The Structure of Politics at the Accession of George III (London, 1929)

Newey, Vincent, 'Pope, Raymond Williams and the Man of Ross', *Essays in Criticism*, 27 (1977), pp. 368–73

Nicholson, C. (ed.), *Alexander Pope: Essays for the Tercentenary* (Aberdeen, 1988)

Nicholson, M. and Mohler, N. M., 'The Scientific Background of Swift's "Voyage of Laputa"', rpt. in *Fair Liberty Was All His Cry: A Tercentenary Tribute to Jonathan Swift (1667–1745)*, ed. A. N. Jeffares (London, 1967), pp. 226–69

Nussbaum, Felicity, *The Brink of All We Hate: English Satires on Women, 1660–1750* (Lexington, KY, 1984)

Orwell, George, *In Front of Your Nose, 1945–1950*, edited by Sonia Orwell and Ian Angus, vol. IV of *The Collected Essays, Journalism and Letters of George Orwell*, 4 vols. (New York, 1968)

Osborn, J. M., 'Pope, the Byzantine Empress, and Walpole's Whore', *Review of English Studies*, new series, 6 (1955), pp. 372–82

Pincoffs, Edmund L., *Quandaries and Virtues: Against Reductionism in Ethics* (Kansas Univ., KS, 1986)

Pinkus, P., 'Mandeville's Paradox', in *Mandeville Studies*, ed. I. Primer (The Hague, 1975), pp. 193–211

Piper, W. B. 'Similitude as Satire in *The Beggar's Opera*', *Eighteenth Century Studies*, 21, no. 3 (1987–8), pp. 40–54

Plamenatz, John, *Man and Society: A Critical Examination of Some Important Social and Political Theories from Machiavelli to Marx* (London, 1963)

Plumb, J. H., *Sir Robert Walpole: The Making of a Statesman* (London, 1956)
Sir Robert Walpole: The King's Minister (London, 1960)
The Growth of Political Stability in England, 1675–1725 (London, 1967)

Pocock, J. G. A., *Politics, Language and Time: Essays on Political Thought and History* (London, 1972)
The Machiavellian Moment: Florentine Political Thought and the Atlantic Republican Tradition (Princeton, NJ, 1975)
Virtue, Commerce, and History: Essays on Political Thought and History, Chiefly in the Eighteenth Century (Cambridge, 1985)

Pollack, Ellen, 'Rereading *The Rape of the Lock*: Pope and the Paradox of Female Power', in *Studies in Eighteenth-Century Culture 10*, edited by H. C. Payne (Madison, WI, 1981), pp. 429–44

Pope, Alexander, *The Correspondence of Alexander Pope*, edited by George Sherburn, 5 vols. (Oxford, 1956)
The Twickenham Edition of the Works of Alexander Pope, edited by J. Butt, E. Audra, N. Ault, F. W. Bateson, M. Mack, J. Sutherland, G. Tillotson and A. Williams, 11 vols. (London, 1939–69)

Price, F. G. H., *A Handbook of London Bankers* (London, 1876)

Price, Martin, *Swift's Rhetorical Art: A Study in Structure and Meaning* (New Haven, CT, 1953)
To the Palace of Wisdom: Studies in Order and Energy from Dryden to Blake (New York, 1964)

Primer, Irwin (ed.), *Mandeville Studies: New Explorations in the Art and Thought of Bernard Mandeville (1670–1733)* (The Hague, 1975)

Probyn, Clive T. (ed.), *The Art of Jonathan Swift* (London, 1978)

Raab, Felix, *The English Face of Machiavelli* (London, 1964)

Rawson, Claude, 'The Injured Lady and the Drapier: A Reading of Swift's Irish Tracts', *Prose Studies*, 3 (1980), pp. 15–43
Gulliver and the Gentle Reader: Studies in Swift and our Time (London, 1973)
Order From Confusion Sprung: Studies in Eighteenth-Century Literature from Swift to Cowper (London, 1985)

Rogers, P., 'Blacks and Poetry and Pope', in *Eighteenth-Century Encounters: Studies in Literature and Society in the Age of Walpole* (Brighton, 1985), pp. 75–92
Grub Street: Studies in a Subculture (London, 1972)
'Gulliver and the Engineers', *Modern Language Review*, 70 (1975), pp. 260–70
The Augustan Vision (London, 1974)
'The Name and Nature of Dulness', *Anglia*, 92 (1974), pp. 79–92

Rogers, R. W., *The Major Satires of Alexander Pope* (Urbana, IL, 1955)

Rousseau, G. S. and Pat Rogers (eds.), *The Enduring Legacy: Alexander Pope, Tercentenary Essays* (Cambridge, 1988)

Rumbold, Valerie, *Women's Place in Pope's World* (Cambridge, 1989)

Said, Edward, 'Swift as Intellectual', in *The World, the Text and the Critic* (London, 1984), pp. 72–89

Schultz, W. E., *Gay's 'Beggar's Opera': Its Content, History and Influence* (Yale Univ., CT, 1923)

Scott, W. R., *The Constitution of English, Scottish and Irish Joint-Stock Companies to 1720*, 3 vols. (Cambridge, 1910–12)

Sherbo, A., 'Swift and Travel Literature', *Modern Language Studies*, 9 (1979), pp. 114–27

Sherburn, George, '*The Dunciad*, Book IV', *Texas Studies in Language and Literature*, 24 (1944), pp. 197–210

Sitter, J. E., 'The Argument of Pope's "Epistle to Cobham"', *Studies in English Literature*, 17 (1977), pp. 435–49

Spacks, P. M., *An Argument of Images: The Poetry of Alexander Pope* (Harvard Univ., MA, 1971)

Speck, W. A., *Society and Literature in England 1700–1760* (Dublin, 1983)
  Stability and Strife: England 1714–1760 (London, 1977)

Spence, Joseph, *Observations, Anecdotes, and Characters of Books and Men Collected from Conversation*, edited by J. M. Osborne, 2 vols. (Oxford, 1966)

Sprat, Thomas, *History of the Royal Society*, edited by J. I. Cope and H. W. Jones (London, 1959)

Steele, Richard, 'A Nation a Family: Being a Sequel to the Crisis of Property', in *Tracts and Pamphlets by Richard Steele*, edited by Rae Blanchard (Oxford, 1944), pp. 573–89

Stephen, Leslie, *English Literature and Society in the Eighteenth Century* (London, 1963)

Straus, Ralf, *The Unspeakable Curll* (London, 1927)

Sutherland, James (ed.), *Alexander Pope: The Dunciad* (London, 1943, rev. 1953)

Swift, Jonathan, *Gulliver's Travels*, edited by R. A. Greenberg (New York, NY, 1970)
  Journal to Stella, edited by Harold Williams, 2 vols. (Oxford, 1948)
  Letters of Jonathan Swift to Charles Ford, edited by D. Nichol Smith (Oxford, 1935)
  The Account Books of Jonathan Swift, edited by P. V. Thomson, and D. J. Thomson (London, 1984)
  The Correspondence of Jonathan Swift, edited by Harold Williams, 5 vols. (Oxford, 1963–5, rev. edn 1965)
  The Poems of Jonathan Swift, edited by Harold Williams, 3 vols. (Oxford, 1958)
  The Prose Writings of Jonathan Swift, edited by Herbert Davis, I. Ehrenpreis, L. Landa and Harold Williams, 16 vols. (Oxford, 1939–75)

Tawney, R. A., *Religion and the Rise of Capitalism* (London, 1948)

Thompson, E. P., *Customs in Common* (London, 1991)
  Whigs and Hunters: The Origins of the Black Act (London, 1973)

Tillotson, Geoffrey, *On the Poetry of Pope* (London, 1938)
  (ed.), *The Rape of the Lock and Other Poems* (London, 1940, rev. edn, 1954)

Toland, John, 'The Secret History of the South Sea Scheme', in *A Collection of Several Pieces of Mr Toland: With Some Memoirs of his Life and Writing* (London, 1726)

Torchiana, D. T., 'Jonathan Swift, the Irish and the Yahoos: The Case Reconsidered', *Philological Quarterly*, 56 (1975), pp. 195–212

Treadwell, J. M., 'Jonathan Swift: The Satirist as Projector', *Texas Studies in Literature and Language*, 17 (1975–6), pp. 439–60

Trickett, R., *The Honest Muse: A Study in Augustan Verse* (Oxford, 1967)

Van Ghent, Dorothy, *The English Novel: Form and Function* (New York, NY, 1953)

Vilar, Pierre, *A History of Gold and Money: 1450–1920* (London, 1984)

Viner, Jacob, 'Man's Economic Status', in *Man Versus Society in Eighteenth-Century Britain: Six Points of View*, edited by J. L. Clifford (Cambridge, 1968), pp. 22–53

Walcott, R., 'English Party Politics 1688–1714', in *Essays in Modern English History in Honour of W.C. Abbott* [no editor] (Harvard Univ., MA, 1941), pp. 81–131

Wasserman, E. R., *Pope's 'Epistle to Bathurst': A Critical Reading with an Edition of the Poem* (Baltimore, 1960)

Watt, Ian (ed.), *The Augustan Age* (Harvard, CT, 1968)
The Rise of the Novel (Harmondsworth, 1973)

Weber, Max, *The Protestant Ethic and the Spirit of Capitalism*, translated by Talcott Parsons (London, 1983)

Weinbrot, H. D., *The Formal Strain: Studies in Augustan Imitation and Satire* (Chicago Univ., IL, 1969)
Eighteenth-Century Satire: Essays on Text and Context from Dryden to Peter Pindar (Cambridge, 1988)

White, D. H., *Pope and the Contexts of Controversy: The Manipulation of Ideas in 'An Essay on Man'* (Chicago Univ., IL, 1970)

Whitworth, Sir Charles, ed., *Works of Charles Davenport*, 5 vols. (London, 1771)

Williams, Aubrey, *Pope's 'Dunciad': A Study of its Meaning* (London, 1955)

Williams, Raymond, *The Country and the City* (London, 1973)

Wilson, Charles, *England's Apprenticeship, 1603–1763* (London, 1965)

Index

Addison, Joseph: celebrates exotic possessions, 49; celebrates merchant class, 26, 42; celebrates Royal Exchange, 56–7; credit imagery compared with Pope's, 48; eulogises trade, 42; finance a literary subject for, 48; named in Pope's poem, 46; on 'interests' in society, 55; personifies credit as inconstant female, 45, 47; praises new riches, 43; promotes market sociability, 3; suggests a prototype for Pope's Belinda, 49; trade the motor of change for, 57; visits a lottery, 58
Aislabie, John, 60–1, 68, 69
Allen, Ralph, 67
Alpers, P. J., 142n
American 'New Criticism', 169
Anne, Queen, 25, 28, 52, 53, 190
Arden, John, 24n
Aristippus, 169
Aristotle, 24, 161: foundation for virtue, 161; notion of autonomy, 113; notion of virtue, 4; *politea*, 24, 87; *Politics*, 172; *zoon politikon*, 24
Ashcraft, R., 20n
Ashton, T. S., xi, 6n
Atterbury, Francis, 67

Bakhtin, Mikhail, 117n, 118–9, 120
Bank of England: and development of trade, 12; and Public Credit, 23; engrossing operations of, 14; floats loan schemes and part-lotteries, 13; founded (1694), 6; Gilbert Heathcote governor of, 143; issues loans in paper at will, 6; new instrument of monetary policy, 4; receiver for government lotteries, 60; receives and lends money at interest, 6; rescues South Sea Company, 103; *Spectator*'s vision of, 47; Steele records lottery at, 57; Swift attacks, 52; Whiggish influence of, 51
Barber, John, 53
Barrell, John, 8n
Bateson, F. W., 142

Bathurst, Allen, 1st earl: celebrated in *Epistle to Burlington*, 172; copyright of *The Dunciad* assigned to, 158; praiseworthy for Pope, 167; style of economy and magnificence, 143
Bell, Ian A., 181n
Benjamin, Walter, 116
Berkeley, George, 3, 4n; *Towards Preventing the Ruin of Great Britain*, 4n, 113
Blackmore, Richard: *Satyr Against Wit*, 193–4
Blunt, John: advises Harley, 52; and Mississippi Scheme, 61; appeals to gambling instincts, 145–6; as scapegoat, 152; leading architect of South Sea Company, 52; memorable figure in *Epistle to Bathurst*, 142, 151; non-conformist origins, 143; proposes incorporation of National Debt into South Sea Company, 62; techniques of manipulation, 138
Bolingbroke, Henry St John, viscount: *Essay on Man*'s opening address to, 167; Gulliver as representation of, 108; identifies *The Craftsman* with Country Interest, 162; influence on Pope, 19; passes Stamp Act (1712), 115; persuades Queen Anne to prorogue parliament, 60; Pope supports his anti-Walpole mobilisation, 153, 173; proprietor of *The Craftsman*, 139; Scriblerians gather around, 18, 71; speculative profits from the Mississippi Company, 61–2; waning influence of, 23
Bond, Denis, 143
Bond, Donald, xiv
Boswell, James, 2n
Bowler, Anne, 153n
Brady, Frank, 109n, 188
Brooks, Cleanth, 41n
Broome, William, 192
Brothers Club, 18
Brown, Laura, 25n, 170n
Budgell, Eustace, 57

212

CAMBRIDGE STUDIES IN EIGHTEENTH-CENTURY
ENGLISH LITERATURE AND THOUGHT